NEW DIRECTIONS
IN ACTION RESEARCH

NEW DIRECTIONS IN ACTION RESEARCH

EDITED BY ORTRUN ZUBER-SKERRITT

 The Falmer Press

(A member of the Taylor & Francis Group)
London • Washington, D.C.

UK   Falmer Press, 1 Gunpowder Square, London, EC4A 3DE

USA   Falmer Press, Taylor & Francis Inc., 1900 Frost Road, Suite 101, Bristol, PA 19007

First published 1996

A catalogue record for this book is available from the British Library

Library of Congress Cataloging-in-Publication Data are available on request

ISBN 0 7507 0579 5 cased
ISBN 0 7507 0580 9 paper

Jacket design by Caroline Archer

Printed in Great Britain by Biddles Ltd., Guildford and King's Lynn on paper which has a specified pH value on final paper manufacture of not less than 7.5 and is therefore 'acid free'.

Every effort has been made to contact copyright holders for their permission to reprint material in this book. The publisher would be grateful to hear from any copyright holder who is not here acknowledged and will undertake to rectify any errors or omissions in future editions of this book.

Contents

Acknowledgements vii

Contributors viii

PART 1   INTRODUCTION

1   Introduction: New Directions in Action Research 3
     Ortrun Zuber-Skerritt

PART II   PRINCIPLES AND PROCEDURES FOR
             CRITICAL ACTION RESEARCH

2   Some Principles and Procedures for the Conduct
     of Action Research 13
     Richard Winter

3   Reflexivity in Emancipatory Action Research:
     Illustrating the Researcher's Constitutiveness 28
     Susan Hall

4   Got a Philosophical Match? Does it Matter? 49
     Mary Jane Melrose

5   Collaborative, Self-critical and Reciprocal Inquiry
     Through Memory Work 66
     Michael Schratz

PART III   PROBLEMS AND SUGGESTED SOLUTIONS

6   Emancipatory Action Research for Organisational Change and
Management Development 83
Ortrun Zuber-Skerritt

7   Towards Empowering Leadership:
The Importance of Imagining 106
Shirley Grundy

8   Emancipatory Action Research:
A Critical Alternative to Personnel Development
or a New Way of Patronising People? 121
Richard Weiskopf and Stephan Laske

9   Becoming Critical of Action Research for Development 137
Graham Webb

PART IV   POSTMODERNISM AND CRITICAL ACTION RESEARCH

10 Exposing Discourses Through Action Research 165
Leonie E. Jennings and Anne P. Graham

11 Managing Change Through Action Research:
A Postmodern Perspective on Appraisal 182
Jack Sanger

12 Emancipatory Aspirations in a Postmodern Era 199
Stephen Kemmis

13 Issues for Participatory Action Researchers 243
Robin McTaggart

Author Index 257

Subject Index 260

Acknowledgements

I wish to thank Griffith University for supporting this project, and Tony Carr for his assistance in the early stages of the project.

I am also grateful to Sue Jarvis, Leanne Wood and Liz Wilson for copy editing, proofreading and desktop publishing the manuscript.

Finally, I wish to thank the authors for discussing their work with me and for contributing their chapters to this book.

Ortrun Zuber-Skerritt
April 1996

Contributors

Shirley Grundy

Dr Shirley Grundy is a senior lecturer in the School of Education at Murdoch University, Western Australia. Her research interests include curriculum theory, policy analysis, organisational leadership and management, school-based research and development, and school–university partnerships for teacher professional development. She is author of a substantial number of academic papers. In 1995 she was president of the Australian Association for Research in Education. For the period 1994–96, she was the joint national coordinator of a large action research-based professional development project: Innovative Links between Universities and Schools for Teacher Professional Development.

Susan Hall

Dr Susan Hall is a lecturer in Academic Staff Development at Curtin University of Technology, Western Australia. She has extensive experience as a consultant and researcher in action research for curriculum development in primary and secondary schools. Her research interests include qualitative research methods, which she currently teaches within the School of Social Science at Curtin, and action research for review and development of work practices. Her PhD thesis (1994) was on making 'working knowledge' explicit within the reflective process of action research.

Leonie Jennings

Dr Leonie Jennings is a senior lecturer in the Faculty of Education, Work and Training at Southern Cross University, Lismore, Australia. Currently she is the program coordinator of postgraduate coursework programs in training and development, organisational development and human resource development. Her research interests include action research in disadvantaged schools, postmodernism, labour market programs and evaluation studies in the training sector.

Anne P. Graham, her PhD student and co-author, is a tutor in the same faculty, whose research interests include action research, public policy and postmodernism. Anne tutors in adult learning, policy, training and research methods.

Stephen Kemmis

Professor Stephen Kemmis is an independent educational researcher and consultant, based in Geelong, Victoria. He is currently Visiting Professor at the Queensland University of Technology in Brisbane. Until 1994, he was Professor of Education and Head of the Graduate School of Education, Deakin University. His publications on action research include *Becoming Critical: Education, Knowledge and Action Research* (with Wilfred Carr, Falmer Press, London, 1986); *The Action Research Planner* and *The Action Research Reader* (both with Robin McTaggart, Deakin University Press, 1988); and the entry 'Action Research' in *The International Encyclopedia of Education* (Pergamon Press, London, 1994).

Stephan Laske

Dr Stephan Laske is Professor of Business Administration, Institute of Business Education and Personnel Management and Dean of the Faculty of Economic and Social Sciences at the University of Innsbruck, Austria. His research interests include: personnel and organisation development, leadership in organisations, labour market research and profes-sionalisation, quality of learning and research in universities.

Robin McTaggart

Dr Robin McTaggart is Professor and Head of the School of Administration and Curriculum Studies in the Faculty of Education at Deakin University, Geelong, Australia. His interests include curriculum, action research and participatory case study approaches to program evaluation. He has extensive experience in each of these areas across a range of fields and in cross-cultural situations and has published widely. He has conducted participatory action research and evaluation training programs for health and community workers, educators, nurses, evaluators and managers in Australia, the United States, Canada, Thailand, Singapore, Hong Kong and Indonesia.

Mary Melrose

Dr Mary Melrose is Principal Lecturer and Professional Development Consultant in the Centre for Staff and Educational Development, Auckland Institute of Technology, New Zealand. Her research interests include adult teaching and learning, quality assurance systems and practices, educational leadership, curriculum development and evaluation, reflective practice, academic staff development and appraisal.

Jack Sanger

Dr Jack Sanger is the Director of the Centre for Applied Research in Management, Education and Training (CARMET) at City College, Norwich. He has extensive national and international experience in public and private sector research and evaluation, as well as organisational development. He has been a consultant in a variety of education settings in Britain and abroad. His work has been funded by, among other things, The British Council, the EU, The British Film Institute, The British Library, LEAs and private industry. He is widely published and the author of *The Complete Observer: A Field Guide to Observation in Social Science* (Falmer Press, 1995).

Michael Schratz

Dr Michael Schratz is Associate Professor of Education at the University of Innsbruck, Austria. His main interests are in educational innovation and change with a particular focus on management and leadership. He has taught in Austria and Great Britain, conducted research at the University of California, San Diego, and worked at Deakin University (Australia). Among his publications are *Bildung für ein unbekanntes Morgen: Auf der Suche nach einer neuen Lernkultur* (Education for an Unknown Tomorrow: In Search of a New Learning Culture) (Munich, 1991) and *Teaching Teenagers* (London, 1993, with Herbert Puchta). He has edited several books, including *Qualitative Voices in Educational Research* (London, 1993), and co-authored a book on school autonomy and development, as well as a book on a new leadership culture for school development.

Graham Webb

Dr Graham Webb is Director of the Higher Education Development Centre at the University of Otago in Dunedin, New Zealand. He has spent over twenty years as a lecturer in higher education, with approximately equal amounts of time at universities in Ireland, the West Indies and New Zealand. His research interests are in the broad area of educational development theory and practice. He is joint author of *Case Studies of Teaching in Higher Education* (Kogan Page, London, 1993), author of *Making the Most of Appraisal: Career and Professional Development Planning for Lecturers* (Kogan Page, London, 1994) and author of *Understanding Staff Development* (Open University Press, in press).

Richard Weiskopf

Dr Richard Weiskopf is Senior Research Fellow in the Institute for Business Education and Personnel Management at the University of Innsbruck, Austria. His research interests include critical organisation and personnel theory, organisational culture and ideology, personnel development, organisational communication and domination.

Richard Winter

Richard Winter is Professor of Education at Anglia Polytechnic University, Cambridge, England. He has been engaged in action research since the late 1970s, at first in the context of teacher education and more recently in social work and nursing. His PhD thesis, a critical study of the theoretical basis for action research, was published by Gower-Avebury (1987) as *Action Research and the Nature of Social Inquiry.* He is also the author of *Learning from Experience: Principles and Practice in Action Research* (Falmer Press, 1989) and co-editor of the international journal, *Educational Action Research.*

Ortrun Zuber-Skerritt

Dr Ortrun Zuber-Skerritt is Associate Professor at Griffith University, Brisbane, Australia, and from 1 February 1996, Professor in the Faculty of Education, Work and Training, Southern Cross University, Lismore, Australia. She has published widely in the fields of literature, higher education and management education and development. She is the editor of several books, a series of monographs on action learning and action research, and the author of *Action Research in Higher Education* (1992) and *Professional Development in Higher Education* (1992, reprinted 1994) both published by Kogan Page, London.

Part I

Introduction

Chapter 1

Introduction: New Directions in Action Research

Ortrun Zuber-Skerritt

Action research has been established as an appropriate research paradigm for educational, professional, managerial and organisational development, and it has been the focus of many books in the last five to ten years. This book aims to present new directions in action research by bringing together leading action researchers who have critically reflected on their theory and practice with a focus on *emancipatory* or *critical* action research, based on the Frankfurt School of Critical Theory.

Briefly, my understanding of emancipatory action research is that it is collaborative, critical and self-critical inquiry by practitioners (e.g. teachers, managers) into a major problem or issue or concern in their own practice. They own the problem and feel responsible and accountable for solving it through teamwork and through following a cyclical process of:

1   strategic *planning*;

2   *action*, i.e. implementing the plan;

3   *observation*, evaluation and self-evaluation;

4   critical and self-critical *reflection* on the results of points 1–3 and making decisions for the next cycle of action research, i.e. revising the plan, followed by action, observation and reflection, etc.

Carr and Kemmis (1986) have distinguished between technical, practical and emancipatory action research which I have summarised elsewhere (Zuber-Skerritt 1994: 113–14) and reproduced in Table 1.1.

Table 1.1   *Types of action research and their main characteristics (Zuber-Skerritt 1992: 12)*

Type of action research	Aims	Facilitator's Role	Relationship between facilitator and participants
1. Technical	Effectiveness/ efficiency of educational practice Professional development	Outside 'expert'	Co-option (of practitioners who depend on facilitator)
2. Practical	As (1) above Practitioners' understanding Transformation of their consciousness	Socratic role, encouraging participation and self-reflection	Cooperation (process consultancy)
3. Emancipatory	As (2) above Participants' emancipation from the dictates of tradition, self-deception, coercion Their critique of bureaucratic systematisation Transformation of the organisation and of the educational system	Process moderator (responsibility shared equally by participants)	Collaboration

Technical action research aims to improve effectiveness of educational or managerial practice. The practitioners are co-opted and depend greatly on the researcher as a facilitator. *Practical* action research, in addition to effectiveness, aims at the practitioners' understanding and professional development. The researcher's role is Socratic and to encourage practical deliberation and self-reflection on the part of the practitioners. Action research is *emancipatory* when it aims not only at technical and practical improvement and the participants' better understanding, along with transformation and change within the existing boundaries and conditions, but also at changing the system itself or those conditions which impede desired improvement in the system/organisation. It also aims at the participants' empowerment and self-confidence about their ability to create 'grounded theory' (Glaser and Strauss 1967), i.e. theory grounded in experience and practice, by solving complex problems in totally new situations, collaboratively as a team or 'community of scholars', everyone being a 'personal scientist' (Kelly 1963), contributing in different ways, but on an equal footing with everyone else. There is no hierarchy, but open and 'symmetrical communication' as described by Grundy and Kemmis (1988: 87):

> Action research is research into practice, by practitioners, for practitioners ... In action research, all actors involved in the research process are equal participants, and must be involved in every stage of the research ... The kind of involvement required is collaborative involvement. It requires a special kind of communication ... which has been described as 'symmetrical communication', ... which allows all participants to be partners of communication on equal terms ... Collaborative participation in theoretical, practical and political discourse is thus a hallmark of action research and the action researcher.

The significance of the contents of this book lies in the fact that the majority of authors, after having written substantive books and/or PhD theses on the subject, distill the essence of their work in their respective chapters. This is of benefit to those readers who are not as yet familiar with the literature on critical action research, as well as to those readers who have read the books/theses and are reminded of the main issues and ideas, but with a new focus: *emancipatory action research*. The book will be of interest to a variety of action researchers in education, higher education, management education, and to consultants in organisational change and development.

Each chapter in this book stands on its own merits and may be read independently from the rest of the chapters. However, the book is designed as a coherent entity structured in three main parts. Part II deals with models, principles and procedures for critical action research (Chapters 2–5). Part III raises some problems and offers various suggested solutions to overcoming these problems and barriers to change (Chapters 6–9). Part III includes chapters which relate critical action research to postmodernism

(Chapters 10–13). The following is a brief outline of each chapter for the reader's preview and possible selection.

Part I: Principles and procedures for critical action research

Richard Winter in Chapter 2 presents a collection of extracts from his book *Learning from Experience: Principles and Practice in Action Research* (Falmer Press, London 1989). He defines action research and provides practical advice on problems and issues, such as finding a focus, selecting action research methods and considering ethical issues, writing up action research, and the question of audience. The author advances six important principles for the action research process: reflexive critique, dialectic critique, collaboration, risking disturbance, creating plural structures, and theory and practice internalised. These principles are further developed implicitly or explicitly in subsequent chapters.

Susan Hall discusses the first of Winter's principles, reflexive critical action research, in Chapter 3. She defines reflexivity in terms of ethnomethodology, critical theory, poststructuralism, and in her own particular interpretation which is based on critical theory. She outlines some purposes for reflexivity in emancipatory action research and obstacles to achieving it. She also gives examples of partial reflexivity (in empirical work and report writing) and of reflexive procedures she has employed in her work. The author argues that the credibility and quality of emancipatory action research can be enhanced through the reflexive research methods she advocates.

Mary Melrose in Chapter 4 presents a tool for reflection and discussion on beliefs and practices in the three areas of curriculum development, evaluation and leadership. She invites the reader to participate and consider focal questions in relation to three main research paradigms — functional, transactional and critical — and to use and critique the tool.

Michael Schratz in Chapter 5 also emphasises the importance of reflection in action research and uses 'memory work' as a collective research method to help participants uncover the hidden aspects of their recollection of past events and actions. The reader again may participate in following the process and procedures of the memory-work method and reading the example of a memory story taken from a research study on personal and institutional racism in everyday settings.

Part II: Problems and solutions

Ortrun Zuber-Skerritt in Chapter 6 summarises her theoretical framework for emancipatory action research and argues that it is an appropriate methodology for education development and organisation development, as well as for the professional development of managers and teachers as action researchers. She then presents an unsuccessful case study with language teachers and discusses the barriers to emancipatory action research and to change. Finally, she demonstrates a step-by-step development of a new model for organisational change and development, adapting and integrating three change models: the classic six-step model of managerial intervention for organisational change (after Beer et al. 1990), Kurt Lewin's organisational change model and the action research model.

In Chapter 7, *Shirley Grundy* focuses on empowering leadership and the importance of 'imagining'. She maintains a critique of 'straight line management' and advocates a strong form of democratic decision-making, drawing on Habermas's ideas of 'communicative competence'. She argues that 'thin-line' (anorexic) management attempts to eliminate uncertainty by taking the shortest route between decision and action, policy and practice, problem and solution. She critiques this kind of management and the personality cult of the 'charismatic leader', and argues for a leadership that privileges debate and contestation, with equal access to opportunities to challenge and information sharing. Grundy concludes that empowering leadership is that which fosters and protects people's confidence and that challenge is interpreted as challenging the idea or evidence, not the person.

Richard Weiskopf and *Stephan Laske* in Chapter 8 also highlight problems associated with emancipatory action research. Based on a concrete project in personnel management, they argue that some of the assumptions of emancipatory action research are rather problematic — for example, the relationship between researchers and the researched, and power being an integral part of the process. The authors propose that action research be seen as an intervention in the political system of the organisation, based on a 'cooperation pact' rather than on consensus.

Graham Webb in Chapter 9 takes a critical view of action research for educational and professional development by tracing the origins of critical theory and its relation to action research. He mounts a critique of action research in terms of emancipation, power, autonomy, democracy, consensus, rationality, solidarity and social justice. He challenges the useful practices of action research and argues for a postmodern stance and practices which are eclectic and pragmatic. Thus this chapter links Part II and Part III.

Part III: Postmodernism and critical action research

Leonie Jennings and *Anne Graham* in Chapter 10 explore the possibilities of dialogue between the modern and postmodern, and between critical action research and the modern/postmodern. They conclude that the use of postmodern theorising and tools may contribute greatly to the process of critical action research and that action researchers may come to realise that their actions might have multiple meanings for their listeners/observers. They point at a particular device which is useful for action researchers in the reflection stage of the process, namely the postmodern tool of discourse analysis.

Jack Sanger discusses a postmodern perspective on staff appraisal in Chapter 11. He challenges the notions of empowerment, emancipation and ownership in action research and introduces the term 'authorship'. Based on a mass action research project on professional appraisal and development with nearly 400 participants, the author describes the cycle of planning a focus, gathering evidence through appropriate research methods, self-evaluation, modification, further planning and reporting the outcomes of the appraisal activities.

Stephen Kemmis in Chapter 12 concisely summarises his previous work on educational action research in the critical tradition. Furthermore, he now challenges the poststructuralists' criticism of critical theory and argues that critical perspectives in education continue to be relevant in the present postmodern era. First he outlines postmodern conditions and postmodernism, then he describes the tasks of education from three perspectives: functionalist, interpretive/poststructuralist and critical. He also presents three perspectives on change as it affects curriculum developers when confronted with rapid, profound and subtle changes. These are technical, practical and emancipatory or critical. Kemmis makes an argument for continuing relevance of critical perspectives in education which engage all action researchers in curriculum as active participants in the process of educational change, and which may still offer them ways in responding to the challenges of the present postmodern era.

Robin McTaggart in Chapter 12 challenges the pessimistic views of social theorists, who see nothing in enlightenment projects but lack of achievement, lack of sustainable ideas and lack of capacity to change things, events or occurrences. He gives examples of success, both new and perennial, as well as of obstacles to emancipatory aspirations in action research. He concludes that, whilst participatory action researchers face considerable practical, theoretical and organisational challenges, new strategic alliances will provide the way forward.

Conclusion

This book is not intended to provide recipes or guidelines on how to conduct action research. Rather, it presents meta-action research, i.e. research and reflection on action research. Referring back to the typology of the technical, practical and emancipatory approach, this book presents a variety of views on emancipatory or critical action research, held by academics who are highly experienced academics in both the practice and theory, action and research of educational, professional, managerial and organisational development and change.

References

Carr, W. and Kemmis, S. (1986) *Becoming Critical: Education, Knowledge and Action Research*. Falmer Press, London.

Glaser, B. and Strauss, A. (1967) *The Discovery of Grounded Theory*. Aldine, Chicago.

Grundy, S. and Kemmis, S. (1982) Educational action research in Australia: the state of the art (an overview). In S. Kemmis and R. McTaggart (eds) *The Action Research Reader*. Deakin University Press, Victoria, 83–97.

Kelly, G. (1963) *A Theory of Personality*. Norton, New York.

Part II

Principles and Procedures for Critical Action Research

Chapter 2

Some Principles and Procedures for the Conduct of Action Research

Richard Winter

Abstract

Action research is seen as a way of investigating professional experience which links practice and the analysis of practice into a single, continuously developing sequence. This chapter explores action research methods, the ethical aspects involved, and the crucial question of how action researchers can claim to be less biased than those they are researching. The author advances six principles which are central to the action research process. They are:

1   *reflexive critique,* which is the process of becoming aware of our own perceptual biases;

2   *dialectic critique,* which is a way of understanding the relationships between the elements that make up various phenomena in our context;

3   *collaboration,* which is intended to mean that everyone's view is taken as a contribution to understanding the situation;

4   *risking disturbance,* which is an understanding of our own taken-for-granted processes and willingness to submit them to critique;

5   *creating plural structures,* which involves developing various accounts and critiques, rather than a single authoritative interpretation;

6   *theory and practice internalised,* which is seeing theory and practice as two interdependent yet complementary phases of the change process.

What is action research?

Action research is used here to refer to ways of investigating professional experience which link practice and the analysis of practice into a single productive and continuously developing sequence, and which link researchers and research participants into a single community of interested colleagues. It is about the nature of the learning process, about the link between practice and reflection, about the process of attempting to have new thoughts about familiar experiences, and about the relationship between particular experiences and general ideas.

Practitioner action research is thus part of the general ideal of professionalism, an *extension* of professional work, not an *addition* to it. The assertion of the viability of practitioner action research is the assertion of a democratic social and political ideal, the ideal of a creative and involved citizenry, as compared to the image of a passive populace, awaiting instruction from above.

Action research provides the necessary link between self-evaluation and professional development. The two important points made are:

1   The process involves reflection, i.e. the development of understanding.

2   The process involves changes in practice, as indicated by the term 'professional development'.

One of the fundamental claims of action research is that, although these two claims can be separated conceptually, they are best achieved together. Hence those affected by planned changes have the primary responsibility for deciding on courses of action which seem likely to lead to improvement, and for evaluating the results of strategies tried out in practice.

Finding a focus

At any one time, we are likely to be aware of countless problems to which our current practices are only questionable and provisional solutions. But, in a way, this range of possibilities creates a difficulty as to which of the many problems to select for the sustained attention which an action research project requires. The simple answer is that we decide what seems 'interesting'. But this merely serves to renew the question: what is the nature of our 'interest'?

Although our own immediate understandings and concerns give us a rich and complex set of resources from which to start, in emphasising these, we are also emphasising such things as emotions, motives, unconscious memories, ambitions, irrational anxieties, overarching beliefs and half-glimpsed insights. This is not an orderly structure: it contains oddities, quirks, ambiguities, contradictions and tensions.

Now it is not possible to rid ourselves of these manifold and contradictory aspects of our interest in a topic. But it is important that we understand them as fully as possible, otherwise, left unrecognised, they will affect decisions as to how we should interpret and evaluate various events brought to light by our investigation. The result may be that we unconsciously make any 'new' insights fit in with our current patterns of perception and so, in the end, the process does not yield much substantial progress.

We need, therefore, to dig down and find the foundations of the interests we bring to a topic. We want to move as quickly as possible beyond what is already familiar, and to find the points where we do have genuine uncertainties, where time spent may more quickly be rewarded with genuine progress.

Action research methods

The first step in the process is the formulation of a general plan. A preliminary checklist of questions would include the following. What is happening already? What is the rationale for this? What am I trying to change? What are the possibilities? Who is affected? With whom must I negotiate? And so on.

Data gathering is the next step and involves gathering information that will tell us more than, as practitioners, we usually know — for example, making systematic records where usually we are content with spontaneous impressions, making permanent records instead of relying upon memory, and collating detailed statements from people whose general opinions we usually take for granted. Data collection methods could include:

1   keeping a detailed diary of subjective impressions, description of meetings attended and lessons learned;

2   collection of documents relating to a situation;

3   observation notes of meetings, perhaps using previously prepared checklists, frequency schedules, etc.;

4   questionnaire surveys, using open or closed formats;

5   interviews with colleagues or others, which allow the many subtle nuances of an unfamiliar perspective to be explored in detail and clarified;

6   tape recording or video recording of interviews or meetings, in order to provide an objective record that can be listened to repeatedly or transcribed, so that patterns of interaction that could go unnoticed are noted and analysed. The distorting effect of recording needs to be taken into account, although this effect can wear off as the people become accustomed to the recording process and see the results for themselves;

7   written descriptions of meetings or interviews which are provided to the other people involved, in order for them to validate or amend such records;

8   triangulation, which is a process by which, when a situation is investigated using a number of different methods, each method partly transcends its limitations, by functioning as a point of comparison with the others. Several different methods may thus seem to converge on one interpretation, thereby giving grounds for preferring it to other interpretations which are suggested by only one method of investigation. Normally at least three methods are needed for comparison, and to allow conclusions to be made, because this avoids simple, polarised oppositions.

Ethical aspects of methods

Action researchers must pay attention to the ethical principles that guide their work. Their actions are deeply embedded in an existing social organisation, and the failure to work within the general procedures of that organisation may not only jeopardise the process of improvement but also existing valuable work.

Proposed principles for action research fieldwork are:

•   Make sure that the relevant persons, committees and authorities have been consulted, and that the principles guiding the work are accepted in advance by all.

•   All participants must be allowed to influence the work, and the wishes of those who do not wish to participate must be respected.

•   The development of the work must remain visible and open to

- The development of the work must remain visible and open to suggestions from others.
- Permission must be obtained before making observations or examining documents produced for other purposes.
- Descriptions of others' work and points of view must be negotiated with those concerned before being published.
- The researcher must accept responsibility for maintaining confidentiality.

The action researcher needs to follow a vigorous intellectual discipline, ensuring that the conclusions of the work are broadly based, balanced and comprehensively grounded in the perceptions of a variety of others. The outcomes of the work are therefore objective and truthful in the sense that the understanding of meaning is directed towards the attainment of possible consensus among actors.

Four practical problems

There are at least four practical problems which arise when seeking to conduct effective action research. They are:

1   How can we formulate a method of work which is sufficiently economical as regards the amount of data gathering and data processing for a practitioner to undertake it alongside a normal workload, over a limited time scale?

2   How can action research techniques be sufficiently specific that they enable a small-scale investigation by a practitioner to lead to genuinely new insights, and avoid being accused of being either too minimal to be valid, or too elaborate to be feasible?

3   How can these methods, given the above, be readily available and accessible to anyone who wishes to practise them, building on the competencies which practitioners already possess?

4   How can these methods contribute a genuine improvement of understanding and skill, beyond prior competence, in return for the time and energy expended — that is, a more rigorous process than that which characterises positivist research?

The six principles discussed below seek to propose an answer to these questions.

Ideology

One of the most important and awkward questions for social research is:

how can researchers claim to be any less biased than those they are researching? One approach is to say that the researcher makes a critique of the ideology of those they are investigating. However, 'ideology' and 'critique' are complex and controversial terms. In particular, how is it possible to be outside ideology, in order to critique it?

All social groups have an ideology, because sharing an ideology is one of the ways by which a group exists. It must follow, therefore, that social researchers cannot be free of ideology, since they also necessarily belong to a social group.

One of the defining characteristics of knowledge in professional areas concerned with understanding people (which includes management) is that it is not a system of accumulated certainties, but is always a matter of interpretation. In order to make decisions, we are forced to choose one interpretation or another. We can therefore easily set up our research so that it confronts one ideology (which we oppose) from the standpoint of another (which we share). In the end, this is somewhat inevitable, but the immediate problem is that we risk not learning anything new; instead, we simply rehearse a familiar debate, armed with fresh evidence from well-worn categories. If research is to be worth the effort, it needs to offer the prospect of going beyond competing ideologies, to offer the possibility of changes in our thinking and practices.

However, ideologies, although powerful influences, are not totally engulfing. One of the reasons for this is that each of us belongs simultaneously to many different groups (family, profession, gender, ethnic group, age group, etc.). Ideology can be like a loose mesh, rather than unseen prison walls, if we make a distinction between two types of thinking:

1   the act of interpreting experience in terms of a set of categories; and
2   the act of questioning the categories in which the interpretations are presented.

It is via critique, as outlined below, that the presence and influence of an ideology can be addressed.

Principle no. 1: reflexive critique

Our working lives are a never-ending sequence of judgments. What is appropriate? What is worthwhile? What is right? We know that all such judgments are open to question, but how can we analyse the process of making judgments without simply imposing a further set of judgments? Positivism claims that, given an effort to define our terms, all statements can be converted into a system of specific labels for phenomena. The thesis of reflexivity, by contrast, argues that most statements rely on complex, interpersonally negotiated processes of interpretation. Individual words only have effective meaning because of the vast array of knowledge of other words and their meanings, brought to bear by speaker and listener, writer and reader, in order to make the process of communication work.

Whereas positivism imagines a single individual using words to label an external reality as he or she perceives it, the thesis of reflexivity suggests that this is a quite misleading assumption: using language is not a private act whereby an individual represents his or her perception. Furthermore, since there is no way of grasping what it is we perceive, except at least partly through language, language structures our consciousness and, at the same time, our relationships with others.

Consequently, the thesis of reflexivity insists upon modest claims: making judgments depends on examples from various personal experiences, not on representative samples of universally agreed categories. These examples will be analysed, but no analysis will be final or complete, because inquiry will take the form of questioning claims, rather than making claims. The result of inquiry will thus take the form of a dialogue between writers and readers concerning possible interpretations of experience, rather than a single interpretation thrust upon a passive reader by a writer expressing certainty. This process of questioning claims provides a dimension of validity. By showing that a statement is grounded in reflexive, interpretative judgments, rather than external facts, I make it possible to review other possible interpretative judgements concerning that statement and thus to envisage modifying it.

An example would be an interviewer giving reasons in favour of one particular applicant for a position:

> There is a continuity in what she wants to do. I mean what she wants to do follows what she has been doing. With others we have interviewed, they have done a bit of this and a bit of that and then something in computing. That worries me, whereas, with this person, there is a kind of progression.

The interviewer claims that 'continuity' is a descriptive fact of this applicant's career. But continuity and discontinuity are unescapably reflexive judgments which necessarily involve the interviewer's own theories and concerns about what is continuity and what is coherence. Also, the interviewer uses 'progression' as an evaluative criterion, but what about if there is a progression, from the point of view of the applicant, in the various roles taken? And what about alternative career patterns such as diversification to avoid narrow specialisation, and diversification to prepare for a future post involving general responsibilities? A highly varied career might as well indicate (positively) an applicant's independence and breadth of concern as (negatively) a lack of focus.

The basic procedure, therefore, is:

1   Accounts such as interview transcripts, written documents, observation accounts are collected and

2   the reflexive basis of these accounts is made explicit, so that

3   claims can be transformed into questions, and a range of alternatives suggested, where previously particular interpretations would have been taken for granted.

Principle no. 2: dialectic critique

Dialectics is a method of analysis which prises apart our familiar ideologies, without suggesting that we have available an infinite choice of alternative interpretations. Dialectics is a general theory of the nature of reality and of the process of understanding reality. We set about understanding the phenomenon being considered by considering:

1   the essential set of relationships which relate the phenomenon to its necessary context; and

2   the essential set of relationships between the elements of which the phenomenon consists.

Any entity we can identify is complex in the sense that it can be analysed into constituent elements — for example, an organisation into its work groups, individuals, tasks, etc. This complexity sets up a contradiction: on the one hand, the phenomenon is a unity, and only the unity can give meaning to the component elements, but on the other hand, this unity can always be broken down into apparently separable parts. To decide what particular separable parts comprise any particular phenomenon is always a matter for empirical investigation and interpretative judgment, and this search characterises the second fundamental in the dialectical approach to the process of understanding, the first being that we can experience reality only by means of our competent participation in the complex structures of language (reflexivity).

The third concept of dialectical thinking is perhaps its single most important contribution. That is, that because of the fundamental contradiction within each phenomenon between its unity and its diversity, we know that the process of change is always latent in it. That the present is different from the past is one of the safest generalisations, hence that the future will be different again from the present is one of the safest assumptions. A dialectical approach urges that any explanation of phenomena that does not explain how and why it has changed and will continue to do so is a poor explanation.

Dialectics proposes that, in order to understand a phenomenon, we treat it as a set of relations between elements which are different and in some sense opposed, yet at the same time interdependent. It is this instability which gives it an inherent tendency to change. Consequently, of the infinite ways in which a phenomenon could be broken down for analysis, the more significant ways are in terms of the internal relationships between constituent elements whose instability creates the likelihood of change.

An example would be that, in investigating the social structure of a work group, a break-up of the group into, say, those who are enthusiastic and those who are cynical may not be significant, if the two groups are socially separate from each other and internally self-reinforcing. Rather, other groupings which include both enthusiastic and cynical members are potentially more interesting, because it is within those aggregations that there is more potential for change of the overall workgroup. The balance of power within the mixed groups will be more helpful in understanding the social psychology of that particular work group.

The dialectical approach asserts that individuals are the product of their social world, but that this social world is structured as a series of contradictions, and is thus in a continuous process of change. Its influence upon individuals is thus both conflicting and varying, and so can never be unambiguous or final. Consequently, individual consciousness is also structured as a set of contradictions, and individuals thus possess a degree of autonomy as to how they will respond to the conflicting and varying pressures from their social context.

Whereas positivist methods suggest that we must observe phenomena exhaustively, and define them precisely, in order to identify specific causes and effects, a dialectical approach suggests we subject observed phenomena to a critique. This entails investigating:

1   the overall context of relations which gives them a unity in spite of their apparent separateness; and

2   the structure of internal contradictions behind their apparent unity, which gives them a tendency to change, in spite of their apparent fixity.

Principle no. 3: collaborative resource

The question here is: what is my role as a researcher? What sorts of relationships does it require me to adopt? Action researchers are part of the situation in question, and it is collaboration among the membership of that situation which creates it and keeps its processes going. Collaboration here is intended to mean that everyone's point of view will be taken as a contribution to resources for understanding the situation, and no one's point of view will be taken as the final understanding of what all the other points of view really mean.

To work collaboratively with these viewpoints does not mean that we begin by trying to synthesise them into a consensus. On the contrary, it is the variety of differences between the viewpoints that makes them into a rich resource. It is by using this resource of differences that our analysis can begin to move onwards from its inevitably personal starting point towards ideas which have been interpersonally negotiated. To treat all viewpoints as a collaborative resource is thus to suspend the conventional status hierarchy which gives some members' viewpoints greater credibility than others.

The interpretative categories we start with are to be treated as data alongside the ideas that we collect. Also, our analysis will not only seek to assemble resources from the differences between viewpoints, but also from the conflicts and contradictions within viewpoints, including our own. The process is one of simultaneously giving weight to the understandings contributed by all members, and at the same time, a process of deconstructing the various contributions so that we can use them as resources for new categories and interpretations. Focusing on the contradictory elements within and between viewpoints enables us to give full recognition to the ideas we may otherwise dismiss as irrelevant, because they don't fit in to our conceptual framework.

There is a link between the collaborative process of mutual challenge between viewpoints and modest claims to objectivity. Objectivity here seems to have four senses:

1   The collaborative process acts as a challenge to, and check upon, one's personal starting point and assumptions, i.e. one's subjectivity.

2   The process involves examining relationships between the accounts of the various necessary members of a situation — those who need to be considered, given the structure of the situation.

3   One outcome of the process is a series of analyses which do not add up to a general law, but which are not just opinions, and which could be illuminating for a range of situations whose structure is similar to the one from which the analyses were derived.

4   The outcome is a practical proposal, the nature of which will (in part at least) be seen when it is put into practice and its conse-quences

noted. It is not necessarily the only or the best strategy, but it is a feasible strategy.

Principle no. 4: risk

The research process can be seen as a threat to all the taken-for-granted processes that we and our colleagues use to function and cope with in our difficult circumstances. Initiators of research must put themselves at risk through the process of investigation. Furthermore, the process is not merely one of exposure to possible refutation, but of exploring possibilities for transformation. What may be transformed, and is therefore at risk, are:

1   researchers' provisional interpretations of the situation, which become mere resources alongside those of other members;

2   researchers' decisions as to the question at issue, and what is and is not relevant; and

3   researchers' anticipations of the sequence of events through which the fieldwork will pass.

Through involvement in the action research process, we not only submit others' accounts to critique, but our own also. We note not only the contradiction in others' viewpoints, but also the contradictions and possibilities for change in our own viewpoints. We are not consultants, advising others how to change, nor unchanging catalysts of others' development. We are part of the situation undergoing change. We have no theoretical basis for exempting ourselves from the processes we set in motion. On the contrary, we want to change, because we want to learn. The only viewpoints we want to support are those which have newly emerged in the course of our fieldwork; those we started out with, we wish to transcend.

Principle no. 5: plural structure

Research reports conventionally summarise and unify. They are linear, presenting a chronology of events or a sequence of cause and effect. They are presented in the single voice of the author, who organises evidence to support his or her conclusions, so that the report will seem authoritative and convincing to others.

But our dialectical, reflexive, questioning, collaborative form of inquiry will create a plural structure, consisting of various accounts and various critiques of those accounts and ending, not with conclusions intended to be convincing, but with questions and possibilities intended to be relevant in various ways for different readers. We therefore need to consider the nature of a plural text to accommodate the plural structure of the fieldwork.

Although the report will seem, at one level, to be a collection of fragments, there will have to be a principle by which some matters are included and others excluded. A plural text needs a structural principle which exists separate from the author's argument, since the author's argument will be only one of various voices in the text. One convenient principle is that of 'the necessary range of data'. A phenomenon to be reported on will have a certain number of elements which must all be included, if the phenomenon itself is to be comprehensible as such.

Data and interpretation will be related as follows. The text will include a plurality of accounts, and also a commentary on each account. To be a reflexive critique, however, the commentaries must address their own contradictions, their own reflexive status. They will therefore contain questions, as well as interpretative statements. The text must give readers the resources with which to disagree.

Readers should be seen as further collaborators in the process, particularly as the first circle of readers must be members of the situation from which the report derives. The report is most appropriately seen as a discussion document through which the dialectic of theory and practice can move back from the moment of theory (the report) to the moment of practice (what is to be done with the report). Our report will suggest to our collaborators a plurality of possible action strategies, and the choice among these possibilities will be a collaborative choice which we, as report writers, have no wish or need to pre-empt by presenting one conclusion or one recommendation.

The suggestion that the primary audience for an action research report comprises the members of the situation from which it was derived may trigger the fear that action research does not lead to the discovery of truths which are of a broader relevance than to the situation from whence they came. However, what enables one specific situation to be relevant to many other situations is a similarity of structure. If our research report has managed to go beyond descriptive detail, and grasped the structure of the situation, there is every chance that the report will be of value to a wider audience than just our immediate colleagues.

Principle no. 6: theory, practice, transformation

The issue here concerns the crucial relationship between theory and practice, between research and action. How can we ensure that the 'findings' can be 'implemented'?

Theory and practice are not two distinct entities, but two different and yet interdependent and complementary phases of the change process. Thus the action researcher is engaged in a set of practical activities.

Conversely, the actors in the situation carry out their activities in the light of a massive corpus of theoretical understanding. Theory and practice are not distinct entities, confronting each other across an unbridgeable gulf: each contains elements of the other.

So how shall we characterise a formal process which links theory and practice within a project? Although action is always reflexive, its reflective basis is always open to question. So the role of theoretical reflection with respect to practical action is not to introduce new and different concepts from outside, nor to present authoritative conclusions. Instead, the purpose of reflection is to question the reflective bases upon which the practical actions have been carried out, to offer a reflexive and dialectical critique whose effect is to recall to mind those possibilities that practice has chosen on this occasion to ignore.

In the above phase, theory questions practice. But this is followed by a contrary movement in which practice questions theory. The theoretical critique is itself open to question: which of these newly recalled possibilities is practically feasible — which of these insights is useable?

Theory and practice need each other, and thus comprise mutually indispensable phases of a unified change process. Together they present the strongest case for practitioner action research as an activity which represents both a powerful, vigorous and worthwhile form of practical professionalism and a powerful, vigorous and valid form of social inquiry.

Writing up action research

The academic norm for research reports — the sequence of literature review, methodology, findings and conclusions — is only one possible format and way for structuring and transforming experience to bring out its significance. We should remember that the conventions and norms as to how writing should be structured have been, and are, continually changing. For example, as late as the seventeenth and eighteenth centuries, both philosophical and scientific writings were often presented in verse or in Latin, or both.

In general, the history of writing shows a continuing process of experimentation, in an attempt to do justice to the always frustrating relationship between the linear sequence of words on a page, the infinite complexities of experience, and the desire to elucidate a wider significance from particular events. Practitioners writing reports on their action research projects should not be overawed by the portentous format and rhetoric of academic journal articles. Instead we should accept and welcome the point that, since our writing emerges from a different set of relationships (collaborative and action-oriented, rather than authoritative and observation-oriented), the format of our writing should also be different.

Although we have as yet no clear-cut set of conventions, some possible starting points are already indicated. Firstly, in view of the link between the social relationships of the research process and appropriate ways of writing, the narrative format can be seen as expressing and recognising the basis of action research — the sequence of practice and reflection. Secondly, the plural text advocated expresses both the collaborative relationships of the research process and the open-endedness of its outcomes. Conversely, certain stylistic features of traditional academic writing could be seen as inappropriate for action research reports. In particular, these are aspects of style, tone and vocabulary which seem to express the expert role, by suggesting a withdrawal from personal involvement and a sustained abstraction from concrete detail.

What sort of style and structure can be both personal and detailed, and yet at the same time, offer general significance? There is an instructive analogy offered by feminist writers who have chosen innovative formats such as the blending of autobiographical reminiscences with interspersed passages of social history, sociology and psychoanalysis, or the weaving of varied themes and general reflections within accounts of everyday life.

Conclusion

The answer to the question 'who are action research reports written for?' is that there are three audiences — each of equal importance.

One audience comprises those colleagues with whom we have collaborated in carrying out the work reported, and with whom the practical continuations need to be negotiated. Action research reports are always situated within a specific professional context, and so include a discussion paper element intended to create a basis for collegiate decisions on changes in that professional practice.

It is important to give equal importance to the second audience. These are interested colleagues in other institutions, or in other areas of the same institution, for whom the underlying structure of the work presented may be similar to situations in which they work. The report is thus intended to help the process of learning among members of a profession, by dealing with critical issues relevant to the process of improving practice.

But the third, and perhaps most important audience, is ourselves. The process of writing involves clarifying and exploring ideas and interpretations. It begins when we start to collect data and to jot down notes on the possible significance of certain incidents. The process of exploration and clarification continues when we first begin to review the whole collection of notes and data, prior to writing. Ideas spring to mind

— questions, links, interpretations — and these develop and ramify as we write the report itself. So writing up a report is an act of learning and, in this sense, we write for ourselves so that, when we read what we have written, we find out what, in the end, we have learned.

Reference

Winter, R. (1989) *Learning from Experience: Principles and Practice in Action Research*, Falmer Press, London.

Note

This chapter is a collection of extracts from Richard Winter's book, *Learning From Experience — Principles and Practice in Action Research,* published by Falmer Press in 1989. This selection was very kindly made by Professor Cliff Bunning, IMC, Australia, whose work in this respect the author gratefully acknowledges.

Chapter 3

Reflexivity in Emancipatory Action Research: Illustrating the Researcher's Constitutiveness

Susan Hall

Abstract

This chapter is an argument and a method for researching reflexively within emancipatory action research and for conducting research about emancipatory action research. It is based on the assumption that researchers in an emancipatory action research context are inevitably constitutive of the data they collect and of the way in which it is interpreted and analysed. Reflexive research practice is advocated in response to the author's criticism that often emancipatory action researchers, like many other researchers, fail to sufficiently display their interpretive work. That is, they fail to show their human influence in the process of selecting, interpreting, analysing and reporting data. This situation raises an issue of credibility which also encompasses political and ethical issues.

These three named issues are addressed by way of an interpretation of reflexivity, as used here; an examination of reasons for and obstacles to engaging in reflexive research practice; and illustrations of reflexivity using examples from the literature as well as the author's applications of it.

Finally, the case is made that the credibility and quality of emancipatory action research, and of research about it, can be enhanced through the reflexive research methods advocated.

Previously (Hall 1990), I made the bold assertion that all educational researchers have ethical and political obligations to be reflexive in their research methods. [1] I now assert that reflexivity is integral to emancipatory action research and is a part which should be made more obvious. It is integral because it epitomises a basic epistemological position underpinning emancipatory action research. This position rests on the following assumptions about knowledge construction that:

1   evidence is derived from authentic data (which resonates the life experience of the researched and researcher);

2   relations between researcher and research participants proceed in a democratic manner; and

3   the researcher's theory-laden view is not given privilege over the participants' views. [2]

The central idea of this chapter is that more reflexive research practice would make the ethics of emancipatory action research more visible, as well as making it more politically effective and credible. Embedded within this *raison d'etre* for reflexivity lies my interpretation of the term which is explained below.

Reflexivity

It should be noted at the outset that the concept of reflexivity is by no means a conclusive one within any of the hermeneutic traditions. It embodies a complex set of problems associated with the researcher's position in relation to the status of knowledge and truth and these problems are constructed differently within each tradition.

•   *Ethnomethodology* aims to elucidate the methods by which cultural groups create and sustain their common sense. The notion of reflexivity used in this tradition has to do with the way in which members recognise, reinforce and create their commonsense knowledge in everyday interactions. It has little to do with reflexivity as used in this paper.

•   *Critical theory* aims to emancipate through engaging participants in self-conscious critique. The focus here is on feedback from the participants in the setting about both the data and treatment of it as well as the researcher's role — as in action research. While there is an emphasis on epistemology and the researcher's personal influence, the criticism can be made that these often appear to be tacked on to the process in reports.

- *Poststructuralism* aims to disrupt current ways of viewing and constructing knowledge in order to make way for and build towards a knowledge viewed as 'contested, temporal and emergent' (Clifford and Marcus in Lather, 1988: 11). The focus here is on discourse — the productivity of language in the process of knowledge construction. With this comes a move away from epistemology and paradigm definition which are seen as restrictive forces upon the construction of knowledge.

  That none of these above traditions is a positivistic one in no way implies that the positivistic approaches are exempt. It simply implies that reflexivity has not been the subject of serious investigation in this field. While many would consider it to be the antithesis of positivism, I suggest that it would provide an enhancing adjunct to positivistic methods of warranting claims for evidence.

As I explore the concept of reflexivity I am working within a broad field of educational research which draws from hermeneutics. My interpretation is more readily matched with that of critical theory than with other traditions but it also incorporates some of the aspects of the poststructuralists' interpretation. More is said about this below (see p. 38) but here it will suffice to say that reflexivity, as I use it, is a deliberate attempt to:

1   monitor and reflect on one's doing of the research — the methods and the researcher's influence on the setting — and act responsively on these methods as the study proceeds; and

2   account for researcher constitutiveness. This process begins with being self-conscious (to the extent that this is possible) about how one's doing of the research as well what one brings to it (previous experience, knowledge, values, beliefs and *a priori* concepts) shapes the way the data are interpreted and treated. An account of researcher constitutiveness is completed when this awareness is incorporated in the research report.

In the following I first define my particular interpretation of 'reflexivity' and locate it within a broader field of educational research which draws from anthropology and naturalistic sociology. Next I outline some purposes for reflexivity in emancipatory action research and go on to cite some of the obstacles to achieving it. From here I advocate some procedures for the kind of reflexivity espoused. Finally, I argue that the credibility and quality of emancipatory action research, and of research about it, can be enhanced through the reflexive research methods advocated.

To elaborate on the definition of reflexivity given above, I borrow from Ruby's (1977) distinction between reflexivity and other terms which are sometimes confused with reflexivity: autobiography, self-reference, self-consciousness. Ruby used these terms to explore the concept of reflexivity in ethnographic film-making. According to Ruby, autobio-graphy requires that the author becomes self-aware, but it does not require that s/he makes that awareness public when presenting the research product. That is, the audience is not usually made aware that there has been a process of selection going on between the acts of self-reflection and the preparation of the material for the final product. The concept of reflexivity incorporates autobiography for, as Ruby (1977: 4) puts it:

> To be reflexive [in reporting] is to be not only self-aware, but to be sufficiently self-aware to know what aspects of self are necessary to reveal so that an audience is able to understand both the process employed and the resultant product and to know that the revelation itself is purposive, intentional and not merely narcissistic or accidentally revealing.

On the other hand, self-reference, according to Ruby, is the use of personal experience as the basis of the product. While this method is rarely used in educational research, it bears mentioning for its relationship to reflexivity. Self-reference is most evident in art forms where the artist uses the self as symbolic of some sort of collective and yet it is evident in many art forms — some would say in all art — in that an artist creates from his/her personal base. However, this form of self-inclusion does not represent reflexivity because it does not attempt to show how the self is constitutive of the process and product.[3] Finally, self-consciousness simply involves being reflective (thinking about) and does not necessarily involve applying those reflections to what is done in the empirical phase or making it known to the audience through the research report. For Ruby, the final point of clarity on reflexivity is:

> Only if a producer decides to make his [or her] awareness of self a public matter and conveys that knowledge to his audience is it possible to regard the product as reflexive. (Ruby 1977: 4)

By taking Ruby's conditions and then adding the necessity for the researcher to use his/her growing self-awareness to gauge and adjust the way in which he or she works during the empirical phase, I have constructed the frame with which I view reflexivity. Within this frame to be reflexive in research is to recognise and work with the notion that the researcher is constitutive of both the data and the final research product. This involves acting reflexively during the empirical and analytical phases of research as well as reporting reflexively in the final product.

This construction of reflexivity incorporates a combination of ways in which reflexivity has been interpreted and applied. However, I concede that it is an ideal rather than a description of practice, for it rarely occurs in its entirety but more often in degrees or partial application which I refer to as examples of partial reflexivity.

Partial reflexivity

Partial reflexivity occurs when the researcher is reflexive about either the empirical or reporting phase but not in both. It is not clear as to whether Ruby (1977: 4) sees reflexivity as applying to both phases, but the following statement suggests that he emphasises reporting over the empirical phase:

> To be reflexive is to structure a product in such a way that the audience assumes that the producer, the process of making, and the product are a coherent whole. Not only is an audience made aware of those relationships but they are made to realise the necessity of that knowledge.

By emphasising reflexivity in the product (reporting), this statement could be taken as an example of partial reflexivity. In contrast to this, much of the partial reflexivity done in the critical theory framework concentrates on reflexivity in empirical work. One such project was the evaluation of the Victorian Transition Education program, conducted by the Deakin Institute of Programme Evaluation at Deakin University, Geelong, Victoria, Australia, which Kemmis (1983: 237) describes as follows:

> the Deakin Institute decided to appoint critical friends for the project who could take a continuing supportive, critical role in relation to the project, scrutinise its operation, help to identify problems with the conduct or reports of the study as they emerged, and check that it operated in accordance with its principles of procedure.

The project described is an example of reflexive reporting in that the report includes a major section on reflecting on the method. Here the exposure to the origins of the project, along with the work of the project team and clients, allows the reader to gain some idea of how in Ruby's terms, 'the producers, the process of making and the product form a coherent whole'. However, by offering the account of the method after it was used, rather than as it was used, the study carries the inherent problems of accounting for process in retrospect. That is, summative accounts of process do not engage the reader in what Silverman (1975: 1) terms *thinking together* with the author to see how the author arrived at his/her conclusions, but rather they give the reader insights to the research process as the author sees it after the event. And after the event is after the interpretative work has been done.

For an example of a more comprehensive approach to reflexive research, I turn to the early work carried out by the anthropologist Carlos Castenada during the 1960s. Castenada's controversial work with the Yaqui Indians in Mexico involved him in undertaking an apprenticeship with the shaman Don Juan. (While there has been much debate as to whether Castenada's work is an authentic or a fictionalised account, that matter is not relevant to the concerns of this chapter. What is relevant here is the contribution that Castenada has made to the construction of knowledge in the social sciences.) David Silverman, in his book *Reading Castenada* (1975), illustrates how Castenada's deliberation and action upon his method in the field, his registering of his contribution to the setting and to the interpretative and analytical work are all incorporated in his style of reporting. The following examples illustrate his deliberation on method and his registering of his personal influence during field work.

Example 1

Castenada comments on his reactions to Don Juan's instructions that he find his 'spot' on the floor where he could sit without fatigue.

> What he had posed as a problem to be solved was certainly a riddle. I had no idea how to begin or even what he had in mind. Several times I asked for a clue, or at least a hint, as to how to proceed in locating a point where I felt happy and strong. I insisted and argued that I had no idea what he really meant because I couldn't conceive the problem. (Castenada 1968: 31 in Silverman 1975: 35)

Here he displays the inadequacy of his Westernised methods of making meaning of the task. He also shows that, by displaying these methods (in asking for clues and insisting on help), he is affirming his position as an outsider.

Example 2

And later, after taking peyote, Castenada comments on his questions to Don Juan about Mescalito, the protector and teacher whom one is supposed to encounter through peyote:

> He seemed to be very annoyed by my questioning. I told him I had to ask all these questions because I wanted to find out all I could.

"Don't ask me!" He smiled maliciously. "Ask him. The next time you see him, ask him everything you want to know."

"Then Mescalito is like a person you can talk ..."

He did not let me finish. He turned away, picked up the canteen, stepped down from the ledge, and disappeared around the rock. (Castenada 1968: 93 in Silverman 1975: 36)

Here we are made privy to a lot about Castenada's influence on his research subject. We get to know of his relationship with Don Juan. For Castenada's part, we see his frustration and his feelings of helplessness and of being mistreated. For Don Juan's part, we see his impatience and annoyance at Castenada's persistence with asking questions.

Later again within the text, we find examples of his deliberation upon classification and analysis and his acknowledgement of his constitutiveness.

Example 3

As the data I had collected were quite voluminous, and included much miscellaneous information, I began by trying to establish a classification system. I divided the data into areas of related concepts and procedures and arranged the areas hierarchically according to subjective importance — that is, in terms of the impact that each of them had on me. (Castenada 1968: 19 in Silverman 1975: 87)

Example 4

Reflecting upon the phenomena I had experienced, I realized that my attempt at classification had produced nothing more than an inventory of categories; any attempt to refine my scheme would therefore yield a more complex inventory. That was not what I wanted. (Castenada 1968: 19 in Silverman 1975: 87)

Example 5

In spite of all the effort I have put forth to render these concepts as faithfully as possible, their meaning has been deflected by my own attempts to classify them. (Castenada 1968: 198 in Silverman 1975: 91)

These three statements (examples 3, 4 and 5) show his reflections on his attempts to analyse. They engage us in his struggle to make sense of

Don Juan's teachings, which, in fact, results in him realising that 'his own sense' is not what he is looking for — or at least, as a social scientist, not what he set out to find. In revealing this, Castenada has illuminated the inherent tendency of social scientists to impose meaning. This imposition is not usually so obvious in educational research because researchers are rarely in a setting which is so totally foreign to them as Castenada's was to him.

Furthermore, Castenada's work is distinct from most educational research in that he has *displayed* his imposition of his own views. As Silverman (1975: 1) says of Castenada's work, one of its most significant features is its facility to engage the reader in the writer's meaning-making process. His work is reflexive.

Degrees of reflexivity in emancipatory action research

If we think of Castenada's work as reflexivity and the other two examples (Ruby's and Kemmis's) as partial reflexivity, then it could be argued that partial reflexivity which concentrates on the doing of empirical work is more appropriate for educational research today. It can be seen to be appropriate because it provides some account of the research process while relieving the reader of having to relive the problematic moments of data collection and treatment. However, I see this situation as symptomatic of a prevailing problem in educational research: what is acceptable (and indeed, required by) research sponsors typically mitigates against researchers revealing their ownership of the knowledge which is constructed and of their authorship in the reporting process. And research practices which conceal ownership and authorship will ultimately jeopardise the achievements of emancipatory action research because they undermine the fundamental component of authenticity.

I turn now to consider the purposes of reflexivity which, when considering the scarcity of actual examples, might be appropriately termed the need for reflexivity.

The need for reflexivity

According to Ruby (1977: 5), the need for reflexivity has arisen in conjunction with a cultural concern with sources of authority which is manifested 'in the growing popular realisation that the world — things, events and people, as well as news, television books and stories — is not what it appears to be'. If one is to give credence to recent research conducted by Dr Kay Bussey at Macquarie University, New South Wales, Australia, this public cynicism is warranted by the propensity of our population to tell lies. No doubt such a statement is potentially disturbing in itself, but what is more disturbing is the similarity between her criteria for lying and the practice we engage in when presenting research findings in a non-reflexive manner.

Bassey says: 'To be a successful liar, you have to convince people that reality is not as it appears to them.' (*The Australian*, 18 October 1989: 19) While I do not accept this as the only definition of lying (and neither do I believe it was intended to be), I do see it as an apt description of non-reflexive research. The process of non-reflexive research is amenable to 'lying' because, in attempting to convince the audience to accept a new construction, we manipulate the evidence to fit with our preferred way of viewing the world and usually fail to acknowledge that this has happened. Reflexivity can provide an internal audit to this process in that it requires us to 'own up' to what we know of our constitutiveness in the knowledge construction process. In writing reflexively, we engage the reader in our meaning-making process, we invite him/her to do what Silverman (1975: 1) calls *thinking together* with us and also offer the evidence and the room for independent conclusions. It goes further than the usual requirements of explaining the methodology and the schema for theorising: it requires the researcher to expose his/her own thought processes. The need, I suggest, is not to avoid 'telling lies', but to provide the opportunity for readers to comprehend the researcher's personal involvement in the knowledge construction process and then decide for themselves.

I contend that, in making this self-disclosure, the researcher faces up to his/her obligations and reveals the status and the ownership of the knowledge. To elaborate, I consider these items in turn. On the matter of obligations I concur with the view that anyone who manipulates a symbolic system has 'the ethical, political, aesthetic and scientific obligations to be reflexive about their work' (Giddens 1976: 8 in Ruby 1977). Given the inevitability that the researcher will always be, in some way, constitutive of the data, it is reasonable to assume that the researcher has ethical and scientific obligations to display (to the best of his or her ability) how this is so. In other words, the researcher should show the particular personal resources as well as the circumstantial resources s/he has used in interpreting the data in the particular way that s/he has. In this sense, reflexivity answers an ethical and scientific need for researchers to stand and be counted about their role in the construction of knowledge. A political obligation becomes obvious when research is used in policy-making. Despite the fact that reflexive reporting is rarely welcomed by task-oriented sponsors, the absence of reflexivity can lead to findings being dismissed; when findings are questioned by sponsors, the interpretation of data also comes under question and too many of the questions about the interpretations are left unanswered.

In regard to the status of the knowledge, reflexive writing can allow the researcher to show how knowledge is socially mediated. For example, by showing relationships between researcher and the researched, he or she can show that knowledge is constructed by people in a dynamic context rather than implying that it is a static entity which is 'out there waiting to be captured'.

On the matter of ownership, reflexivity can serve to offset the dominant or privileged position which a researcher assumes in order to theorise. A 'privileged position' is that position which all researchers take when theorising as outsiders to a situation. We use our own theory-laden view — that is, we use our knowledge of the relevant literature and our reflections upon the subject to assume that we are somehow more qualified to account for what is happening than those who are participating in the situation. While we work hard to produce a warranted account, we must nonetheless admit that it is distorted by our own position. As Lather (1988: 9) has pointed out, 'Self-reflexivity becomes essential in understanding how empirical work is selective, partial, positioned.'[4]

Obstacles to reflexivity in educational research

In view of the fact that reflexivity is not a highly developed practice in emancipatory educational research, any move to rectify the situation should benefit from a consideration of the major obstacles. I argue below that prevailing attitudes to social science within our society, such as the pervading mechanistic and scientistic world view, manifest in a demand for the kind of research reports which exclude reflexivity.

Firstly, the current mechanistic world view denies the connection between the researched and the researcher (Capra 1983: 23) and this connection is central to reflexivity. The mechanistic world view which Capra refers to implies that the researcher is a mechanistic being in which the mind can operate independently from previous experiences, personality, values and beliefs. Furthermore, it implies that the various constituents of a research project — researcher, topic and subject/s — are separate and isolated components.

In light of this mechanistic world view, it is not surprising that the qualities of natural science have been superimposed upon social science. Scientism has both contributed to and been sustained by this world view. Consequently, social science has inherited the aspirations for objectivity which should more rightfully apply to natural science. Some of these are: reification — treatment of people and events as objects; researchers attempting to adopt a neutral, disinterested position; and researchers avoiding admission that they are constitutive of their data. These aspirations for objectivity are pursued on the grounds that to be subjective by revealing the self in research is self-indulgent or, at worst, even narcissistic.

These two conditions, the mechanistic world view and the superimposing of natural science on social research, have certainly been at the centre of the ongoing paradigm debate within social science circles. And, subtly, their influence is one which contributes to the situation where research sponsors do not look for reflexive research practice. In fact, despite Ruby's claim about there being a cultural trend towards critique, research sponsors do not always embrace research with an attitude of inquiry but, rather, tend to use it primarily as a means of legitimating or extending pre-formulated ideas. They want their reports to be brief and conclusive so that dispute about authority will be minimised. Furthermore, while research report writers continue to aspire to 'objectivity', sponsors can continue to dismiss them by finding that this aspiration has not been achieved — an inevitable outcome of researchers being human. With these points in mind, it is understandable that 'objective', non-reflexive reports best suit the requirements of sponsors.

These obstacles suggest that nothing short of a radical turnaround in the way knowledge is viewed and taught in the field of education would bring about a demand for reflexive reporting. Despite this situation, I maintain that progress can be made in small measures and we should follow the path of other social disciplines, such as film making, in exploring more and better ways of making emancipatory action research more reflexive.

I have already mentioned that those educationalists who do engage in reflexive research practice draw from one or more of a variety of research traditions, and that my own approach is more consistent with critical theory than with the other previously mentioned traditions. However, I want to acknowledge my empathy with many of the poststructuralist ideals which I have attempted to incorporate in my procedures as outlined below.

Some procedures for reflexivity in emancipatory action research

As can be noted from my earlier reference to Castenada's work, procedures for reflexivity are necessarily linked to the particular purpose and nature of each study. They cannot be universally prescribed. The following procedures are designed for a piece of critical ethnographic educational research which I conducted for my PhD dissertation. In the study, I (as researcher) monitored a teacher's (Ellen's) collaborative process of formatively evaluating an aspect of her own teaching. In doing this, I was participating in the teacher's classroom, in some of her more general school activities and in some of her personal and professional life outside of the school to try to gain an holistic understanding of her work. Ethnographic descriptions of this participatory experience were accumulated and problematised in an ongoing production of grounded theory.

. The task of designing reflexive practices to suit the purposes and nature of this study involved reconciling ideals with what was pragmatic. The tasks which I took on were those of:

1   systematically reflecting on the research method and modifying my practice according to the purpose and context through the empirical phase;

2   writing myself into the story of the case study and noting my perceptions of the way in which my values and ideological and epistemological positions influenced the selection, interpretation and analysis of data. This is a practice supported by both critical theorists and poststructuralists;

3   documenting (with Ellen) the growing relationships between myself (researcher) and Ellen (the researched) — a poststructuralist notion; and

4   recognising and attempting to offset the 'privileged position' (see Lather, below) in my style of theorising.

I did not, however, address the pillar of poststructuralism: the productivity of the researcher's language in the knowledge construction process — which would have enhanced the depth of my reflexivity.

Five specific reflexive procedures were used in the study. They are described, and in some cases illustrated, in the excerpts below.

The reflexive procedures employed

1   In the report, I declared my experiences and knowledge base which I brought to bear on the data collection, interpretation and analysis:

   a   democratic ideological/epistemological leanings;

   b   relevant personal and professional background experiences (these are also registered within the case study text where they influence particular hypotheses);

   c   lessons gained from experience at co-researching with the participants of settings.

2   I adopted a style of hypothesising which interrupts and problematises the text as well as incorporates the information about my experiences

and knowledge base. This information was recorded (in interrupted text) by way of displaying the theorising process within the case study.

Procedures 1 and 2 can be observed in the following excerpt. In the following excerpt from the case study (Hall 1994, vol. 2: 53–54), regular print depicts the main text and bold print depicts my hypothesising as interrupted text.

I accepted her offer of a seat this time and began drawing up a classroom seating plan and inserting the names of any children whom I could identify with a particular seat. I would describe the room as traditional in appearance with the neatly formed rows of desks angling in to face the blackboard in the centre of the front of the room. The student teacher, I assumed, was adopting Ellen's usual position, in front of the blackboard and facing the students. This seating structure and attentive listening contributed to my impression that the classroom was run on a fairly teacher-directed line. I also wandered around the room looking at work displayed on various pin-up boards. I thought the pieces of written work were varied in topic and structure (even when they seemed to be based on a class activity or exercise) and that they were also indicative that the children were practised at expressing themselves individually. It struck me as being an unusual phenomenon in a classroom where interactions are mainly directed to and through the teacher.

Although by appearances, this classroom fits the description of a cohesive group (Classroom Development Project 1979) and, therefore, of one which curbs freedom of expression, the samples of work suggest that the students are practised at expressing themselves individually. This anomaly provides evidence for further investigation.

I was curious to explore this anomaly. [To this Ellen wrote: 'a lot depends on the subject/activity. Also, some of this work results from Sandra's lessons. We probably need to talk more about this; it's a bit complicated. (addendum) School, parental expectations come into this.' Ellen's overall comment at the end of this piece provided some elaboration: 'Yes, the pattern of interaction is still, at this stage, controlled by me, but this is part of the overall (long range) plan of having the children become more self-directing and, ultimately, responsible for their own advancement. I want them not to need me. We also have, surprisingly as it may seem, a lot of fun.' When I took this up with Ellen, she explained her long-range plan as having the students develop self-responsibility from a secure and caring classroom environment. Within this plan, a teacher-directed approach was used to establish the secure environment.]

I sensed from Ellen's written responses that my comment could have been taken as judgmental. For this purpose alone, the procedure of talking to Ellen about her written comments gave me a chance to check out such hunches and attempt to resolve any problems which had occurred. In this case, while Ellen did not respond to my suggestion that my comments sounded judgemental, she seemed glad of the opportunity to ensure that I understood her long-range plan for classroom control. Furthermore, my comment prompted Ellen to explicate her plan for classroom control.

It is likely that reflecting on my feedback also provided data which Ellen will use in her own evaluation study.

These comments suggest that Ellen does not attribute most of the classroom ethos to her influence but rather she attributes some of it to the fact that Sandra takes the class in the afternoons. She also recognises that parental expectations guide her own contribution to classroom ethos.

3   I engaged in regular feedback sessions with Ellen on both the data collected and on my influence on the settings in order to construct shared meaning. The following excerpt from the study elaborates this (Hall 1994, vol. 1: 80–84).

The feedback sessions

Turning a feedback session into a reflexive research procedure is, from my perspective, largely dependent on attitude and intention. In this case my attitude and intention were to look for ways in which my actions brought reactions and to alter those actions if and as I deemed necessary for the smooth running of the study. To achieve this in the feedback sessions, I thought it was absolutely necessary that I did not control the talk. The way in which I carried out this intention has been described elsewhere (Noddings 1984 in Belenky et al. 1986, p.116):

> 'I let the object act upon me, seize me, direct my fleeting thoughts … My decision to do this is mine, it requires an effort in preparation, but it also requires a letting go of my attempts to control. This sort of passivity … is not a mindless, vegetable-like passivity. It is a controlled state that abstains from controlling the situation.' (Noddings 1984, in Belenky et al. 1986: 116)

In retrospect, I propose that it is this attitude of intention more than any particular strategy that makes the feedback sessions a part of my reflexive process.

Different feedback procedures were used for each phase of the study. In Phase 1, feedback to Ellen was given at the end of the phase and took the form of my written ethnographic descriptions of the observation visits between March and June. This feedback also included a category of hypotheses headed 'The Researcher's Part in the Setting'. Ellen read and responded to these in writing. From these responses, I not only gained more data and more insights with which to interpret existing data, but I also gained some insights into the way in which Ellen viewed my work. For example, at one point in the responses, Ellen expressed disagreement with my interpretation of her approach to classroom control. This not only provided me with more data (another view) but it also alerted me to the possibility that my interpretation may have offended Ellen. I considered this and decided to follow it up with Ellen by asking for clarification and elaboration on what she had written (see Case Study 1987: 53–54). The consequences of following this up were that Ellen explicated her short and long term plans for classroom control, I began to see Ellen's classroom behaviour in a new light, and she appeared to feel more comfortable in knowing that I was prepared to see the matter through her eyes.

At another point, Ellen's response suggested that one of my written insights had caused her to question the scope of her own data collection and reflection, specifically, whether or not to include her sustained attention to students' emotional well-being as part of her data. This time Ellen pursued the matter with me. She had not previously thought of the idea and wanted to discuss it as a possibility. Although Ellen did not change her foci for data collection at this point, I could see that my mentioning this in the description had caused her to reflect on and further articulate her evaluation design and I, in turn, took this as my cue to begin monitoring any changes in Ellen's topics of data collection. In this way, using the feedback enabled me to change my hypotheses about what was going on and to develop new foci as well as to gauge and adjust my participation in the setting. In other words, it became a reflexive procedure within the empirical work of the study.

During the second phase of the study, wherein I aimed to intervene in Ellen's explication of working knowledge, feedback was given weekly and in two different forms. Ellen read and responded to my rough observation notes immediately after each lesson and then, usually the week afterwards, she would read and respond to my full ethnographic description of the lesson along with my hypotheses which were sorted into categories and then into groups of categories: Ellen's evaluation, the method, the researcher's part in the setting, and the history of interactions between the researcher and the participants. Particular emphasis was placed on three procedures during feedback sessions: (i) negotiating the rough observation notes; (ii) constructing the draft ethnographic descriptions; and (iii) negotiating the ethnographic descriptions. Each of these activities is described below.

Negotiating the rough notes

These sessions began with oral feedback based on the rough observation notes which I deliberately placed on display between us. This was done not only because the notes were not fulsome enough to provide a comprehensible account but also because I wanted Ellen to know that she was viewing all that I had recorded. Furthermore, I wanted her to respond to their accuracy. My intention was to be non-judgmental; the notes would be a record of the content and procedure of Ellen's lessons rather than provide any comment about the value of the lessons.

As I spoke about my observations, I was mindful that I was both relating a list of items for Ellen to check and creating an opportunity for Ellen to explicate, and so I would pause after each item. While some items were quickly scanned by Ellen, she frequently paused to go into explanation of other items, expanding upon what she had done and why. I, in turn, jotted down these explanations as samples of explicated knowledge. They included additional insights, new information, and any of Ellen's interpretations which differed from mine.

Constructing the ethnographic descriptions

To construct the descriptions in the case study I followed two steps. First, I used the brief notes and the memories which they triggered about the context to produce a thick description (Geertz 1973) . . . Second, when recording my hypothesising in the case study, I inserted Ellen's responses to the description (in squared brackets). This enabled me to identify some of her newly explicated knowledge and to show where Ellen's and my interpretations differed. It also enables the reader to follow how Ellen and I gradually moved towards shared perceptions.

Negotiating the ethnographic descriptions

Ellen read the ethnographic descriptions at the beginning of the feedback sessions. The procedure was the same as was used for the rough notes and it gave Ellen a chance not only to check again what I had observed but to see and react to how I was interpreting the data. As the sessions went by she was able to see and comment on the hypotheses I was developing and again these comments were added to my data set. Obviously this process could be ongoing, but in order to draw closure I settled for two sessions per lesson.

As a reading of the ethnographic descriptions will show, in the early sessions I gathered a lot of data about my participant observer methods. By June, as predicted, we had begun to reach a shared perception of Ellen's knowledge about her lessons and the action taken within them. As this happened data about the researcher's role assumed secondary importance to data about the explication of Ellen's knowledge. In other words, as the research procedure was developing, the data bank about Ellen's explicated knowledge was growing.

4   I described in the case study the ongoing history of relationships between Ellen and myself. An example of this can be seen in the following excerpt from the case study (Hall 1994, vol 2: 96–97):

2   Ellen's reactions to my observation notes

Ellen checked my notes of today's lesson and made comments and explanations as she reflected on the lesson. Last week I asked her whether she felt any discomfort with being exposed in my ethnographic reporting. She said she didn't — at least not in a way which disturbed her. I recollected then that teachers with whom I had worked with in previous studies were not so comfortable at this early stage of a project. I attributed the difference mostly to Ellen's being a student of ethnography herself — she had more understanding and interest in my reporting process. As mentioned earlier, Ellen's comments and explanations have been inserted in my observation notes (above) and, in some cases, constitute samples of what I took to be Ellen's explicated knowledge.

The fact that Ellen was a student of ethnography assisted our working relationship in that her interest allowed me to explain my procedures to her in more depth than usual and this minimised confusion and insecurity on her part. Ultimately this meant less effort for me.

Ellen's comments within my data are at times explications of previously unexplicated knowledge.

There is now a two-cycle process occurring between feedback and explication. Each feedback session produces explication of Ellen's knowledge which, after being recorded in my descriptions, becomes further feedback. This feedback, in turn, brings about further explication.

5   I kept a research diary and discussed items of deliberation about method and analysis with my supervisors. The following excerpt provides an example (Hall 1994: 84–85).

The Research Journal

The journal began as an ongoing account of my initial thoughts and deliberations during the fieldwork and it continued as I proceeded through the various stages of analysis and report writing. I used it to clarify my thoughts and to make them explicit to my supervisors. I also intended that it would help map my path of understanding and

45

provide a way of maintaining a sense of control over my learning process. Having started, I began to think of other purposes for the journal as well as the sorts of things I might write in it. These are listed below.

Excerpt from Research Journal, 20/8/86

Items to enter

• ideas that occur to me;

• feedback and input from my supervisors;

• pronounced feelings which I experience during the course of my inquiry.

Purposes for these entries

• to help my inquiry develop in a spiralling fashion as in action research, rather than let it lead me round and round in circles which go nowhere;

• to allow me to acknowledge my progress and discoveries (this will be much needed in times of despair!);

• to assist me with periodic reviews of directions to be followed;

• to enable me to keep close tabs on my method during the field work stage. (This will contribute to my account of the method in the final report and may also provide material for a paper somewhere along the line.)

As it transpired, the journal served all of the four purposes listed. In summary, the journal, in conjunction with the giving and receiving of feedback, contributed significantly to the empirical parts of the study being carried out reflexively.

At the beginning of this chapter, I referred to some underpinning assumptions about knowledge construction in emancipatory action research. The reflexive procedures described here were designed to address those assumptions. They address them by making research more authentic and more democratic. These procedures also work towards making emancipatory action research more readable to the research participants (clients) and to researchers in the same field who recognise its authenticity in terms of their won positions. In other words, it is more meaningful to readers who are able to 'borrow the lenses' worn by the researcher. Finally, and just as significantly, the reflexive procedures described should assist those who do not share or accept the researcher's lenses in making their criticisms more explicit. The intention of all of this is to make the research more credible.

Conclusion

In this chapter I have explored and described something of the nature of reflexivity, put up a case for it and provided some examples from a recent study. In conclusion, I suggest that in emancipatory action research our obligation to 'own up' to our personal contributions in the process of our knowledge construction also enhances the credibility of the emancipatory research enterprise. Moreover, when we show that our research methods are devised and carried out by people, rather than by 'science', we are no longer vulnerable to the scientistic whims of sponsors. They can no longer accept or dismiss our work on the basis of its level of 'objectivity', which can itself be constructed and reconstructed according to whether or not the findings suits their ends. Far from suggesting that the single act of owning up to our constitutiveness will change that situation, I proffer it as a minimal prerequisite in the struggle to make emancipatory action research and research about it more honest and eventually more useful to practitioners about whom and for whom we conduct research. Furthermore, I suggest that reflexive research practice, which includes some reflexive reporting, will also be more useful to research sponsors. However, the level of reflexive reporting will need to be chosen according to the social and political nature of the research assignment.

Acknowledgements

I am grateful to a number of people for critical discussion and input to ideas during their reactions to drafts of this chapter: thanks to Nado Aveling and Anthea Taylor for reactions to an early draft, as well as to Cherry Collins for facilitating that discussion; and to Alison Lee and John Hall for reactions to and editorial assistance with a later draft.

References

Capra, F. (1983) *The Turning Point: Science and Society and the Rising Culture*. Fontana Paperbacks, London.

Hall, S.H. (1990) Reflexivity in Educational Research, invited paper presented to the Network of Conversational Analysis, University of Calgary, Alberta, Canada, October.

Hall, S.H. (1994) The Explication of Working Knowledge Within a Teacher's Self-Evaluation of Her Teaching. Unpublished PhD thesis, Volumes 1 and 2, Murdoch University, Western Australia.

Kemmis, S. (1983) Reflections on method. In S.Kemmis, D. Dawkins, L. Brown, B. Cramer and T. Reilly, *Transition and Reform in the Victorian Transition Education Program*. The Final Report of the Transition Education Case Study Project, Transition Education Advisory Committee, Melbourne .

Lather, P. (1988) Ideology and Methodological Attitude. Paper prepared for an Invited Symposium on Ideology and Methodology, American Education Research Association Conference, April.

Ruby, J. (1977) The image mirrored: reflexivity and the documentary film. *The Journal of the University Film Association*, 24 (1), Fall, 3–11.

Silverman, D. (1975) *Reading Castenada: A Prologue to the Social Sciences*. Routledge and Kegan Paul, London and Henley.

The Australian (1989) The honest truth is we're liars. An article on research on lying conducted by Dr Kay Bussey, Macquarie University, New South Wales, Higher Education Supplement, 18 October.

Endnotes

1   This chapter draws on a paper presented to the annual conference of the Australian Association for Research in Education, Adelaide, 28 November–2 December 1989 and also on a revised version presented to the Network for Conversational Analysis, University of Calgary, Canada, September 1990.

2   The act of writing in the first person is in keeping with this aim in the sense that it helps to portray the researcher's presence in what is being reported. In doing so, it also helps to offset the notion of the researcher being in the 'privileged position' as 'objective outsider'.

3   Constitutive, not only because he or she will influence the setting, but also because his/her personal constitution (knowledge, experiences, values , beliefs, attitudes and epistemological leanings) will contribute to the way in which the data is selected, interpreted and analysed.

4   Within the way in which I use the term reflexivity, the *self* in *self-reflexivity* is a redundancy.

Chapter 4

Got a Philosophical Match?
Does It Matter?

Mary Jane Melrose

Abstract

This chapter is a brief exploration of the theory and practice of curriculum development, curriculum evaluation and leadership theory and practice within three underlying paradigms (functional, transactional and critical), together with a tool to assist reflection on beliefs and practices in these areas.

Introduction

This chapter focuses on three paradigms — functional, transactional and critical — and their underlying philosophical bases which are commonly recognised in many fields of education, including educational research, program development, program evaluation and educational leadership. I have consulted some literature in these areas and I have reflected on what I believe and what others value.

I am a staff developer at the Centre for Professional Development and Auckland Institute of Technology where I also coordinate the curriculum development of the Diploma in Adult and Tertiary Education. Currently I am particularly interested in research (especially action research), collegial review, recognition of prior learning, program development and evaluation, staff appraisal systems and the monitoring of union/management contracts.

I have developed ideas about various teaching and learning approaches, explored a range of evaluation tools and methods and considered the leadership models which one would expect, if groups of tertiary educators were following different paradigms. Now I am inviting you to explore whether you see these paradigms as real or imaginary. You will have the opportunity to use and reflect on my descriptions. As you read, you are asked to consider these focus questions:

• What is *your* underlying paradigm as you work within an educational setting?

• Does the paradigm change as you practise curriculum development, curriculum evaluation and educational leadership?

• Does it matter if a teaching and management group has a match in their practices and beliefs within an underlying paradigm?

Research paradigms

In the last few years, I have become increasingly interested in the concept of educational research as an activity within three major paradigms: functional (technical), transactional (interpretive) and critical (emancipatory). The positivist, hermeneutic (interpretist) and critical world views have been discussed, and the implications of the adoption of these philosophically different bases for educational research explored in the writings of Habermas (1972), Guba (1985), Candy (1989), Webb (1991), Kemmis (1991) and Bawden (1991).

Positivists value concrete and factual bodies of technical knowledge and generalisations, arrived at by repeated and confirmatory experimentation and observation. Research in this paradigm usually begins with a particular hypothesis about how the experimental subject will behave, given a set of predetermined variables. A researcher with this world view is likely to believe he or she can 'objectively' discover cause and effect, or recognise means and ends, in any situation by examining a tight deterministic relationship or correlation between experimental factors. Positivists, searching after new, absolute truths, set their own aims and agendas yet frequently believe these to be value-free. They also believe that they can use the results to control or predict the outcome in similar situations (Candy 1989). Educational researchers with this world view tend to be instrumentalists, reducing teachers and students to 'treatments' and 'objects' for research (Webb 1990). Positivists tend to ignore human values and beliefs in their equations, but intend that their research findings will be applied in order to improve the 'technology of schooling' or in order to 'mould the individual for a given form of social life' (Kemmis 1989: 7).

The hermeneutic world view recognises multiple interpretations of events, based on the different understandings, motives and reasoning of unique individuals (Candy 1989; Webb 1990). Just as there are many languages and 'texts' in the world, there are many and varied meanings for the individuals using them as they act and react with their environment. Each individual has their own construction of the world and creates their own reality and their own learning pathway through it. There is no objectively 'correct answer' to any educational research question and it is therefore not necessary, or even desirable, to begin with a definite hypothesis about an educational situation.

The research aims or questions and the methodology are themselves value laden, as they were constructed by a researcher or a group of researchers with a particular set of beliefs and past experiences. The value positions of the stakeholders are acknowledged by the researcher. There is a probability of increasing understanding about the research topic by investigating how various individuals perceive their educational experiences and their own learning. Transactional educational researchers search for an understanding of individual cases rather than sweeping generalisations. They recognise that causes and effects are mutually interdependent and that context as a whole, not as a series of artificially separated variables, is important (Candy 1989). Educational researchers working within this paradigm utilise their findings to inform the judgment and enlighten the practice of other educationalists as they in turn develop educational processes which assist the self-actualisation of others (Kemmis 1989). The knowledge from transactional research gives some insight into how individuals perceive their world and interact socially within it (Webb 1990). Many transactional researchers share with positivists the desire to be objective and detached from the subjects of their research as they observe and describe them, as if this detachment ensures validity (Candy 1989).

The critical world view has been developed through the beliefs of some philosophers and educational researchers that neither the positivist nor the hermeneutic world view goes far enough in transforming and improving individual learning, educational systems or societal norms.

Critical theory developed out of structuralist explanations of social relations which stress the effects of the predominant structures of society in forming and determining the actions of individuals. The main criticism of such arguments concerns the lack of importance which is placed on human agency. Human beings not only inherit roles and functions, but also act to change and reform structures.

While acknowledging the importance of structures in controlling and limiting human action, critical theory expresses confidence in the collective actions of people to change their social conditions by removing obstacles to their freedom. (Webb 1991: 36)

Critical theory has regenerated the Aristotelian concept of praxis, the idea that personal theory and practice grow, develop and adapt in unison and are not artificially separated (Webb 1990). A critical practitioner is in effect a researcher into his or her own practice who develops and redevelops personal theories cyclically, as a consequence of putting these theories, as they arise, into active practice and then reflecting on that practice and the learning which has taken place. Critical educational research formalises the efforts of reflective practitioners (Kemmis and Hughes 1979). Any knowledge gained by critical researchers is emancipatory, utilised in rational discourse about the structures within which people find themselves, with the aim of collaboratively changing and improving these and transforming the environment for learning and living. Knowledge is, however, always open to critical question and debate (Webb 1990; Kemmis 1989). Relative truths are set within the human and political context of the research. Educational researchers working within the critical paradigm do not merely describe individual perceptions but encourage individuals and groups to examine and question their perceptions of the structures and control mechanisms of society or organisations, with the aim of empowering them to reconstruct their interpretations. Critical research is value laden. Not only is the researcher interested in the value positions and beliefs of the group, but the researcher abandons any pretence of neutrality and often evokes specialist knowledge to stimulate the group into examining the ethics, morality and politics of their situation. The goal of critical researchers is personal or social transformation (Candy 1990). The critical approach seeks explicitly to identify and criticise disjunctions, incongruities and contradictions in people's life experiences (Candy 1990: 7).

Problems for investigation arise in context and as a perceived reality for a group of people and critical research often has this real, problem-solving focus. Because researchers working in the critical paradigm, and to some extent in the transactional paradigm, treat the group of educators in the educational situation as the focus for participation and involvement, often writing about their research in the first person rather than the second or third (Kemmis 1990), research within these paradigms should result in immediate learning for the participants or co-researchers as well as for the researcher. In contrast, researchers working in the functional paradigm tend to treat others as a data source and do not provide them with research findings, other than in a research paper to which they may not have access.

In the transactional and especially in the critical paradigms, research as an action and reflection and learning from research are ideally linked for all the research stakeholders and participants (Carr and Kemmis 1983; Zuber-Skeritt 1992). Research is conceptualised as a value-laden activity, influenced by the values of researchers, who are involved not detached from the research environment, as well as by the values of others. These values may be changed by learning during the research. Bawden (1991) has explored the learning/research link in the context of action research and action learning. Communicating as historical perspective is valued particularly by critical theorists who believe that a historical perspective helps people to understand and change the structures and systems within which they operate (Freire 1972; Kemmis and Fitzclarence 1986).

Foci for educational researchers include curriculum development, curriculum evaluation and curriculum leadership. My observations and research results confirm that the curriculum, evaluation and leadership models and paradigms described by previous researchers are recognised by and acted upon by tertiary teachers as practitioners across a wide range of subject areas. I provide below some of the key ideas and the influential researchers who generated them in three theory areas: curriculum, leadership and curriculum evaluation. I have found these summaries useful in staff development workshops, when staff are reflecting on their own models and theoretical position.

Curriculum paradigms

The functional (or technical) paradigm is based on previous 'moral' (eighteenth century and early nineteenth century) curriculum codes which trained 'the masses' for their duties to the state and which produced highly skilled workers to assist the economy. Curriculum developers working within this paradigm are concerned with prescribing what and how something (a body of knowledge) is taught by teachers who faithfully reproduce the curriculum developer's ideas. Researchers and proponents of this paradigm include Tyler (1949), Taba (1962), Wheeler (1967), Nicholls (1978) and Lundgren (1983).

The transactional (or practical or process or interpretive) paradigm is based on liberal ideas about humans as members of society, education as involving judgments about educational and social values and teachers as making decisions and solving problems, along with their students, within a complex context for learning. Curriculum developers working within this paradigm are concerned with who teaches, who learns, and how 'attitudes' and 'values' as well as a knowledge base can be learned. Researchers and proponents of this paradigm include Schwab (1971), Walker (1971), Skilbeck (1976), Print (1988) and Sheehan (1986).

The critical (or emancipatory) paradigm is based on critical theory involving dialectical reasoning. The teacher or student tries to stand outside a situation in order to critique it, to illuminate debate and to act for change. Curriculum developers and teachers working within this paradigm are concerned with how and when the learning occurs, and whether and why curriculum should be changed for the benefit of an improving society.

Researchers and proponents of this paradigm include Habermas (1972), Kemmis and Fitzclarence (1986), Aronowitz and Giroux (1986), Kelly (1986) and Altricher (1990).

Evaluation paradigms

The functional paradigm developed in the early twentieth century during the arms and space races. It pervades the present educational climate as the New Zealand government strives to standardise curricula at a national level on a data base of learning units, produce skilled workers and improve the economy — goals which seem to be linked at government policy level. Evaluators working within this paradigm evaluate alone or as part of a team of visiting experts, searching for an answer to the questions of whether the pre-set goals of the curriculum have been met and whether the program and the teachers produce learners who have the correct, measurable and observable skills to meet the needs of society and industry at the present time. Judgments are made by the evaluators and reported to decision-making authorities. Evaluators who are proponents of this paradigm include Tyler (1949), Scriven (in his early work, e.g. 1967), Stenhouse (1970) and Popham (1988).

The transactional paradigm is based on ideas about liberal humanism and subjectivist ethics (House 1978), which acknowledge the variety of experiences and values underlying perspectives and perceptions for teachers and learners in the same program. Evaluators working within this paradigm frequently involve a group of program stakeholders (especially students and teachers) in the development of criteria and in the enactment of the evaluation process. Evaluators investigate the unexpected and evolving aspects of the educational events and the context of these, and recognise that the people participating in the program and the context at that time make it unique. Evaluative reports are illuminative, descriptive and targeted at the stakeholders. Judgments and decisions are made by the stakeholders in response to the evaluation. Evaluators who work within this paradigm include Parlett and Hamilton (1972), Adelman and Alexander (1982) and Rolph and Rolph (1989).

The critical paradigm is based on ideas about learning communities as self-evaluating and critically reflecting entities which are empowered to set their own standards. Program stakeholders initiate and control the evaluation process which is ongoing, cyclic and change-orientated. Initially, the reporting, judgments and decision-making are internal to the group which is developing its own praxis, but meta-reflection on the whole experience can be disseminated — for example, by publication — to others who gain ideas about evaluation and learning to adapt and apply to their own learning community. Evaluators who work in this paradigm include Marshall and Peters (1985) and Kemmis and Hughes (1979).

Leadership paradigms

The functional (or technical or skills-based) paradigm is based on ideas which arose in a class-based society at the time of the Industrial Revolution. Leaders in this paradigm are required to specialise and conform to an established, hierarchical structure and to uphold the present goals and values of an organisation. Leaders develop skills in order to carry out tasks efficiently and effectively. Researchers and proponents of this paradigm include Selsnick (1957), Hershey and Blanchard (1972) and Iococca (1982).

The transactional (or interpretive) paradigm originated in the social context of the great depression. Leaders in this paradigm recognise multiple realities of organisations depending on the perceptions of the different people within them, who are moulded into a cooperative team. Leaders practise negotiation and encourage staff development to maximise contributions to the team. Researchers and proponents of this paradigm include Gron (1983) and Limerick and Cunnington (1987).

The critical (or transformational) paradigm is set within the future shock and culture shock concept (Toffler 1977; 1990) of the twentieth century, with its increasing rate of change and its increasingly complex and large organisations. The premise embedded within the literature about future shock is that individuals are faced with the greatest rate of change in systems of living and learning in history and that this rate of change is itself continually and exponentially increasing. Leaders working within the critical paradigm empower individuals and groups to change with the changes in technology, organisations and society. They also question and criticise present systems within organisations and society with a view to changing and improving them and increasing justice and equity in society in the future. Researchers and proponents of this paradigm include Burns (1978), Aronowitz and Giroux (1986), Codd (1989) and Smyth (1989).

A tool for reflection and discussion

Appendix 4.1 consists of a tool which I have developed to assist a self-reflective practitioner (or an observer) to identify different philosophical positions about curriculum evaluation, development and leadership. At the 1992 Sydney HERDSA conference, I presented a more detailed description of a workshop on self-identification of curriculum and leadership models (Melrose 1993). Data from research interviews and workshops with polytechnic staff has indicated that there is usually some match in the underlying paradigm(s) for an individual's self-identified models of curriculum development and leadership. Those who have no match or have a conflict between their models and the models of those around them are likely to move to a new role in the organisation or to leave it altogether. In the tertiary sector, adult students frequently have different philosophical positions and beliefs about teaching and learning from the staff. Some understanding by adult students about their own models and those of the staff who teach them may also assist learning on a program.

It is expected that further research in these areas will show that paradigm agreement and a match across the three fields of curriculum development, curriculum evaluation and curriculum leadership is important for a team approach to teaching and learning in an educational organisation.

The critical view of research as an activity within a critical learning community, which itself changes as a result of research, can be extended to view curriculum leadership in an educational environment as an holistic research endeavour. Critical transformation is possible through the transmission of research findings so that they may be added to a changing pool of knowledge and theory readily accessible to others. I hope that this summarising and linking of previous theory may contribute to a greater understanding of the conceptual links for other practitioners as researchers, curriculum developers, teachers, curriculum evaluators and leaders in educational settings.

References

Adelman, C. and Alexander, R.J. (1982) *The Self Evaluating Institution.* Methuen, London.

Altricher, H. (1990) Towards a theory of action research. *Proceedings of the 1st World Congress on Action Research and Process Management*, Brisbane.

Aronowitz, S. and Giroux, H.A. (1986) *The Conservative, Liberal and Radical Debate over Schooling.* Routledge and Kegan Paul, London.

Bawden, R. (1991) Towards action research systems. In Ortrun Zuber-Skerritt (ed.) *Action Research for Change and Development*, Gower-Avebury, Aldershot.

Burns, J. (1978) *Leadership*. Harper and Row, New York.

Candy, P.C. (1989) Alternative paradigms in educational research. *Australian Educational Researcher* 16 (3).

Carr, W. and Kemmis, S. (1983) *Becoming Critical: Knowing Through Action Research*. Deakin University Press, Victoria.

Codd, J. (1989) Educational leadership as reflective action. In J. Smyth (ed.) *Critical Perspectives in Educational Leadership*. Falmer Press, Deakin University, Victoria.

Friere, P. (1972) *Pedagogy of the Oppressed*. Harmondsworth, Penguin.

Gron, P. (1983) Accomplishing the doing of school administration: talk as the work. *Administrative Science Quarterly* 20 (2).

Guba, E.G. (1985) Chapter in Y.S. Lincoln (ed.), *Context of the Shift in Organisational Theory and Enquiry: The Paradigm Revolution*. Sage, Beverly Hills.

Habermas, J. (1972) trans. J.J. Shapiro, *Knowledge and Human Interests*. Heinemann, London.

Hershey, P. and Blanchard, K.H. (1972) *Management of Organisational Behaviour*. 2nd edn. Prentice Hall, Englewood Cliffs, New Jersey.

House, E.R. (1978) Assumptions underlying evaluation models. *Australian Educational Researcher*. 7(3), 4–12.

Iococca, L.A. (1984) *Iococca, an Autobiography*. Bantam Books, Toronto.

Kelly, A.V. (1986) *Knowledge and Curriculum Planning*. Harper Education Series, Harper and Row, London.

Kemmis, S. (1989) Metatheory and Metapractice in Educational Theorising and Research. *Proceedings of the International Symposium on Action Research in Higher Education, Government and Industry*, Brisbane.

Kemmis, S. (1991) Improving education through action research. In Ortrun Zuber-Skerritt (ed.) *Action Research for Change and Development*. Gower-Avebury, Aldershot.

Kemmis, S. and Fitzclarence, L. (1986) *Curriculum Theorising: Beyond Reproduction Theory*. Deakin University, Victoria.

Kemmis, S. and Hughes, C. (1979) Curriculum evaluation in higher education: self reflection in a critical community. *Proceedings of the Fifth Annual Conference of the Higher Education Research and Development Society of Australasia*, Brisbane.

Limerick, D. and Cunnington, B. (1987) Management development, the fourth blueprint. *Journal of Management Development* 6 (1), 54–67.

Lundgren, U.P. (1983) *Between Hope and Happening: Text and Context in Curriculum*. Deakin University, Victoria.

Marshall, J. and Peters, M. (1985) Evaluation and education: the ideal learning community. *Policy Sciences* 18, 263–88.

Melrose, M. J. 1993, Identifying models of curriculum and leadership for reflective proactive and the implementation of change. *Research and Development in Higher Education* 16. HERDSA, Sydney, 329–33.

Nichols, A. (1978) *Developing a Curriculum: A Practical Guide*. Allen & Unwin, London.

Parlett, M. and Hamilton, D. (1972), E*valuation as Illumination: A New Approach to the Study of Innovatory Programmes*. Occasional Paper 9, Centre for Research in the Educational Sciences, University of Edinburgh.

Popham, W.J. (1988) *Educational Evaluation*. Prentice Hall, Brookvale.

Print, M. (1988) *Curriculum Development and Design*. Allen & Unwin, Sydney.

Rolph, J. (1989) Evaluating courses: assessment and evaluation. *Higher Education* 14 (2), 117–31.

Schwab, J.J. (1969) The practical: a language for curriculum. *School Review* 78, 1–23.

Scriven, M. (1967) The methodology of evaluation in curriculum evaluation. In R.E Stake (ed.) *American Educational Research Association Monograph Series on Evaluation, No. 1*. Rand McNally, Chicago.

Selsnick, P. (1957) *Leadership in Administration: A Sociological Interpretation*. Row, Peterson and Co., Illinois.

Sheehan, J. (1986) Curriculum models: product versus process. *Journal of Advanced Nursing*, 11 (6), 671–78.

Skilbeck, M. (1976) *School-based Curriculum Development and Teacher Education*. Mimeograph, OECD.

Smyth, J. (ed.) (1989) *Critical Perspectives on Educational Leadership*. Falmar Press, Deakin University, Victoria.

Stenhouse, L. (1970) Some limitations in the use of objectives in curriculum research and planning. In S.J Eggleston (ed.) *Paedogogica Europea VI,* George Westermann, Braunschweig.

Taba, H. (1962) *Curriculum Development Theory and Practice*. Harcourt, Brace and World Inc., New York.

Tyler, R.W. (1949) *Basic Principles of Curriculum and Instruction*. University of Chicago Press, Chicago.

Walker, D.F. (1971) A naturalistic model for curriculum development; synchronising models of curriculum development and curriculum evaluation. *School Review* 80, 51–65.

Webb, G. (1990) Putting praxis into practice. In C.J. Collins and P.J. Chippendale (eds) *Proceedings of the 1st World Congress on Action Research, Vol. 1: Theory and Practice Frameworks*. Acorn Publications, Brisbane, 33–42.

Wheeler, D.K. (1967) *Curriculum Process*. University of London Press, London.

Zuber-Skerritt, O. (1992) *Professional Development in Higher Education — A Theoretical Framework for Action Research*. Kogan Page, London.

Appendix 4.1
A tool for self-identification of curriculum development, evaluation and leadership models

Instructions

Read the descriptions of the three different models in Part 1 (below). Consider your own beliefs and practices. Construct your own individual code for curriculum development and write it in the table below. You may use between 1 and 3 letters for your code. Each letter may be capital or lower case.

Use: F or f for Functional
T or t for Transactional
C or c for Critical

Note

There are no 'correct' answers. People have constructed many different codes, e.g. T or fTc belong to people with a similar outlook but the second person switches from one model to another at times (depending on context) while still preferring a transactional approach.

Move on to construct your codes for Part 2 and Part 3 and add these to the table.

Table of codes

Area of Practice	Code	Comment
1. Your curriculum development		
2. Your curriculum evaluation		
3. Your leadership		

Now consider the following:

Do your codes match? If not, why not? Do you think that your codes match those of the rest of your education team or your organisation? What implications do your answers have for:

- curriculum re-development (especially at different levels and for different groups of students);
- curriculum evaluation;
- assessment methodology;
- staff appraisal and staff development;
- career development;
- team building?

Clues to identifying the code

Part 1: For curriculum development

- *Functional:* Is set in the present. Fits what the industry or society needs now for that person to take up that job. Reproductive. Technical. Task- and skills-based for a specific occupation. Content of subject area is very important. Has objectives that are often set by an external body or an industry group with some input from teachers. Sometimes referred to as practical. Methodology often involves set lectures and teacher-directed demonstrations, workshops or laboratories.

- *Transactional:* Based on the needs of the individual students or group who happen to be doing that course. Often transferable skills are involved. Process- rather than product- or content-orientated. Negotiated objectives and criteria (for individual and/or group) evolve. Methodology often involves facilitation of group discussion. People-centred. Student-centred. Experiential learning is valued. Democratic.

- *Critical:* Based on predictions of future needs, visions of a better, fairer world. Education for the future is a focus. Learning to learn is important. Developing critical thinkers is a goal. Methodology often involves teacher asking critical questions, shaking previously held beliefs, querying current systems, acting as change agent, emancipatory. Objectives are often broad.

Part 2: For curriculum evaluation

- *Functional:* Focuses on whether the present, pre-stated, educational goals, aims and objectives of the curriculum/program have been met and whether the prescribed program outline has been delivered.

  Methods are likely to include quantitative measurement of student/participant behaviour before (less frequently during) and after the program, often by tests or examinations. Student assessment and curriculum evaluation therefore overlap in this model. Productivity of teachers, the cost efficiency of the program, and outputs of various types (compared with resource inputs or stated goals) may also be measured. Performance of students/participants and teachers during or after similar programs may also be compared or contrasted.

Typically carried out by one or more external expert evaluators, by a committee appointed by management or by a group of external peers. The evaluation plan is set and approved by management beforehand. The evaluation report is formal, often includes judgmental statements by the evaluators, and is directed to decision-makers within the upper management structure of the educational organisation or in government. Such evaluation, because it involves this level of decision-making, is usually summative. The evaluators and the decision-makers often maintain that the evaluation is as value-free and objective as possible.

Transactional: Focuses on how the program or curriculum is perceived by different people who are stakeholders in the process of learning. Often the focus is whether or not the current expressed needs of stakeholders, especially students/participants, have been met and whether negotiated learning events seem to have resulted in stakeholder satisfaction.

Methods are likely to include analysis of stakeholder needs, especially needs of potential or actual students or their actual or potential employers. Methods also often include detailed observations and descriptions of the process of the curriculum as it is enacted. Transactional formative evaluation results in changes to planned programs while they are in progress. Favourite methods of data collection are individual interviews and focus groups, where students, teachers or employers are asked about their feelings and perceptions and whether they believe that individual or group learning goals have been met as a result of the curriculum.

Reflective diaries, case studies and videos about a program are other popular methods for data collection.

Evaluation may be carried out by invited educational experts chosen by the stakeholders, by a group of stakeholders (often staff and students on a program) or by a mixed group of internal and external peers. The evaluation plan is flexible, negotiated and often based on the evolving concerns of the stakeholders, especially teachers and students, and on emerging issues rather than on the interests or biases of the evaluators or of upper management. However, the values of all those who seek or contribute data influence the selection of investigative foci, the methodology and the interpretation of results. The reports may be formative or summative, formal or informal, and each report is tailored specifically for a particular stakeholder group. Decisions about curriculum change are typically made by the teachers or by curriculum managers. Monitoring the results of the changes is a part of the evaluation process.

Critical: Critically examines the value systems of the stakeholders and the historical, political and social context of the curriculum, in an attempt to explain why and how that curriculum operates and in order to identify changes which will empower groups to improve that curriculum. Focuses on whether the present goals, aims and objectives of the curriculum/program are likely to be appropriate for the society of the future as well as focusing on whether they are appropriate for the society of the present. Often seeks to describe the impact (perceived or predicted, short-term or long-term) of a program curriculum on individuals and groups, for example on those who have gone to work since completing a program and on those who employ them.

Evaluation may serve a formative or summative function and the process is typically cyclic and continuing. Evaluation is goal-free in that all processes, perceived outcomes or effects are sought which are believed by stakeholders to be attributable to the program. The systems which form the educational environment for the program are often investigated as well as the learning events. The interaction of personal theory and practice for teachers in the context of a particular curriculum can also be a major focus for evaluation.

As many stakeholders as possible are consulted and actively involved during the evaluation. Ideally the values of these stakeholders and the evaluators are also investigated and described. The evaluation process is typically carried out by a group of teachers (and students) within a program. An educational expert may help to begin the process with the group. Self-evaluation of values, theory and practice is often the starting point. Changes in goals, content, process and context are documented as the curriculum evolves. The evaluative results, judgments and effects of decisions are reported at least to other stakeholders and ideally published as educational research.

Evaluation results in cyclic, collaborative investigation and reporting and continual decision-making by the whole educational community, by people driven by a desire to improve group or individual practice by critical thinking, whether this leads to small or large changes in that practice. This emancipated educational community accepts a collective responsibility to plan and carry out evaluations, report data, make judgments about the curriculum based on the evaluation, implement and monitor changes for improvement and re-evaluate.

Part 3: For leadership

- *Functional:* Basically acts on what hierarchy wants and demands at present. Administration efficient, tasks and skills carried out to meet deadlines set mostly by others or imposed by the systems in place. Task-orientated. Gets on with the work in order to free others to teach, etc. Communicates after the event. Approval of upper hierarchy most important. Likely to believe that there are leaders and followers; that leadership rests in individuals and is conferred by status within the hierarchy, often because the leader has superior knowledge and skills. Needs of management have priority. Directive, dominant, autocratic, controls resources. May be charismatic and philosophically competent in structure and ideals, be efficient and improve productivity at best. May be static, dictatorial and paternalistic at worst. Main concern is for the organisation.

- *Transactional:* People-orientated, consultative, balances needs and wants of upper hierarchy and own staff and communicates from one group to the other, decisions made at staff meetings, collaboratory, group-centred. Needs of group have priority. Acts as agent for group, negotiates conditions, mediates disputes and clashes in interests, concerns and values.

    Involves and includes others in achieving collective interests and goals. Reflective action guided by democracy. Organises opportunities for dialogues. Multidirectional, multidimensional. Dynamic, enabling, empowering at best, bogged down in the process at worst. Main concern is for the group of people.

- *Critical:* Visionary, leads group into a brand new world, tries to communicate this vision to others. May make decisions unilaterally or discuss them first. Needs of all humans in society have priority. Values progress towards betterment of the human condition, social justice, progress towards a universal ethics of brotherhood. Searches for truth. Encourages others to take risks and takes them herself, emancipatory, empowering, enabling, reflective. Questions established systems before responding to many requests. Future-orientated. Acts as change agent. Contests and reformulates goals. Dynamic. Has holistic views. Action based on moral preferences. Tends to use collective deliberation. Subversive, reformational, informed militant. Main concern is for society in the future.

Chapter 5

Collaborative, Self-critical and Reciprocal Inquiry Through Memory Work

Michael Schratz

Abstract

In action research, reflection plays an important (according to Donald Schön, the *most* important) aspect in the desired improvement of social situations in which people work. Reflection processes rely a lot on the way practitioners remember certain actions and how they evaluate them with a view towards changing future patterns of behaviour. Underlying this 'theory of action' is the fact that anything a person remembers constitutes a relevant trace in his or her construction of personal and/or professional self. Remembering actions, episodes and events from the past makes certain aspects of those processes accessible. Using memory work as a collective research method helps in uncovering the hidden aspects in the way a person evaluates his or her actions.

In this chapter I want to show how students use memory work as an emancipatory action research method to uncover and lay bare earlier understandings of social behaviour in personal and professional situations in the light of current understandings. By presenting parts of a memory story, its discussion and its final revision, I present an insight into how memory works in an institutional setting. It has its origin in a course, with university students dealing with the difficult situation of living together interculturally, which aimed at developing a method to research into personal and institutional racism in everyday settings.

Introduction to 'memory work' as a research method

Within memory work, which was first used by a group of feminist researchers and scholars, amongst them Frigga Haug and her colleagues, there is a continual underlying conflict between the radical and the conservative, between memories of the past, inevitably tinged with a degree of nostalgia, and a need to find in this past keys to the locks that constrain our actions, and our sense of self, in the present. Their exploratory work led them to the method of starting from their *writing of stories* about situations or events which they had experienced in the course of their lives. From this starting point, Frigga Haug argues that it is important to *work historically* if we want to find out the social construction, the mechanisms, connections and meanings of our actions and feelings. It became crucial, however, to ensure that memories of everyday life not be seen through an individual perspective but be rendered in a form that encouraged a different form of analysis. As a first step, the group chose to work *collectively* on their written sketches. The emphasis is equally emphatic on each word: *collective, memory* and *work*. For Haug (1990: 47) the result is a necessary, enjoyable, new, great social research methodology.

Over the years, Frigga Haug and her colleagues have developed a set of procedures for collective memory work which is best treated as a set of rules. Some of the rules might seem strange or unnecessary at first, but they have been shown to work in practice and they have survived significant tests of experience. The rules for memory work we outline here are derived from Haug (1987) and Crawford et al. (1992).

1   Each member of the group writes a memory.

2   The group meets and analyses each written memory.

3   Members of the group rewrite their texts.

4   Analysis of the texts is related to other theories.

In the first phase, as in any research work, the starting point is to find adequate research questions for the memory work to follow. In memory work, no less than in any other form of research, the substantive content of the research is of critical importance and the way in which the problem is framed, while it will keep changing, determines much of what follows.

Once a theme has been agreed, in small groups of four to five, each member/researcher writes a memory which relates to the chosen theme. This memory is usually of an everyday, but particular episode, event or action from their experience. The text is always written in the third person, which may initially seem strange but distances the actor in the event from the person who remembers the experience. The written text should illuminate the scene(s) in as much detail as possible, including even inconsequential or trivial detail, but without offering any interpretation or explanation for what is described. Usually the process will work better if participants write one of their earliest memories rather than something recent.

In the second phase, the texts are exchanged and analysed by the group. It is important to emphasise that this process is very different from that used by conventional discussion groups organised around the reading of a text, even though memory work groups often evolve from reading groups. Since interpretation does not figure in the text, and since the author has anyway adopted the convention of writing in the third person, there is little heed given to stylistics or to literary or expressive form. In addition, the conventional authority of the 'author' in relation to the reader hardly figures at all. By analysing each other's memory texts, all authors become co-researchers and as such each becomes part of the research process, acting both as subject and object in a process of knowledge production.

In the next phase, the members of the group rewrite their original memory texts, paying particular attention to the questions raised by their co-researchers in the analytical phase. By modifying the texts, the authors engage in a reflective process which brings to light new 'data' from their memory. These are things which might have been suppressed in their identity formation process and which often suggest reinterpretations of the construction of self.

The new memory texts are discussed again among the co-researchers. This time the original versions of the memories are compared and contrasted with the second ones and examined further. Common themes are discussed in view of a new understanding of the overall topic. If there are other memory work groups involved, the findings and discussions are exchanged across the groups. This process of collective theorising is a powerful feature of memory work and often involves relating to other theoretical positions and other kinds of research.

Memory work in the making

Memory work has so far been mainly developed and used in the investigation of feminist topics, like female sexualisation (Haug 1987) or emotions and gender (Crawford et al. 1992). It has also been used in a more directly applied form by Susan Kippax (one of the co-authors of the

Crawford book) in the investigation of the memories men and women (hetero and homosexual) have of sexual contact as part of a project in HIV/AIDS research (Kippax et al. 1990) and by Lindsay Fitzclarence as a way of helping student teachers understand the nature of authority as they attempt to manage the difficult transition between the roles of student and teacher. In my own work, I have successfully used it with students in a course on intercultural learning and, with Rob Walker, in a research methodology course in a peace studies program (cf. Schratz & Walker 1995).

In a written format, it is not really possible to reproduce the sometimes exciting and stimulating life of a memory work group. Nevertheless, I will try to convey some of our experience of this work by giving an example of a memory story, its discussion and its final revision. It is taken from a course with university students dealing with the difficulties of living together in culturally diverse groups (Fuchs and Schratz 1993). The aim was to use memory work to help students develop an understanding of their own racism in an everyday institutional setting.

In a first step, the whole group brainstormed the topic of racism and, after considerable discussion, agreed on a theme that served as a starting point for small memory work groups, each consisting of four to six co-researchers. One of the themes chosen was that of encountering someone with another skin colour, a theme to which everybody could contribute. Moreover, this theme seemed important because we all knew and understood the importance of external appearance and the role that skin colour plays in racism.

The first version of one memory story is presented as an example, followed by a summary of the discussions in the memory work group and finally the revised, second version of the memory text.

Encountering a person of another colour

(first version, translated from the German original)

As often on his long journey around the United States he was waiting at a filthy Greyhound bus station for the bus to arrive. He used to spend most of the day sightseeing and tried to sleep on the bus while getting to the following destination. Otherwise he would not have been able to cover the long distances on his trip, and by doing so, he saved accommodation expenses. His journey had taken him from Washington DC, where he had worked as an au-pair boy for six weeks, up north along the East Coast, right across Canada to the

West Coast, down south along the West Coast and across the States back east again. He always used to choose routes which took him to the well-known sights of the respective areas. This time he was travelling south through the state of Mississippi to meet an American he had gotten to know during his stay in the US.

This area left a poorer impression with him than the other places he had seen so far. He could not see any tourists around there, there were mainly exclusively poor people who seemed to live there. Nevertheless, waiting at the bus station there was not much different from having done it anywhere else. He was surrounded by rather poor people who could only afford the bus as the cheapest means of transport. Among them there were lots of homeless who could be found in the country of unlimited opportunities in the same way as in any other country. For them the bus station seemed to be the meeting place as is the case with train stations in European countries. He only stuck out from the local people because of his mountain rucksack, which rendered him the character of a tramper. Moreover, in this area of the US, also being Caucasian was rather the exception so that he even stood out more from the group of people waiting for the buses.

After the bus had arrived and the passengers had boarded, the usual Greyhound ritual started: the driver walks through the rows of seats and checks the tickets, then he announces on the loudspeaker: "This is a non-smoking ...". He had found a seat in the rear third of the bus and prepared himself for a longer trip across the state. Slowly he realised that he was the only white person on the bus. It was the first time this had happened to him during his trip. To make sure his impression was right, he looked back and eventually took it for sure. The other passengers did not take any notice of him, while he started becoming aware of the unusual situation. He looked at the different physiognomy in the form of the black people's heads and was reminded of the figure of the "Little Black Nigger Boy" *[Schwarzes Negerlein]* which had been standing on the primary teacher's desk for the purpose of collecting money for missionary activities by the church when he first went to school. Every time somebody put in a coin, the "Nigger Boy" would nod.

When he was watching the black passengers on the bus, however, he did not have that neat perception any more. On the contrary, some heads seemed quite clumsy, almost threatening, although he only saw them from behind. After some time he started noticing a strange smell in the bus, which reminded him of a particular spice which he had come across for the first time when he was invited for lunch by a black family on his trip. It was not a pleasant smell; in its intensity he found it quite penetrating. Is it sweat or mouth odour, he wondered. On his journey, he always had some packed lunch with him, but the strange smell did not let his appetite arise. He would rather not eat anything this time until he got to the next stop. Instead, some passengers started opening their own lunch packets and began eating the food in a noisy way. He then noticed the strange smell of that spice even more intensively in the bus. (Even nowadays, many years after, he can identify the former smell and associates it with negative feelings.)

He also had always something to read with him in order to bridge the travelling time if he was not able to sleep on the bus. This time he did not even succeed in doing some reading on this trip. Next to him sat a black woman with a voluminous body. She needed more than just her own seat and her buttocks reached over on to his seat. He was slim and therefore had enough room, but he rather lent towards the aisle, in order to avoid too close a body contact. Generally, he quite liked body contact, but in this particular situation he did not feel like it. The more so as the woman had meanwhile unpacked her knitting-needles and, apparently without paying attention to her seat neighbour, had begun moving her left needle up and down in rough movements in front of his body. He tried to lean towards the aisle even more so as not to be incidentally hit by the needle. She did not seem to pay any attention to him.

When the sun started rising outside, a strange feeling overcame him. He did not know whether it was fear or simply a dull feeling of strangeness: for the first time he completely felt in the minority. And although he had regarded himself as a very tolerant person, he caught himself in thoughts like 'What happens if ...?' He felt not only disturbed by the penetrating smell, but also by the sight that the black passengers also simply threw their rubbish on the floor. Then he eventually fell asleep. He was happy when he had reached the destination, where he was met by the white peanut farmer whom he had met previously on his journey through the States. For the first time he felt conscious of belonging to somebody of the same skin colour.

Discussion of the memory text

The above memory story was actively discussed by the co-researchers in the memory work group. It is only possible to reproduce a short summary of the discussion here. In order to differentiate the discussion in the group from the memory story, I have chosen the present tense for its reproduction. The plural forms of the personal pronoun (we, us, our) are used to stress the importance of the collective work among the co-researchers in the group.

The person is described as a person travelling extensively, which means he does not really have an interest in staying long enough in one place to be confronted by its particular culture. Therefore, real intercultural encounters do not often take place for the traveller, even though here the narrator gets into close contact with the local people on the bus. In our memory group we talk about the German saying *'Reisen bildet'* [travelling educates], since the writer legitimises his journey as an educational trip: he had first worked as an 'au-pair boy' in order to visit the 'well-known sights'. We asked if travelling had not hardened the prejudices the person had already. Otherwise, the sights would not have been worth the visit and so well known that he could plan his routes accordingly.

Travelling as a tourist always means being outside the places you visit. The tourist can come and go when s/he pleases, a freedom which separates the visitor from the local inhabitants. Although in the scene described, the writer's experience is of being in the minority, as a tourist he is a person who is free to move. We asked him how old he was at the time of the story. He was a student in the Tyrol at that time, which also explains his mountain rucksack, which made him distinct, not only from the local people waiting there but also from other travellers.

Differentiating himself from others is a theme that runs through the whole text like a thread. The white colour of his skin makes him aware of his minority position on the bus and affects his feelings. ('Generally, he quite liked body contact, but in this particular situation he did not feel like it.') The very nature of the environment seemed to change; the writer says that the places he had visited before seemed to be less poor and therefore more frequented by tourists, whereas here he found 'mainly people who seemed to live there', 'rather poor people who could only afford the bus as the cheapest means of transport' and 'among them there were lots of homeless'. Richer areas, we assumed, are rather more frequented by white people than this area, where 'his white skin colour was rather the exception'. He further demarcates himself from the people around him by describing how far he had already travelled and by highlighting the differences which make him distinct from the others 'so that he stood out'.

We notice that in the story it is the main actor, the white tourist, who shows 'active' interests. We experience him as an 'au pair' boy (we want to know how a male student gets a summer job of that kind), as a culturally interested and intellectual person and somebody who reads, whereas the African Americans on the bus have attributed to them rather deprecative qualities. Like the homeless at European train stations, they meet at the bus station, on the bus they eat in a way that does not stimulate his appetite, and the woman next to him knits 'in rough movements' and prevents him from falling asleep.

The example of the knitting woman shows further divisions between the people who are referred to, this time hierarchically. The (higher) level of the intellectual (reading) as opposed to the (lower) level of the technical and manual (knitting), the person of white skin as opposed to black, the male as opposed to the female. There is also the demarcation marked by smell, which has a high emotional impact on the writer. Incidentally, he mentioned in the discussion group that usually he was not so sensitive to smell. Since he could not withdraw from it on the bus, he experienced it as repulsive: 'It was not a pleasant smell; in its intensity he found it quite penetrating . . . Even nowadays, many years after, he can identify the former smell and associates it with negative feelings.'

We were struck that the narrator associates this unpleasant smell, which he attributes to a particular spice, with excretions of the body (sweat or mouth odour). Associations with food and the body exist within a binary opposition (clean/dirty) within which strong and barely controlled emotions are usually invested and implicitly associated with moral judgments. In cultures in which hygiene and training in cleanliness are highly valued (like Austria), smells are vigorously hidden away or avoided. Therefore, dirt, smells and noise can generate strong feelings when people from different cultures live together.

The narrator loses his appetite because of the 'eating noises' and 'the penetrating smells', which he experiences as unpleasant and threatening. How strongly those impressions have been imprinted in his subconsciousness shows in the passage that 'even nowadays, many years after, he can identify the former smell and associates it with negative feelings'. In a similar way, he feels threatened by the close contact of the 'voluminous body' of the black woman sitting next to him with 'her buttocks' reaching over to his seat. One member of the memory group thinks of the image of the fat black woman in movies who is depicted as the 'good mammy' rather than as a threatening person from whom one withdraws. We did not venture further as this seems to touch the boundary between memory work and therapy to which Frigga Haug refers. Nevertheless, we came to the conclusion that questions of body contact, eroticism and sexuality seem to play an important part in intercultural encounters and we looked at this in another series of memory texts in our work which we have not included here.

It also interests us that the narrator not only experiences the black woman's body as threatening, but that he also presents the needle as a kind of 'weapon' with which he could be hit, even if by accident. Somebody also points out that, from a feminist perspective, knitting as a skill and as a means of female productivity could also be seen as an instrument of domination over men. The only thing he can hold against her is his escape into an intellectual act because he 'always had something to read'. It is interesting that in the second version the narrator 'was taking out a book and holding it demonstratively in front of his head when reading it' (as a weapon of defence?) so that he 'could at least get her to narrow the radius of the movements of the needles'. In the first version he tries to escape this 'threat' by moving his body from her towards the aisle of the bus 'so as not to be incidentally hit by the needle'.

When asked about the contradiction inherent in the different reactions in the two versions, the writer explained that he had at first tried to turn away from her, as described in the first version. After some time he used the book, as described in the second version; otherwise he would have had to remain with his body in an awkward position. What was striking in our discussion was the common trait in both versions that intercultural communication between the people or cultures did not really take place. We are confronted with avoidance rather than communication.

Regarding the contrast between the 'black woman with a voluminous body' and the emphasis on the intellectual capacities of the 'slim white man', we asked whether the narrator had been influenced in his perception by ethnocentrally desirable beauty ideals. For Wolf (1990: 12):

> 'Beauty' is a currency system like the gold standard. Like any economy, it is determined by politics, and in the modern age in the West it is the last, best belief system that keeps male dominance intact. In assigning value to women in a vertical hierarchy according to a culturally imposed physical standard, it is an expression of power relations in which women must unnaturally compete for resources that men have appropriated for themselves.

The man seemed to have difficulties in getting in contact with the black woman, although he spoke English. This was a period when fashion models were all slim, young and white and the memory work group suggested that he would not have had any problems if a young, slim (white) woman had sat next to him.

We got a similar impression when discussing the writer's description of the other 'black' people on the bus. For the narrator they only appear shadowy and threatening as is indicated in the sentence: 'Some heads seemed quite clumsy, almost threatening, although he only saw them from behind'. We started discussing the important part that the shape of the head played in the theory of race. Phrenology (the scientific study of the head form) was a decisive force in the emergence and dissemination of the idea of racism (cf. Miles 1989). We asked if the passengers on the bus did not have any other characteristics and traits which attracted the narrator's attention and asked some other questions like 'Was there no contact or conversation at all between him and the others?' 'Was there not even any kind of eye contact?'

In contrast to the description of the black passengers on the bus is the 'Little Black Nigger Boy', who represents his first encounter with black people. Compared with the people on the bus, that figure was 'neat' and unthreatening. However, even then there was no intercultural communication with the 'child' from the foreign culture but only a mechanical nod, thanking you for your gift to the missionaries. The situation on the bus is characterised by the same lack of speech and creates another demarcation between the narrator and the other passengers. We do not know from the text, however, whether the latter had communicated with each other at all. The only expression of language appears in the announcement of the bus driver by means of one-way communication — apart from that, language is absent. It was interesting to notice that in other texts, too, missing or interrupted verbal communication played an important part. In no case was this a matter of language barriers but always a problem of people from different cultures getting into contact with each other.

We discussed in detail the meaning of the phrase 'And although he had regarded himself as a very tolerant person, he caught himself in thoughts like "What happens if …?" This stirred up an intense discussion on the term 'tolerance'. We asked questions like: 'What lies behind the tolerance of the narrator?' 'Why doesn't he show feelings and emotions?' 'Does he suppress or repress them and by doing so does he think he is being tolerant?' The memory text contains several hints that certain aspects of the passengers' behaviour seem to disturb him but the emotions (aggression) we expected in his own behaviour are faded out or distorted.

Later in the memory work process, when we talked about general theories of racism, we noted that Devereux (1973) argues that distortion is particularly developed where the (research) material under inquiry arouses fear. Researchers who deal with this kind of material seem to safeguard themselves against this fear by either suppressing certain parts of their material or by mitigating — not analysing or wrongly interpreting — it, but by describing it in an ambiguous way or by arranging it in a new and different way. He further argues that suppression and repression appear when someone is threatened in his or her own identity and leads to fear of the other, of strangeness.

The description of the rising dawn on the bus reminds us of the feelings young children have when they must go to bed. Just as children experience insecurity and anxiety when confronted with night coming, so we interpret the narrator's 'dull feeling of strangeness', the feeling of being alone or being left alone, as a possible form of regression into (early) childhood. His thought of 'What happens if ...?' reminds us of the 'incendiary compositions' *[Brandsätze]* (Jäger 1992), which ignite racism through verbal phrases like 'Who's afraid of the Black Man?', which appears in the second version of the text (see below). Whereas in the children's game it is possible to run away, the narrator has to stay on the bus all night. He is only free from fear when he falls asleep, and when he is met by the white farmer, to whom he feels a sense of 'belonging' because of 'his skin colour'.

Encountering a person of another colour
(second version, translated from the German original)

> He was then in his early twenties and had used his university summer holidays to explore the 'locations' of his American Studies course. By doing so he, on the one hand, was interested in improving his language competence; on the other hand he wanted to get to know the country and the people. For the first six weeks he had arranged to stay as an au pair boy with an American family at the West Coast, where he was intensively confronted with the American vernacular. For the second part of his stay he had bought a bus pass on the Greyhound system, which entitled him unlimited travelling around the States and Canada for two months so as to get to know as much as possible about the people and country.
>
> He had already been on his way for a couple of weeks and had got used to the routines doing the sightseeing during the day and sleeping on the bus during the night. Although it was quite tiring, it enabled him to cover as many miles as possible and to live on little money. During his trip he was often invited by people he had met on the way to stay with them, which made it possible for him to

clean himself properly and recuperate. Once again he was on the way to meet one of the people he had met, a peanut farmer in the south of the US, who had invited him for such a visit.

After a long journey from the East Coast up north, across Canada to the West Coast, down south to the Mexican border and all the way back towards the south east he entered the southern states for the first time. As often, he was waiting at the Greyhound Bus Station, which was situated in a rather neglected part of the city and therefore quite filthy, and made use of the time he had to wait for the connecting bus to experience the atmosphere around there. It was not without reason that he was travelling on his own because he wanted to have as many authentic encounters with people who lived in the particular area as possible. By doing so, he thought he would get the best chance to get to know the country and the people.

Although he had experienced this situation of waiting many times during his trip, this time it was different. Most of the people waiting were Americans of African origin, so he stood out markedly, being Caucasian with a mountain rucksack on his back. He was happy that the other people did not take any notice of him. He had often been warned by other people that the areas around bus stations were dangerous since there were 'all kinds of people' hanging around there. He had not been deterred by those warnings, but he had become more cautious since his rucksack with its whole contents had been stolen at one bus station during his journey.

After the bus had arrived and the passengers had boarded, the usual Greyhound ritual started: the driver walks through the rows and checks the tickets, then he announces on the speaker: 'This is a non-smoking ...' As always, he had found a seat in the rear third of the bus so as not to be dazzled and woken up by the headlights of approaching cars during the night. The other passengers had begun to make themselves comfortable for the night. Afterwards it became loud on the bus, as the people who knew each other started talking to each other. He noticed that their vernacular differed from the one he had previously heard in the States: it was somehow different and louder. It was only then that he realised that he was the only white person on the bus, which had happened to him for the first time on his journey. To make sure he was right, he looked back and eventually confirmed it. The other passengers did not take any notice of him, whereas he started to become aware of the unusual situation.

Previously he had met several black people at different occasions on his trip, but always out of a majority position. This time he was only surrounded by Americans of African origin, which provided him vividly with the 'authentic experience of the people'.

He had found a seat next to a black woman with a voluminous body, since he rather chose to sit next to a woman in this unusual situation. However, she needed more than just her own seat and also used some part of his. As he was slim there was enough room for both of them. Although he usually found it easy to get in contact with other passengers sitting next to him, he found it difficult that time. In fact, he greeted her in a friendly way, but they never got into further talking during the whole journey. However, he felt disturbed by her when she started unpacking her knitting needles and began moving them up and down in front of his head. She did not seem to bother that he could feel disturbed by that. It even made him aggressive, but he did not want to let her know. Somehow he thought that it was the way black people did it and hence he subjected himself to that cultural behaviour. He could at least get her to narrow the radius of the movements of the needles by taking out a book and holding it demonstratively in front of his head when reading it. He thanked her for that and she answered with a nodding gesture, which he interpreted as 'OK'.

When thinking about the situation he remembered his early school days when they had a collecting box carrying a black little boy with little clothing on the teacher's desk. It carried a text saying 'Collections for mission in Africa'. Like all the other friends at school he had always asked his parents for coins to give to the 'poor little Nigger Boy'. Once one put the coin in the box, the 'little black Nigger Boy' would nod with its head, which had had a very motivating effect on the children. Thinking back he found it very absurd.

By looking closer at the black passengers on the bus, the perception of the neat child on the mission box disappeared in his memory in favour of the perception of the real people who were adults of different ages. The form of their heads appeared rather clumsy and seemed almost threatening to him. He could not make out why they appeared to him that way. Perhaps it was also the smell which soon filled the inside of the bus. It reminded him of a particular kind of spice he had come across for the first time when he was invited for lunch in a suburb of Chicago by a black family on his trip, and which he did not particularly like.

He recognised that smell again and found it unpleasant in the closed area of the bus and quite penetrating in its intensity. Trying to check up on it, he noticed that a couple of rows in front of him some passengers had unpacked their lunches and had started eating them. That intensified the smell on the bus even more. Still today, many years after, he can identify the former smell and associates it with negative feelings. Besides, he noticed that they were eating their sandwiches with loud noises and that they threw the wrapping paper on the floor, which he found disturbing as well. In any event, the smell and the noises spoilt his appetite so that he himself did not unpack his lunch and rather tried to get distracted by reading a book.

It had meanwhile got dark outside, which made the atmosphere on the bus even more peculiar. He was caught by a strange feeling. He did not know if it was the fear that something could happen. He remembered the game 'Who's afraid of the Black Man?' from his early childhood memories and was surprised how strongly this image had become resident in his memory. It was probably also a feeling of strangeness, since it was the first time for him to ethnically belong to the minority. From this experience he also became conscious what it must mean for somebody to be in the minority. He was happy when they had reached their destination the following morning, where he was met at the bus station by his friend. For the first time he felt that he belonged to somebody of his own skin colour.

Developing shared ownership of memories

It is important not to read these two pieces of writing as 'before' and 'after' texts and to search for evidence of reformed racism in them. In the second text the writer remembers new things, puts a different emphasis on aspects of his account but does not try to expunge his racism from memory or rephrase things in a politically correct form. What is important is what the group learns from the discussion: the text is provided as a means of provoking and disciplining the discussion, not as evidence of pre-test and post-test achievement.

This example of a memory and its reworking by the group does give an idea of the nature of the research processes within a memory work group. Such work does not have to be seen as self-contained, and often members of the group use the experience to write about the topic in ways that draw on the discussion but make little reference to the memories. One of the reasons that the group can engage in critical discussion is the fact that the person who wrote it is not made vulnerable and does not need to be protected by the other members of the group. What is under scrutiny are the shared responses of each group member in the face of those facets of the memory that transcend idiosyncracy.

References

Crawford, J., Kippax, S., Onyx J., Gault, U. & Benton P. (1992) *Emotion and Gender*. Sage, London.

Devereux, G. (1973) *Angst und Methode in den Verhaltenswissenschaften*. Suhrkamp, Frankfurt/M.

Freud, S. (1901/1964) The psychopathology of everyday life. In J. Strachey (ed.) *The Standard Edition of the the Complete Works of Sigmund Freud, Vol. XIV*. Hogarth Press, London.

Fuchs, G. and Schratz, M. (eds) (1993) *Interkulturelles Zusammenleben, aber wie? Auseinandersetzung mit alltäglichem und institutional-isiertem Rassismus*. Österreichischer Studienverlag, Innsbruck.

Haug, F. et al. (1987) *Female Sexualisation: A Collective Work of Memory*. Verso, London.

Haug, F. (ed.) (1990) *Erinnerungsarbeit*. Argument, Berlin.

Kippax, S., Crawford, J., Waldby, C. and Benton, P. (1990) Women negotiating heterosex: implications for AIDS prevention. *Women's Studies International Forum* 13 (2), 533–42.

Miles, R. (1989) *Racism*. Routledge, London.

Schön, D. (1983) *The Reflective Practitioner*. Maurice Temple, London.

Schratz, M. and Walker, R. (1995) *Research as Social Change: New Opportunities for Qualitative Research*. Routledge, London.

Wolf, N. (1990) *The Beauty Myth*. Vintage, London.

Part III

Problems and
Suggested Solutions

Chapter 6

Emancipatory Action Research for Organisational Change and Management Development

Ortrun Zuber-Skerritt

Abstract

This chapter argues that emancipatory action research is organisational change 'best practice' and that it fosters organisational learning and the development of the 'learning organisation'. A new model for organisational change and management development is created by combining emancipatory action research with adaptations of Lewin and Beer et al.'s organisational change models.

Introduction

The aims of any action research project or program are to bring about practical improvement, innovation, change or development of social practice, and the practitioners' better understanding of their practices. This chapter addresses the problem of how to achieve effective change and why many change programs do not produce real transformational change.

Argyris (1990) and Bunning (1993) have identified organisational defences and barriers to introducing change and action research into organisational systems, and examined how to overcome these defences and barriers through 'double-loop learning'. I have shown elsewhere (Zuber-Skerritt, in press) that resistance and barriers to emancipatory action research can be explained in terms of Argyris' and Schön's (1974) action theory (i.e. espoused theory versus theory-in-use; Model 1 and 2 values, strategies and behaviour) and Carr and Kemmis's (1986) typology of action research (technical, practical and emancipatory).

The purpose of this chapter is to draw on the literature on change and innovation, and in particular on the organisational change model by Beer et al. (1990), to demonstrate that emancipatory action research is organisational change 'best practice', and that it fosters organisational learning and the development of the 'learning organisation' (Senge 1990).

Although Beer et al. do not refer to action research in any way, I wish to argue that the same barriers to and managerial interventions for effective organisational change which they identify also apply to emancipatory action research, and that in fact this integrated research and development methodology is the most effective way to achieve management and organisation development.

This argument is developed by first describing an existing model of emancipatory action research and its application in various scenarios, including a case study of unsuccessful emancipatory action research. Then emancipatory action research is shown to foster organisational learning, innovation, change and the 'learning organisation'. Finally, Beer et al.'s (1990) model is adapted and used as the basis for creating a new model of emancipatory action research for management and organisation development.

Emancipatory action research

In the tradition of the Frankfurt School of Critical Theory, I have described emancipatory action research as collaborative, critical and self-critical inquiry by practitioners (e.g. teachers, managers) into a major problem or issue of concern in their own practice. They 'own the problem' and feel responsible and accountable for solving it through teamwork and through following a cyclical process of (1) strategic planning, (2) implementing the plan (action), (3) observation, evaluation and self-evaluation, (4) critical and self-critical reflection on the results of (1)–(3), and making decisions for the next cycle of action research — that is, a revised plan, followed by action, observation and reflection, and so on. (Zuber-Skerritt 1992a).

More precisely, action research is *emancipatory* when it aims not only at technical and practical improvement, the participants' transformed consciousness, and change within their organisation's existing boundaries and conditions, but when it also aims at changing the system itself or those conditions which impede desired improvement in the organisation. Emancipatory action research also aims at the participants' empowerment and self-confidence about their ability to create 'grounded theory' (Strauss and Corben 1990) — that is, theory grounded in experience and practice — by solving complex problems in totally new situations, collaboratively as a team or 'community of scholars', everyone being a 'personal scientist' (Kelly 1963), contributing in different ways, but on an equal footing with everyone else. There is no hierarchy, but open and 'symmetrical communication' (Zuber-Skerritt 1992a).

A model for professional, education, management and organisation development

In my previous work (Zuber-Skerritt 1992b), I have argued and demonstrated that emancipatory action research is an appropriate methodology for education development and organisation development, as well as for the professional development of managers and teachers as action researchers. Table 6.1 and Figure 6.1 represent a simplified summary of this theoretical framework.

The CRASP model of action research is extended in Figure 6.1 for management and organisation development and explained as follows. In recent years there has been increasing pressure for accountability in all sectors. This accountability is often defined, determined and based on external values, including values of bureaucratic reasoning. Therefore, a critical attitude towards government and bureaucratic systematisation is an important responsibility of leaders and professional practitioners in management and higher education.

Table 6.1   *The CRASP model of action research for professional development*

Action research is:

Critical (and self-critical) collaborative enquiry by

Reflective practitioners being

Accountable and making the results of their enquiry public

Self-evaluating their practice and engaged in

Participatory problem-solving and continuing professional development

Source: Zuber-Skerritt (1992b: 15)

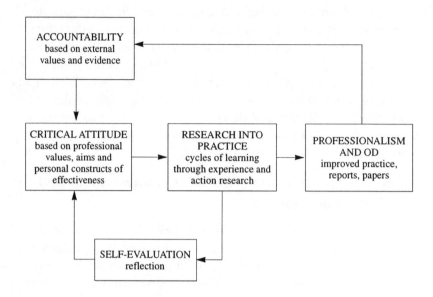

Figure 6.1 *The CRASP model of action research for management and organisation development*

This critical attitude towards the status quo in practice and context is mainly based on their intrinsic professional values and aims and related to their personal constructs of effective and ethical professional practice (Kelly 1963). Professionalism in management and higher education can be achieved through collaborative, critical research into practice through cycles of continuous learning through experience and action research. Important requirements for action research are self-evaluation and reflection based on evaluation and invited critical feedback from stakeholders. Such a reflective practice will lead to the practitioners' critical attitude as well as professionalism, organisation development *and* accountability evidenced by improved practice, quality performance, public reports and other publications.

Examples of successful applications of this model to action research projects, aimed at improving learning and teaching at the undergraduate and postgraduate levels at Griffith University are described in Zuber-Skerritt (1992b; 1992c), and at the University of Queensland, for senior administrative and academic staff, in Zuber-Skerritt (1994a; 1994b; 1994c). Some of the examples include the following topics:

- The Development of a Multi-media Personal Safety Awareness Program to Maximise Personal Safety within the University of Queensland Community (UNISAFE);

- Gaining Greater Staff Understanding and Support of the University's Annual Appeal;

- The 'Quest for Quality' — Improving Central Administration's Services to the University;

- Developing a New Paradigm for Teaching Management Studies at Gatton College;

- The Challenge of Maintaining Quality of Learning in a Class of 800–1200 (Anatomical Sciences Department);

- Improved Teaching and Learning in Large Classes (Biochemistry Department);

- A Pilot Study of Integrated, Active Learning in the Postgraduate Preparation of Guidance and Counselling Professionals (Education Department);

- The Facilitation and Development of Professional Praxis (Human Movement Studies Department);

- Fostering Excellence in Teaching and Learning in Medicine (Medicine Department);

- Excellence in Clinical Learning Outcomes (Physiotherapy Department);

- The University of Queensland Communication Clinic: A Quality Clinical Education Program for the Department of Speech and Hearing (Speech and Hearing Department).

For example, the departmental team of six academics in Physiotherapy summarised the results of their action research project entitled 'Excellence in Clinical Learning Outcomes' within the Excellence in University Education (DEUE) program at the University of Queensland as follows (Zuber-Skerritt 1994: 62–63):

> In order to maintain and pursue a vision for excellence, the DEUE team in the Department of Physiotherapy at the University of Queensland responded to the challenge of restructuring the clinical program so that the existing high quality of physiotherapy graduates be at least maintained, and if possible improved, within a framework of diminishing human and financial resources. The collaborative problem-posing, problem-solving processes of action research have

been used to effectively address existing complex issues and the emerging issues of the major restructuring proposed. The process of action research, while focussed strongly on the project itself, has also impacted significantly on the learning and development of the DEUE team. What was initiated with enthusiasm, energy and commitment has, in its unfolding and development, generated a new depth of thinking and understanding about the teaching and learning processes in the Department of Physiotherapy which will lead to excellence in professional practice. It will now be possible to structure a quality clinical program which is also cost effective.

The main insights I gained from coordinating and evaluating numerous action research teams and projects are that action research only works successfully if all members of a team own the problem and are interested in solving it; if they work on the project collaboratively and voluntarily, rather than being co-opted, manipulated or forced on the team by a sponsor or superior; and if they are open for change, critical review, reflection and self-evaluation. Another important factor affecting the success of action research is the support from top management and sponsors (Zuber-Skerritt and Howell 1993).

Although most of the above conditions did apply to a case study with Chinese teachers at Griffith University, aiming at their language curriculum development and improving the institutional research culture of language education (Zuber Skerritt, 1996), this is an example of emancipatory action research which was both successful and unsuccessful.

Case study

This study was part of a project entitled 'Raising Student Proficiency and Meeting Industry Needs in Chinese Language Education at the University Level', funded by the National Priority (Reserve) Fund 1993. The project consisted of three components:

1   assessment of industry's Chinese language needs;

2   investigation of student proficiency and student needs;

3   action research and curriculum development.

The project results were published in Farquhar and McKay (1996). The case study under discussion relates to the third component which was both successful and unsuccessful depending on the criteria used for evaluation. According to the language teaching team, it was successful.

Team members appreciated:

- having a skilled facilitator;
- collaborating with colleagues;
- working on important and practical issues;
- planning and taking systematic and strategic action;
- gaining new knowledge, skills and insights;
- a sense of excitement and renewed motivation.

However, being involved in action research brought a lot of problems to the surface for the project team members, problems which were related to their different assumptions and expectations about the process and outcomes and which were related to some members' lack of commitment, communication and cooperation.

Using the criteria for emancipatory action research, as outlined above, the project was not successful, because of barriers related to the team's aims, values and world views. With reference to Table 6.2, most of the team members adhered to paradigm 1 of action research, other research and leadership, and some to paradigm 2, rather than 3. This was confirmed in a study of their personal orientations using an instrument designed by Bunning (1993). This tool and technique is useful for eliciting people's paradigms of action research. Therefore, it is included in the Appendix.

Table 6.2   *Comparative paradigms*

Paradigms	1	2	3
Action Research	Technical	Practical	Emancipatory
Research	Positivist	Interpretive	Critical
Leadership	Functional	Transactional	Transformational

Participants varied in their responses to the questions about personal orientation for members of an action research group. The Personal Orientations Questionnaire (see Appendix) was completed by eight participants: six language teachers and two facilitators.

Respondents were asked to consider each of the following questions:

1   What do you think is an ideal personal orientation for members of an action research group?

2   What do you think is the overall orientation of the group you are a member of?

3.   What do you think your own orientation is?

For each of the above questions, respondents were asked to consider the following list of paired options, and to select the appropriate orientation from each pair.

a   outer or inner directed;

b   survival or developmentally oriented;

c   short-term doer or reflective practitioner; and

d   efficiency or effectiveness oriented.

In summary, through their responses to these three questions, respondents demonstrated that they had different attitudes to authority and hierarchy, different assumptions about action research, and had different perceptions about the process that they had been engaged in. Accordingly, for the question on the ideal orientation of an action research group (question 1), respondents had no difficulty choosing which option they thought was appropriate; for most respondents it was the opposite of how they perceived their own group (question 2). Interestingly, when it came to nominating their own personal orientation (question 3), respondents found it more difficult to make such stark contrasts — to place themselves clearly as being oriented either one way or the other. There was certainly a strong tendency to identify one's own personal orientation as the ideal orientation, and as not being the orientation of the group. However, there was also a tendency for respondents to perceive their own orientation, on at least one of the options (a)–(d), as combined rather than adhering so strictly to one orientation or the other. It would appear that most respondents felt that the group had not done 'action research' *properly,* as they understood it. However, while they could clearly identify what they perceived to be 'less than ideal' orientations within the group (i.e. the orientation of others), they found it more difficult to label their own orientation in such clear terms.

Barriers

I conclude from this case study that the main barriers to emancipatory action research are:

*   *Single-loop learning* instead of double-loop learning. This means: 'Single-loop learning is any detection and correction of error that does not require change in the governing values' (Argyris 1980:

14), whereas double-loop learning does. Single-loop learning is technical, functional and short-term oriented. Most participants in the case study did not change their governing values, strategies and behaviour.

- *Dependence on experts or seniors* instead of independence of thought and expression. Most participants in the Chinese case study relied heavily on the facilitator.

- *Efficiency orientation* instead of effectiveness orientation to research and development. Most participants in the case study wanted 'to get on with the job', rather than spending time on reflection, team building and group discussion. They were interested in short-term results in minimum time instead of long-term effectiveness.

- *Interested mainly in operational issues* instead of being interested in strategic organisational issues. Most participants resented the facilitators' attempts to guide them through a process of strategic planning, experiential learning and understanding the basic philosophical assumptions underlying educational and organisational change.

It is a most difficult task in organisational and staff development to effect transformational change and a shift in people from single- to double-loop learning, from dependent to independent thinking, from efficiency to effectiveness orientation, and from an operational to a strategic approach to organisation development. It is at least equally difficult and time consuming to achieve this shift for a whole group or a whole organisation to become a double-loop 'learning organisation' (Senge 1990). The next section explains the meaning of this term.

The learning organisation

The quality improvement programs at the University of Queensland mentioned above had the main aim: to *build a 'learning organisation' with a culture for innovation and change.* The area of building learning organisations is relatively new. Senge's (1990) book *The Fifth Discipline* is a breakthrough. The fifth discipline refers to systems thinking and building new types of organisations which are decentralised, non-hierarchical and dedicated not only to the success of the organisation, but also to the well-being, growth and development of its members. Senge (1990: 4) predicts:

> The organizations that will truly excel in the future will be the organizations that discover how to tap people's commitment and capacity to learn at all levels in an organization.

He defines a learning organisation as a place where people are continually discovering how they can create and change their reality. This requires an attitude that learning should be life-long and cooperative. It should be learning through discussion and dialogue. Senge refers to the original Greek meaning of *dialogos,* i.e. sharing of ideas and meaning within a group that is able to discover insights which are not attainable individually.

The discipline of dialogue also involves learning about group processes that support or undermine learning. We are living in a time of rapid change. In order to recognise and adapt to change, and moreover to learn faster than the rate of change, we must develop a capacity to create new conditions, strategies and methods for solving new problems in unknown future situations.

We have evidence that effective ways of building learning organisations are quality improvement programs using action learning and action research (Bunning 1992; 1993; Zuber-Skerritt 1994b; 1995). Quality and excellence are of great importance, not only to business and industry for a country's economic survival in growing international competition, but also to educators charged with the responsibility of educating people to become responsible citizens of the world. This means to have a global view and see the total picture, to strive continually for the best achievements and for a peaceful, sustainable future. This also means to satisfy our 'customers' in the widest sense, including future generations, through quality management and assurance processes.

On the basis of his action research in a major government department, Bunning (1992: 53) concludes that the success or failure of a quality management program depends on issues such as:

- top management's degree of courage and vision;

- understanding the process of empowerment of staff, believing in it and actually doing it;

- knowing how to design and manage a large organisational change project;

- knowing how to build cybernetic loops so that the program and all its various parts are self-correcting;

- valuing learning and growth in the medium term over pain avoidance, traditional benefit and ego in the short term;

- understanding that what you have taken on is not a limited direction program for organisational improvement, but a new way of life. The goal is never to be the same again.

A very important condition for innovation and change is the appropriate organisational culture. The literature on organisational culture has repeatedly identified the following salient features of a culture encouraging innovation and change:

- more receptivity to new ideas;
- faster approval, less red tape;
- more collaboration between departments;
- abundant praise and recognition (which is often missing or lacking in academia);
- advance warning of changes;
- open circulation of information;
- extra resources available;
- the attitude that we are always learning.

To sum up, the literature on quality management and organisational innovation, change and development provides plenty of advice and guidelines for change and quality improvement programs. However, many such programs do not have the desired effect.

Why change programs don't produce change

This is the title of a classic article by Beer et al. (1990) in the *Harvard Business Review.* In their four-year study of six large corporations (with revenues of US$4–10 billion), these researchers identified three major interrelated factors required for corporate revitalisation: *coordination* or teamwork (e.g. among marketing, product design and manufacturing departments, as well as between workers and management); a high level of *commitment* necessary for coordinated action; and new *competencies* for problem-solving as a team (e.g. analytical and interpersonal skills and knowledge of the business as a whole).

These researchers have also found that the greatest 'fallacy of programmatic change' is the textbook idea that corporate revitalisation and renewal processes come about through company-wide change programs including a mission statement by top management, the employment of human resource managers, a new organisational structure, a performance appraisal system, and training programs to turn managers into 'change agents'. Instead, they advocate an approach to change which is based on work and task alignment, starting at the periphery with general managers and moving gradually towards top management. They maintain that 'successful change efforts focus on the work itself, not on abstractions' (p. 159). This is in line with the principles of action research.

They also suggest a move 'from the hierarchical and bureaucratic model which has characterized corporations since World War II to what we call the taskdriven organization where what has to be done governs who works with whom and who leads' (p. 158). Action research is also non-hierarchical and aims at 'symmetrical communication' (Carr and Kemmis 1986).

On the basis of indepth analysis, Beer and associates recommend a sequence of six steps ('the critical path') to achieve task alignment. Table 6.3 is a summary of their six-step process of managerial interventions for organisational change.

Table 6.3 *A six-step model of managerial interventions for organisational change*

Steps	Tasks
1	Joint definition and diagnosis of a business problem. This mobilises the general managers' and their staffs' initial commitment to the change process.
2	Developing a shared task-aligned vision of the organisation and creating consensus for the new vision among stakeholders.
3	Strong leadership in facilitating team building and learning, as well as replacing managers who cannot function in the new organisation.
4	Spreading the new vision to all departments without pushing it from the top, letting them apply the concepts of coordination and teamwork to their particular situation, even if it means 'reinventing the wheel'.
5	Institutionalising the revitalisation and change by general managers through formal policies, systems and structures, so that the process continues even after they have left.
6	Monitoring and adjusting strategies in response to problems in the revitalisation process. This leads to the learning organisation capable of learning to learn and of adapting to a changing competitive environment.

Source: After Beer et al. 1990.

These steps develop a self-reinforcing cycle of coordination, commitment and competence. It is important that CEOs and senior managers themselves practise what they preach. This means that they themselves must adopt the same team behaviour, attitudes and skills which they have been encouraging in their general managers. Beer et al. (1990: 166) conclude from their research:

> Companies need a particular mind-set for managing change: one that emphasizes process over specific content, recognizes organization change as a unit-by-unit learning process rather than a series of programs, and acknowledges the payoffs that result from persistence over a long period of time as opposed to quick fixes. This mind-set is difficult to maintain in an environment that presses for quarterly earnings, but we believe it is the only approach that will bring about successful renewal.

A new model for emancipatory action research

As stated earlier, although Beer et al. have not at all mentioned action research, it is an appropriate and complementary methodology to their findings and conclusions. For action research, too, emphasises process over a specific content; it recognises change as a continuous, cyclical, lifelong learning process, rather than a series of programs; it is based on team collaboration, coordination, commitment and competence; and it needs to foster critical, double-loop learning in order to effect real change and emancipation, not only for the participants themselves, but also for the organisation as a whole.

Therefore, I wish to compare the key processes of the two models: the task-alignment model and the action research model of organisational change, and then suggest a new model of emancipatory action research for management and organisational change, developed in a five-stage argument.

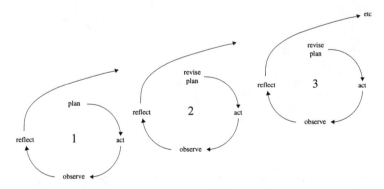

Figure 6.2 *The spiral of action research cycles*

First, the task-alignment model summarised in Table 6.3 is a linear process, whereas the process of action research is cyclical. Figure 6.2 represents the classical spiral of action research cycles, each cycle consisting of a *plan* (including problem definition, situation analysis, team vision and strategic plan), *action* (i.e. the implementation of the strategic plan), *observation* (including monitoring and evaluation) and *reflection* on the results of the evaluation, which usually leads to a revised or totally new plan and the continuation of the action research process in a second cycle, then a third and so on. Second, I wish to change Beer et al.'s (1990) linear model into a cyclical process, as suggested in Figure 6.3, because it can be argued that organisational and business management problems cannot always be clearly defined at the outset, but are often vague and have to be revised several times through trial and error.

It can also be argued that change is not necessarily linear with a beginning, process and end, but that it is evolving and ongoing.

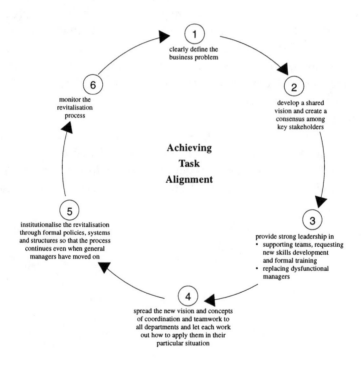

1 clearly define the business problem

6 monitor the revitalisation process

2 develop a shared vision and create a consensus among key stakeholders

Achieving Task Alignment

5 institutionalise the revitalisation through formal policies, systems and structures so that the process continues even when general managers have moved on

3 provide strong leadership in
• supporting teams, requesting new skills development and formal training
• replacing dysfunctional managers

4 spread the new vision and concepts of coordination and teamwork to all departments and let each work out how to apply them in their particular situation

Figure 6.3 *Achieving task alignment for organisational change*

Third, the cyclical models of task alignment and action research may be overlapped, as suggested in Figure 6.4 as a tentative model. This clearly shows that the task alignment model lacks an important part of the action research process: reflection.

Fourth, it is interesting to add Lewin's (1952) model of organisational change to the above two models and to show the three stages of unfreezing, moving and refreezing. *Unfreezing* means creating the motivation to change in an organisation through a disturbance — for example, an innovation. *Moving* means changing and developing new beliefs, values, attitudes and behaviours on the basis of new information and insights. *Refreezing* means stabilising and integrating the new beliefs, values, attitudes and behaviours into the rest of the system and reaching a new equilibrium, until there is a need for a new cycle of unfreezing, moving and refreezing.

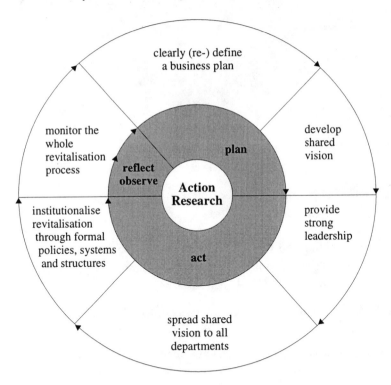

Figure 6.4 *The overlapping process models of achieving task alignment and action research*

The three overlapping models of organisational change in Figure 6.5 result in a new model of emancipatory action research for organisational change and development. However, Figure 6.5 (like Figure 6.4) is still a tentative model, for it shows that an important part of the action research process remains missing: reflection.

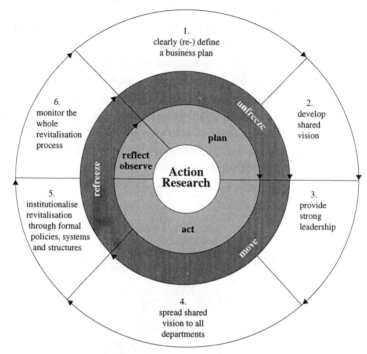

Figure 6.5 *A tentative model of emancipatory action research for organisational change*

By integrating the three models in Figure 6.5, it becomes clear that there is an overlap of moments or stages in the process of organisational change as shown in Table 6.4.

Table 6.4 *Comparison of three organisational change models*

Task alignment model	Lewin's model	Action research model
Steps 1 and 2	Unfreezing	Planning
Steps 3 and 4	Moving	Acting
Steps 5 and 6	Refreezing	
Step 5		Acting
Step 6		Observing, reflecting

It is important to note that a key element in the action research model is critical and self-critical reflection on the whole process, which is emancipatory, empowering, transformational and therefore effective only if subsequent steps are taken to transform the system and to make changes to those conditions in the organisation which impede real change and improvement. Hence, a fifth and final adaptation to the model of emancipatory action research for organisational change is necessary to achieve a coherent integration of the three models in Figure 6.6. This means Lewin's model has to be extended by one step (revise) and the task alignment model by two steps (get *feedback* on *draft* policies and *reflect* on the results).

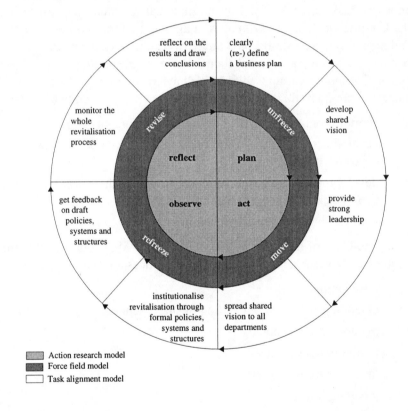

Figure 6.6 *A model of emancipatory action reseach for organisational change*

This is the model of emancipatory action research for organisational change, developed in a five-step process of adapting and extending two classical organisational change models and integrating them into the action research model. Although this model provides a general and broad framework for understanding organisational change, the process is often less structured in practice. For example, the process may not start with planning/unfreezing, but may be entered at any point.

Management education and development

How can managers be prepared to understand, model and operate in this model of professional and organisational development? Management education, and especially Master of Business Administration (MBA) programs, has been heavily criticised for being too theoretical and irrelevant to the needs of industry, not only in Australia, but elsewhere in the world (Industry Task Force 1995). The international research program of the 'Task Force on Leadership and Management Skills', funded by the Commonwealth of Australia, has come to the same conclusions and recommended a more organisational focus. For example, Carter et al. of the Boston Consulting Group (1995: 1274) have recommended four types of changes in programs for developing the next generation of senior managers:

1   shorter programs (less time away from the organisation);
2   development programs more focused on an individual company's needs (customisation);
3   development programs more closely linked to the workplace rather than the classroom (experiential);
4   a project-based approach to learning.

On the basis of a survey, Wawn et al. (1995: 551) conclude that the most effective management development practices are (in this order):

1   job rotation;
2   external providers — including business schools;
3   mentoring and coaching;
4   on-the-job experience;
5   'action learning' programs;
6   job assignments;
7   in-house training and development programs;
8   work with other organisations.

In contrast, and quite independently from these studies, research at Griffith University has shown that action learning and action research are the most appropriate methods for developing managers for the twenty-first century (Limerick and Cunnington 1993; Zuber-Skerritt 1992a). On the basis of our research, we have developed an MBA–Executive program by action learning and action research which develops senior managers as leaders of 'The High Performing Learning Organisation'. This program has the following characteristics, as summarised in Table 6.5.

Table 6.5 *Main features of the MBA–Executive course by action learning*

•   *Flexible delivery mode:* Two residentials of two weeks each instead of regular timetabled classes on-campus; two subjects by distance education with regular meetings of action learning groups; two work-based projects.
•   *Duration:* 13 months (high density) or two years (option).
•   *Course individually structured* to suit the needs of the managers and their organisations through work-based assignments and projects.
•   *Academic faculty* with international reputation and industry experience.
•   *Use of action learning and action research,* strategic alliances, networking and the latest information technology with global reach.
•   *Excellent staff–student ratios,* groups of five to six.
•   *Recognition of prior learning* and credit for relevant prior management development programs
•   *Flexible exit possible:* after one-third of the course, a *Graduate Management Qualification;* after two-thirds, a *Graduate Diploma of Management.*

Conclusions

The objectives of this chapter have been to draw on selected models of organisational change and innovation in the literature and to demonstrate that emancipatory action research is organisational change 'best practice', and that it fosters organisational learning and the learning organisation. These objectives have been met by reference to the literature and my own work and by developing a new model of emancipatory action research for management and organisation development. This model represents a cyclical, ongoing process of managerial intervention and learning for organisational change and the development of a learning organisation.

It is hoped that this model (Figure 6.6) may be useful to and adapted by action researchers, change agents, managers, teachers and students for their own purposes, when introducing interventions and processes of action research for management and organisation development. More research and development work is needed to resolve the problem of dealing with people and organisations having positivist mindsets and being resistant to the notions of action research, change and empowerment of people.

I conclude that emancipatory action research is the most effective way to achieve organisational change and that it concurrently facilitates organisational learning. Orchestrating a company-wide process of revitalisation, change and renewal is the prime responsibility of senior management. Development of effective change leaders, however, cannot occur in the classroom. Rather, development needs to occur in an organisation where teamwork, high commitment and new competencies are practised — competencies such as knowledge of the business as a whole, analytical skills, interpersonal skills, and skills to identify and solve practical problems. The design of an MBA–Executive program by action learning is an example of leading-edge management education for the future, fully integrating work and study.

Organisations need a particular mindset for managing change and bringing about successful renewal or revitalisation. This mindset includes emphasis on process over specific content, seeing organisational change as a by-process, rather than a series of programs, and long-term outcomes as opposed to short-term benefits. Emancipatory action research also requires a move from the old model of the hierarchical, bureaucratic organisation to the new model of a problem-oriented, task-driven action learning organisation.

References

Argyris, C. (1990) *Overcoming Organisational Defenses – Facilitating Organisational Learning.* Allyn and Bacon, Boston.

Argyris, C. and Schön, D.A. (1974) *Theory in Practice: Increasing Professional Effectiveness.* Jossey-Bass, San Francisco.

Beer, M., Eisenstat, R.A. and Spector, B. (1990) Why change programs don't produce change. *Harvard Business Review*, November–December, 158–66.

Bunning, C. (1992) *Total Quality Management: Applying it in the Public Sector and to Professional Services.* In O. Zuber-Skerritt (ed.) Series of Occasional Papers, No. 1, International Management Centre, Brisbane.

Bunning, C. (1993) *Learning Organisation Systems*. DBA dissertation. International Management Centre, Buckingham, accepted for publication by Gower-Avebury, Aldershot.

Carr, W. and Kemmis, S. (1986) *Becoming Critical: Education, Knowledge and Action Research*. Falmer Press, London.

Carter, C., Nicholson, J. and Barlow, M. (The Boston Consulting Group) (1995) The Australian manager of the twenty-first century, *Enterprising Nation*, Research Report Volume 2. Industry Task Force on Management and Leadership Skills, Australian Government Publishing Service (AGPS), Canberra, 1223–88.

Farquhar, M. and McKay, P. (eds) (1996) *China Connections: Australian Business Needs and University Language Education*. National Language Literacy Institute of Australia, Melbourne.

Industry Task Force on Leadership and Management Skills (1995) *Enterprising Nation*. Research Report, AGPS, Canberra.

Kelly, G.A. (1963) *A Theory of Personality*. Norton, New York.

Lewin, K. (1952) *Field Theory in Social Science*. Selected theoretical papers edited by D. Cartwright. Tavistock Publications, London.

Limerick, D. and Cunnington, B. (1993) *Managing the New Organisation. A Blueprint for Networks and Strategic Alliances*. Business and Professional Publishing, Chatswood.

Senge, P. (1990) *The Fifth Discipline*. Doubleday/Currency, New York.

Strauss, A. and Corben, J. (1990) *Basics of Qualitative Research. Grounded Theory, Procedure and Techniques*. Sage Publications, London.

Wawn, T., Green, J. et al. (Barraclough and Co.) (1995) Experienced insights: opinions of Australian managers, ideals, strengths and weaknesses, *Enterprising Nation*, Research Report Volume 1. Industry Task Force on Leadership and Management Skills, AGPS, Canberra, 521–68.

Zuber-Skerritt, O. (ed.) (1992a) *Professional Development in Higher Education: A Theoretical Framework for Action Research*. Kogan Page, London, reprinted 1994 as a paperback.

Zuber-Skerritt, O. (ed.) (1992b) *Action Research in Higher Education: Examples and Reflections*. Kogan Page, London.

Zuber-Skerritt, O. (ed.) (1992c) *Starting Research: Training and Supervision*. TEI, University of Queensland, Brisbane, Chapters 11–13.

Zuber-Skerritt, O. (ed.) (1994a) *Departmental Excellence in University Education (DEUE): Action Research Case Studies*. TEI Occasional Papers No. 3. University of Queensland, Brisbane.

Zuber-Skerritt, O. (1994b) Learning and action research. Chapter 6 in P. Nightingale and M. O'Neil (eds) *Achieving Quality Learning in Higher Education*. Kogan Page, London, 99–117.

Zuber-Skerritt, O. (1994c) *Academic Staff Development in Australia in the 1990s: A Government-Driven Quality Agenda*. GIHE Occasional Papers No. 3. Griffith University, Brisbane.

Zuber-Skerritt, O. (1995) Developing a learning organisation through management education by action learning. *The Learning Organisation* 2 (2), 37–47.

Zuber-Skerritt, O. (1996) Action research and Chinese curriculum development. In M. Farquhar and P. McKay (eds) *China Connections: Australian Business Needs and University Language Education*. National Language and Literacy Institute of Australia, Melbourne.

Zuber-Skerritt, O. and Howell, F. (1993) *Evaluation of MBA and Doctoral Programs Conducted by the International Management Centre, Pacific Region*. Tertiary Education Institute, University of Queensland, Brisbane.

Appendix 6.1

Personal Orientations

Please respond to the following questions:

1. What do you think is an ideal personal orientation for members of an action research group?

2. What do you think is the overall orientation of the group you are a member of?

3. What do you think your own orientation is?

A	**B**
(a) **Outer directed** (Looks to others particularly seniors, guidance)	(a) **Inner directed** (Tends to independence of thought and expression)
(b) **Survival oriented** (Interested, at the moment, in meeting current work demands)	(b) **Developmentally oriented** (Busy, but always open to something new that is important)
(c) **Short-term doer** (Task-oriented, short-term perspective)	(c) **Reflective philosopher** (Willing to step back and reflect regularly)
(d) **Efficiency oriented** (Interested mainly in operational issues)	(d) **Effectiveness oriented** (Interested in strategic issues for the organisation)

Please insert your selected orientation (A or B) in the blank boxes.

Question	a	b	c	d
1				
2				
3				

Cliff Bunning, 1993

Chapter 7

Towards Empowering Leadership: The Importance of Imagining

Shirley Grundy

Abstract

The metaphor of 'line management' forms the theme of this chapter. A critique is mounted of 'thin, straight-line' management which is often valued within modern management theory and practice because of its promise of efficiency and effectiveness both in relation to decision-making and accountability. Habermas' theory of communicative competence is employed to explore the basis for the re-privileging of participative decision-making. What is argued, however, is not just that the 'lines' of management should be 'thickened' (while remaining essentially 'straight') but that they should be developed more discursively. Hence a form of 'storyline' management is argued for. 'Storyline' decision-making is not a form of gabfest which results in all voice and no action. Rather, a rigorous form of discursive decision-making is advocated in which Habermas' stipulation that the 'force of the better argument' should alone prevail as the justification for action is extended to incorporate 'the art of imagining' through which the possibilities for challenge are widened. Valuing challenge grounded in imagination as much as in information sets up liberating possibilities for the development of fluid, responsive and 'empowering' forms of management and decision-making.

Introduction

Everywhere within the management and leadership literature, one runs up against either advocacy or critique of so-called efficient management approaches which emphasise results-oriented organisational and administrative practices. Yeatman (1990: 14), for instance, argues with respect to public-sector management:

> With [the emphasis] on results-oriented management, the purposes of public administration and public service tend to be reduced to the effective, efficient and economic management of human and financial resources.

To argue against 'efficiency' or 'effectiveness' as desirable attributes, particularly of public service organisations, would be nonsense. Of course we want actions we take to have an 'effect'; of course we want to work in ways that do not dissipate our energies, but instead employ them 'efficiently'. The trouble is that, within the fields of public-sector management and administration, the concepts of 'efficiency' and 'effectiveness' have taken on particular meanings which have dislocated them as terms in a human discourse of desire or even reasonableness and instead have imbued them with the dehumanised overtones of technical processes. In fact, Nobel Prizes have been awarded for management theories which advocate formulaic management practices. Corbett (1992: 62) described the distinction that H.A. Simon (winner of the 1978 Nobel Prize for Economics) drew between what he termed 'programmed' and 'non-programmed' management decisions. The former are decisions which occur in numbers and frequency which permit them to be made formulaically and which are hence amenable to automation, while the latter rely upon human judgment.

> Simon argues . . . that progress will be made when managers reduce the number of non-programmed decisions and increase the number which can be made in a programmed fashion . . . As he puts it, 'the automated factory of the future will operate on the basis of programmed decisions produced in the automated office beside it'. In the automated office, managers would analyse the outcomes of future decisions by simulating the future decision-making environment in the form of computerised models and injecting into these models a range of possible decisions to see what results will follow.

While two decades later our faith in 'automated' decision-making capacities, be it for the factory or the human service organisation, may have waned, the desire for streamlined management processes has not. However, rather than process streamlining of the assembly line variety (Williams, Haslam & Williams 1992, cited in Watkins 1994: 6), more recent advocates of management efficiency and effectiveness stress 'flexibility'. Functional, numerical and financial flexibility are the ingredients of efficient and effective organisation and management practices (Watkins 1994: 20). Flexibility, however, is not to be valued in and of itself. Rather, it must always be tied to 'outcomes'. Since 'ends' are now privileged above 'means', efficient and effective management and administrative systems are to be evaluated in terms of their results or 'outcomes' (Grundy 1992).

While flexibility may be the management orientation which is currently valued, the effective achievement of results (outcomes-based management) is understood as the shortest distance between decision-making and outcome, while efficiency is signalled by the slimness of the decision-making chain. The metaphor of the 'thin, straight line' of decision making is an attractive one for the restructuring of organisations to improve outcomes (often called 'line management'). That is, an organisation which requires a reduction in the number of levels of decision-making ('flat' management structures) and a reduction in the numbers at each level involved in decision-making will not dissipate energy, but will harness it for the production of desired outcomes. Watkins (1992) identifies this 'thinning' and 'straightening' of means/end management practices with a reduction in consultation processes and a loss of democracy. Referring to developments within public-sector management in Victoria, Australia, Watkins argues:

> Since 1986, the pendulum has swung away from the advocacy of democratic decision-making processes towards the more repressive techniques of scientific management. [There has been an] abandonment of the rhetoric of collaboration and consensus through the development of documents which . . . employ the rhetoric of business management. (Watkins 1992: 241)

Within this way of understanding management practices, collaboration and consensus seeking waste time. I have heard it argued on university committees (usually by those who hold leadership positions) that the vast majority of people within the organisation are demanding: 'Let the leaders lead. Don't ask us what to think — you are paid to do the thinking, just tell us what to do.' Indeed, the rapid rise in salaries of managers within public and private-sector organisations reinforces the division between those who are paid to decide and those who are paid to produce.[1] Thus consultation and collaboration appear no longer to be key terms in the discourse of efficient and effective management.

This trend towards 'thin, straight line' management is evident even in the face of the advocacy of devolved decision making (such as is the case within Australian schools). I will argue below that devolution does not necessarily mean democratisation. Indeed, forms of participatory decision making, theoretically made possible by the devolving of responsibility to the site of the school, are often resisted by the leaders of those organisations (school principals). Moreover, the establishment of 'lines of accountability' (upwards) in conjunction with the (downwards) devolution of responsibility means that each organisational unit becomes subject to the same line management practices that prevail in large corporations.

In this paper, I want to maintain a critique of what I have called 'straight line management' and continue to advocate democratic decision-making processes. However, I want to extend the ideas of participative decision-making to argue that we need to go beyond a weak form of democratic consultation, driven by the question 'is this the best/right/most defensible course of action?' Instead I will argue for a strong form of democratic decision-making, the fundamental principle of which is the question 'could it be otherwise?'. In moving from the privileging of rational defensibility to privileging the opening up of alternative possibilities, I want to affirm 'the art of imagining' not just 'the science of reasoning'. In doing so, I will make reference to schools as a particular example of a public service organisation, for it is with the organisation and management of schools and schooling that my interests and experience lie.

In making this argument, I draw upon Habermas' ideas of 'communicative competence', which are, in turn, grounded in an understanding of the nature of human action.

Management and human action

It is interesting to trace the conceptual continuities in Western thought. 'Thin line' management practices can be interpreted as attempts to overcome the uncertainties of human interaction. Within this view, which Benhabib (1986) argues is a strong theme in Western philosophy, the social world is regarded as somehow flawed because of the uncertainties inherent in interaction. This, according to Benhabib (1986: 87), was Hegel's view:

> Human action . . . remains perpetually caught in a dialectic where the discrepancy between intention and consequence is never eliminated. . . . [T]he discrepancy between action and consequence arises through the misunderstanding, misinterpretation, and misconstrual of our acts by others.

If the social world is so uncertain, one way of dealing with it is to treat it as if it were the physical world; to act upon the social world rather than interacting within it.[2] This elimination of uncertainty is what 'thin line management' attempts; the shortest route between decision and action, between policy and practice, between problem and solution. If interaction can be curtailed, if defined lines of consultation and decision making can be identified, then the uncertainties of the world of interaction can be controlled, if not eliminated. This then allows the managers to 'leave their mark', to leave an impression upon what they understand to be 'their' world.

Habermas (1984; 1987), along with others such as Hannah Arendt (1958), argues against this attempt to see the uncertainties of human action as problematical (what Hegel called 'bad infinity': Benhabib 1986: 243). According to Benhabib (1986: 243), Habermas celebrates rather than denigrates the uncertainties associated with human action in the social world:

> The interpretive indeterminacy of social action is not an ontological shortcoming, but its constitutive feature. The model of communicative action . . . emphasises that social action always entails linguistic communication, and that interpretive indeterminacy is a constitutive feature of social action.

This means that the social world is not just to be dealt with communicatively, but the social world is constituted linguistically — that is, through communicative practices.

One of the implications of this is that the social world as it is manifested in human service organisations, for instance, is not simply a 'system' that can be managed in a way that eliminates uncertainty and contradiction, but it is a form of social life which is constituted through the communicative practices of the members of the school community.

Beyond the gabfest

This is not to suggest that social organisations or institutions should be organised and managed as perpetual 'gabfests', characterised by all talk and no action. When Habermas advocated communicative practices as constitutive of the social world, he had in mind a particular form of what he calls 'communicative competence'. This means that the communicative practices within the social world need to take cognisance of three realms of understanding. These are the external or empirical world, the social world of norms and values and the subjective world of personal feelings, desires and intentions.

Communicative practices need to encompass principles in relation to each of these realms. Firstly, with respect to the empirical world, statements need to be able to make claims to 'truth' on the basis of empirical evidence. With respect to the inter-subjective world of values, claims need to be able to be made that can be defended in terms of 'rightness' or 'appropriateness'. With respect to the subjective world, it is important that the speaker speaks 'sincerely' and 'authentically'.

However, we should not assume that these various validity claims (that is, 'truth', 'rightness' or 'sincerity') can be established outside the communicative site itself. Indeed, Habermas argues that the validity claims can only themselves be established discursively (that is, through discussion, debate, etc.), but that certain conditions need to prevail. These conditions are grounded in freedom, equality and justice. That is, not only must assertions, observations and intentions be able to be tested against the validity claims of 'truth', 'appropriateness' and 'authenticity', but they must be able to be tested in conditions of freedom and equality. This means that everyone must have equal chances to assert and challenge, to put forward reasons and arguments and to demand reasoned arguments from others.

It should be noted that in this communicative view of the social world, there is no resiling from contestation or from multiple interpretations. Indeed, multiple interpretations are the essence of this social world. But it is also the case that not all interpretations are to be accepted simply because they are voiced. It is the force of the better argument that must prevail, but not simply the arguments based on evidence from the so-called 'empirical' world. Inter-subjective and subjective interpretations take their place alongside empirically based argument. Moreover, the 'force of the better argument' does not mean the arguments of those with most power. All must have equal chances to assert, to defend and to challenge.

Expanding the concept of communicative competence

So what does this all mean for a social organisation or institution, such as a school or a hospital, if we think of it not as a system to be managed, but as a communicative community? How might such a community be organised? What might management practices look like in such a community? How might we interpret 'leadership' here?

Habermas' idea of communicative competence suggests that, far from the concept of 'thin line management' which seeks as far as possible to streamline and formalise communicative structures into decision-making systems, a robust, highly 'textured' form of management and organisation suggests itself. This is a form of organisation that privileges debate and contestation. It is a form of organisation that critiques the personality cult of the 'charismatic leader' and instead values rational argumentation carried out in conditions of equal access to opportunities to challenge. This does not mean the end of leadership. Indeed, those officially charged with leadership responsibilities have opportunities to open up possibilities of communicative decision-making. The 'equality' principle does not necessarily entail the end of leadership, although it may well mean the end of leadership being understood as invested permanently in particular persons. Instead, multiple opportunities will be opened up for leadership by numerous members of the organisation. Leadership would become associated with particular tasks and strategies rather than particular positions.

It is precisely here, however, that there is room for further exploration of Habermas' ideas of communicative competence. The notion of the 'force of the better argument alone' and the validity claims, particularly the 'truth' claim, are grounded in principles of rationality. That is, the better argument becomes the one for which reasons and supportive evidence can be given. This means that the equality conditions become suspect. It is all very well to assert equal access to making claims, but the better argument will be able to be made by the one who has access to supporting evidence or data. And those who are most likely to have access to such information are those with information networks and access to formal information dissemination structures (in sites like schools, these are most likely to be school principals and other members of the executive).[3] Thus demanding that consultation and contestation be grounded in the force of the 'better argument' alone may well negate the equality conditions. So a rationalist interpretation of communicative competence is not as empowering as it may at first appear.[4]

But what if we were to broaden the validity claims a little to encourage, not only the meeting of challenges to provide supportive evidence, but the exercising of imagination? That is, the question around which the validity claims are contested becomes not just 'can this be supported or defended?' but 'could it be otherwise?' The ability to challenge, in this case, is not so much determined by access to information, but by the exercising of imagination.

Let us first explore what this opening up of the justificatory demands does to the validity claims. Firstly, it opens up the possibility that there may be multiple 'truths'. The question 'could it be otherwise?' makes it necessary to seek other evidence. The question might not simply be able to be 'is this true?', but rather 'is this true in every instance; for all members of this organisation or for all whom this organisation serves?' Such questions ought to particularly focus our attention upon those on the margins — not to speak on their behalf, but to open up the possibilities for their contribution and contestation.

The same applies for the validity claim of rightness and appropriateness. Again, the scope of the question is expanded. It is not just 'is this appropriate from the shared understandings of this group of people?' but 'is it appropriate for all those whom the policy or practice might touch?' Such questions demand more than simply a dispassionate consideration of a range of views. They require an act of imagining: 'Imagine that I am an Aboriginal child in this school, will this policy be appropriate for me or for my family?'; 'Imagine that I am a non-English speaker in this hospital, will this policy or practice promote my health care?'

Of course, it is quite easy to place limits on our imagining. But here too the validity claim of appropriateness is apposite. What is appropriate imagining? The 'equality and justice' conditions within which the validity claims are to be established provide a clue here. These conditions are designed to give a voice to those who, in other communicative circumstances, might have their voices drowned by the voices of authority. The proviso that all should have the opportunity to challenge, however, can apply only to those in the communicative group. And these might well be those who share power already in the organisation. Moreover, if, as we noted above, some of these are the 'information rich', then they are difficult to argue against.

But if we overlay here a privileging of imagining, then through the act of imagining, others can vicariously be drawn into the debate. And the justice provision would suggest that those for whom truth and authenticity should be questioned are those whose voices are marginalised.

Of course, we need to be careful here lest we simply substitute empathetic imagination for 'voice' — that is, we just make sure we have 'thought about' those on the margins. The 'truth' validity condition reminds us that we do need evidence of some form ultimately to support our acts of imagining. Moreover, the 'sincerity' validity claim requires that we privilege authentic, subjective experience. Speaking on behalf of another will not suffice. However, privileging imagining within communicative practices reminds us of the need to seek evidence from 'the other', from the marginalised, from those whose voices have not and cannot be given access to or space within the debate. It also opens up possibilities for the 'voicing' of experience by other means than through scholastically presented argumentation. Ellsworth (1992: 111) notes some of the ways in which she and her students experimented with voicing the subjective experiences of the marginalised and, hence, interrupting established forms of debate, dialogue and disputation.

Leadership and the art of imagining

At the beginning of this paper, I argued that current management trends represent a move away from democratic decision making and towards straight-line management. I asserted that this was the case even within forms of devolved decision making. The argument presented above for a form of administration grounded in communicative competence clearly offers a challenge to such trends. In what follows, I wish to substantiate the claim that devolved decision making does not necessarily entail communicative decision making practices (even when it operates in quasi-participative forms). I also further explore the implications of communicative competence for leadership and management. In doing so, I refer to quoted comments from school principals about (devolved) participative decision making. These comments were contained in a report entitled *Devolution: The Next Phase* (hereafter called the Devolution Report), published by the Western Australian Secondary Principals' Association (Chadbourne and Clarke 1994).

In the report, 'participatory' and 'devolved' decision making are equated:

> Since 1987, principals have been required to adopt participative decision-making processes in the running of their [sic] schools. In some cases the requirement takes the form of official [policies] ... In other cases, the requirement takes the form of a virtually non negotiable expectation held by superordinates and subordinates. (Chadbourne and Clarke 1994: 29)

Participative decision making appears to counter 'thin line management' where decisions are handed down the line (and accountability reporting handed back up the line) through individuals. The requirements for consultation and participation in policy formation at the school level appear to embody some of the principles of communicative competence, at least to the extent that it is accepted that decision making should be shared within the organisation with the right to involvement being broadly recognised. In many cases, however, the notion of 'straight line' management is not necessarily replaced: the line is simply thickened. That is, 'committees' are substituted for individuals. The authority structure is not fundamentally challenged; the authority has simply been vested elsewhere than in an individual.

One of the quotes in the Devolution Report (Chadbourne and Clarke 1994) is quite interesting in demonstrating that the line management structure has not been fundamentally altered. It has, if anything, become simply a 'thicker line' (i.e. a line of committees rather than individuals). But this example also demonstrates that, in this instance, the underlying thin line management structure has not really altered at all:

> A lot of policy at present is being generated in committees that I'm not actually sitting on and they report to me ... One of our committees has just generated a policy on drugs in the school, which, it turns out, was quite draconian but it passed through. I now have to say 'Well look, you have been working on this policy for twelve months and you've put hours ... into it, but I am going to chip this bit out and that bit out.' So straight away there is a degree of resentment ... The expectation is that they'll have all the say, not just some of it ... (Chadbourne and Clarke, 1994: 32)

This is, of course, a decontextualised quote, and we cannot know the actual circumstances to which it refers. As a piece of text, however, the quote raises a number of issues from the standpoint of a communicative competence approach to leadership. In the first place, it does not appear that there has been a real redistribution of power here. The power of the principal has been nominally handed to a committee. It is evident from the quotation, however, that even this level of sharing of power is in name only. The power is retrieved by the principal whenever it suits her/him. The references to 'them' and 'me' also suggest that power is not being 'shared' here; it is being 'given' and 'taken back'. We must ask whether relocating power with committees rather than engaging in a wider distribution of power is a form of participative decision making that is any more than 'thick line' rather than 'thin line' management.

But does the theory of communicative competence have anything to suggest to us about how the 'lines' of management might become more inclusive? I would argue that it does. On the one hand, the concern for equal access to make suggestions and to challenge is clearly important. In the example quoted the principal felt excluded from the process. He/she had become the outsider, the 'other'. It is likely that others might also have felt just as excluded. There is no mention of wider consultative procedures. Moreover, the validity criteria of 'truth', 'appropriateness' and 'sincerity' provide a means for engagement with proposals and policy. Rather than simply chopping things out because one claims the ultimate authority to do so (no matter how rationally defensible the argument for doing so might be — in this case the draconian nature of the policy), a process of arguing through the justification for the policies seems preferable to autocratic censorship.

However, given the above argument, the idea and process of justification needs to extend beyond asking the question 'is this position defensible?' A form of communicative competence which extends challenge beyond rational argumentation is grounded in the art of imagining. This is a form of imagination which asks such questions as: 'Could it be otherwise?' and 'If it was otherwise, would this policy be more appropriate for one or other groups, particularly taking into account those who have not had a voice in the decision making process?' The opportunity to exercise the art of imagining in this way must extend beyond those formally designated as 'decision makers'. Seizing the opportunity to challenge on the basis of imagining, however, is likely to be encouraged if those with formal responsibility for leadership actively divest themselves of the responsibility of being the only or, indeed, the principal enquirers. Conversely, participative decision making is not served when power or control is simply handed over. Forms of power and information 'sharing' need to be developed.

Storyline management

The development of such a form of management might still entail a form of 'line' management, but it will not be straight line (whether thin or thick line) management. Rather, I prefer to think of it as 'storyline' management. That is, the lines develop and change with the development of the issue under consideration. But the communicative lines don't just go on for ever; the 'story' must reach its conclusion (however temporary that might be) at some time.

The leader in this form of management facilitates the development of the storylines, keeps them moving forward, opens up creative possibilities for the development and insists that the 'plot' be tested against the validity claims. The leader is not the author. 'Authorship' is collaborative. The leader is more like an 'editor', organising, negotiating, etc., but not 'authoring'. Moreover, such 'editorial' leadership may change from time to time. But neither is the leader excluded from participation in the 'authorship' of the 'storyline'. A particular responsibility of the editor/ leader is to foster, indeed ensure, inclusive authorship, including the voices of the marginalised.

Such a form of management does not eliminate the 'power' of the leader. But it transforms it from authoritative power to power sharing (or 'empowerment'). As has been noted above, some forms of participative decision making simply relocate power, divesting one person or set of persons of power and investing power in others. One principal who is quoted in the Devolution Report complained of what she/he perceived of as a total loss of power:

> Well I think I've lost autonomy with practically every school policy. Once upon a time it was perceived that policy would emanate from the principal's office, or from the administrative team anyway. I think there is an expectation now amongst teachers that policy will start at the bottom and come up and then be rubber stamped by the principal. (Chadbourne and Clarke 1994: 32)

This is an interesting example of a dichotomised notion of power. That is, power is finite and is possessed by one set of people or another. If one set has it, the others do not, and if power is transferred to these others, then there will be a loss of power by those who used to have it. As was noted in relation to the earlier quotation, this is not 'shared' power.

Communicative competence challenges this notion of the finite existence and exercising of power. Where communicative practices such as those discussed above are opened up, there are possibilities for empowerment — that is, exercising some degree of power or control in a situation.

Here I want to sound a cautionary note about substituting one management/leadership metaphor for another. Metaphors of 'thin, straight line' (anorexic) management practices have a hard edge to them. It is easy to respond negatively to such images. Conversely, the image of 'storyline' management evokes feelings of warmth and humanity. We should not, however, be glib about the idea of power sharing or 'empowerment', or expect that the opening up of communicative practices will be comfortable. Anyone who has attempted collaborative authorship will know that it is hard, sometimes distressing, frequently stressful. Privileging 'challenge' within communicative management practices will not create a tranquil work environment. There is nothing comfortable about the notion of challenge. Moreover, when the challenges go beyond simply asking for justification to asking 'could it be otherwise?' then the threats of challenge increase rather than diminish.[5] This sense of threat is implicit in the following quote from the Devolution Report:

> I thought if staff were involved in the decision making, then things would be more meaningful for them and they'd have a greater stake in the school … Even just informing people becomes a bit of a nightmare because you've got some people saying, I wonder how

> biased this information is, is it objective information, is it right information, where do you get the information from, can we check the information. (Chadbourne and Clarke 1994: 31)

This is a significant quote, because it illustrates the problems identified above with respect to the requirement for rational justification. It may well be an example of people saying 'could it be otherwise?' 'Is this the only "truth"?', 'is this the most "appropriate" information?'

Note, however, that such questions are regarded as both frustrating and threatening. The right to question the information is, however, absolutely fundamental to a communicative theory and practice of leadership and management.

Coping with the threat of challenge

One answer to the question of how we might cope with such threats is 'trust'. In the Devolution Report (Chadbourne and Clarke 1994), 'trust' is provided as an answer to the difficulties of 'thick line' management (i.e. management by committee).

> It really comes back to trust. Lack of trust. If we could get to that stage where everybody's pulling together, looking for student outcomes and trust people until they make a mistake.

Another principal noted:

> I get worried that we've got 21 standing committees and we've got *ad hoc* committees and we're getting representation from all sorts of sources, but it's not necessary if we've got trust.

The issue of trust needs to be recognised as problematic. 'Trust' alone does not necessarily redistribute power, 'trust' does not necessarily lead to power sharing, nor does 'trust' ensure that the validity conditions of 'truth', 'appropriateness' and/or 'sincerity' are met. 'Trust' does not demand that stringent conditions of justice grounded in equal opportunities to challenge are met. Trust might well eliminate challenge.

At least, that might well be the case for the sort of leave-things-as-they-are trust that appears to be advocated in the quotes above. This is not to say that trust should be eliminated from the discourse. However, a richer and more fruitful concept might be 'confidence', that is, the confidence that everyone and everything can be challenged; confidence that our challenges will be met with argument and evidence and that we will, in turn, be appreciated for providing imaginative challenges. What is needed is confidence that when we challenge we will be interpreted as challenging the idea, the assertion, the evidence, not the person.

Empowering leadership will be that which fosters and protects such confidence.

References

Arendt, H. (1958) *The Human Condition*. University of Chicago Press, Chicago.

Benhabib, S. (1986) *Critique, Norm and Utopia: A Study of the Foundations of Critical Theory*. Columbia University Press, New York.

Chadbourne, R. and Clarke, R. (1994) *Devolution: The Next Phase*. Report of the Western Australian Secondary Principals Association, Perth.

Corbett, D. (1992) *Australian Public Sector Management*. Allen & Unwin, Sydney.

Ellsworth, E. (1992) Why doesn't this feel empowering? Working through the repressive myths of critical pedagogy. In J. Gore (ed.) *Feminisms and Critical Pedagogy*. Routledge, New York, pp. 90 –119.

Grundy, S. (1987) *Curriculum: Product or Praxis?* Falmer Press, London.

Grundy, S. (1992) Beyond guaranteed outcomes: creating a discourse for educational praxis. *Australian Journal of Education*, 36 (2) 157–69.

Habermas, J. (1984) *The Theory of Communicative Action,* vol. 1. Beacon Press, Boston.

Habermas, J. (1987) *The Theory of Communicative Action,* vol. 2. Beacon Press, Boston.

Watkins, P. (1994) The Fordist/post-Fordist debate: the educational implications. In J. Kenway (ed.) *Economising Education: The Post-Fordist Directions*. Deakin University Press, Geelong, 1–42.

Watkins, P. (1992) The transformation of educational administration: the hegemony of consent and the hegemony of coercion. *Australian Journal of Education*, 36 (3), 237–59.

Yeatman, A. (1990) *Bureaucrats, Technocrats, Femocrats: Essays on the Contemporary Australian State*. Allen & Unwin, Sydney.

Notes

1   At my university, for instance, at a time when the management of the university was demanding productivity pay-offs for a 2 per cent salary rise for the majority of staff, the Vice-Chancellor was awarded a 25 per cent rise with no productivity increase requirements.

2   I have explored this idea of the elimination of uncertainty in human action in a 1992 paper entitled 'Beyond guaranteed outcomes: creating a discourse for educational praxis' (Grundy 1992).

3   Even with the explosion of access to information through the Internet and the World Wide Web, it is interesting to note that in schools the computer with Internet access is often in the principal's office and it is the principal who has the flexibility of work organisation to allow exploration of the medium and access to information.

4   Elizabeth Ellsworth has presented a powerful critique of the failure of the principles of critical dialogue to ensure equality of communication within groups despite the best intentions to do so. (See Ellsworth 1992.)

5   The obvious question, then, is: 'Why bother?' The answer to that is complex and it is pursued through the volumes of Habermas' work. In short, the case for 'empowering leadership' rests upon the same arguments as those for emancipatory action research. These arguments are pursued in other chapters of this work. In my own work I have explored arguments in support of emancipatory action research in *Curriculum: Product or Praxis?* (Grundy 1987).

Chapter 8

Emancipatory Action Research: A Critical Alternative to Personnel Development or a New Way of Patronising People?

Richard Weiskopf and Stephan Laske

Abstract

This paper attempts to discuss some of the problems associated with emancipatory action research. In particular, the idea of reducing the sphere of power via communicative action is critically examined. We draw on our experience from a concrete project, in which we tried to use action research as an alternative to traditional approaches to the development of organisations or the people concerned, and to initiate a mutual learning process between workers and scientists in a cooperative. We argue in this paper that consensus-orientated research tends to overrate both the possibility and value of consensus and mutual understanding of the problems. Thereby it tends to oversee that power is reproduced in various ways rather than reduced. We propose to see action research as an intervention in the political system of the organisation — that is, based on a 'cooperation pact' rather than on consensus.

Introduction

The field of personnel management is rather broad, and normally includes planning, recruitment and selection of employees; 'reward' systems; performance appraisal and so on. In particular, training and development of 'human resources' during the 1980s and 1990s has become one of the central topics in the field of personnel management. Internal or external experts have been engaged to discover the gap between the qualification demands of the organisation and the actual performance of individuals. Accordingly, training strategies have become important tools for reducing or closing this gap in order to provide the organisation with appropriate people who can help the organisation achieve its output goals.

One of the central criticisms of the traditional approaches to development has been that people in organisations are seen as 'personnel' rather than as human beings. The training (qualification) of human resources seems a means for disciplining the people concerned rather than developing their personal capacities (Gorbach & Weiskopf 1993). The basic problem seems to be the constitution of a subject/object dualism or a monological relationship based on distance between those who decide the 'objective' needs and demands for qualification and those 'to be developed'. The basic idea behind the more technical concepts is that personnel (or 'human resources') are *objects* to be 'prepared for success' rather than human beings valued for themselves.

The idea of emancipation

In the field of business administration, *personnel management* has been seen as being strongly connected to the employees' interests: as the 'soft' end of the 'hard' economic concepts. The human relations idea and the rhetorical shift from 'personnel management' to 'human resource management' (Storey 1991) emphasised the importance of learning, personal growth and development in organisations. Corporate training programs and strategies have been claimed to be the 'vital component' of modern human resource management. 'If the training and development of its employees is not afforded high priority, if training is not seen as a vital component in the realization of business plans, then it is hard to accept that such a company has committed itself to HRM.' (Keep 1991: 125) According to the ideas of many contributors, there is no inherent contradiction between the rationality of economic organisations and the rationality of individuals. Organisations can both fulfil the needs of personnel and achieve the economic goals of the organisation. Many organisations stress the importance of an 'investment in human resources', which are often ticketed as the 'enterprise's most important capital'. Of course the idea of 'investing in people', of treating people properly and so on, has nothing to do with emancipation. Rather '[t]he discourse of welfare and the human relations school clouds personnel's role in providing a nexus of disciplinary practices aimed at making employees' behavior and performance predictable and calculable — in a word, "manageable"' (Townley 1994: 143). Critical theory has always criticised both the objectifying practices of management and the managerial ideology of the harmonious relationship between managerial and employees' interests. Especially in the German tradition, action research was seen as a 'critical social science' (Moser 1975) — and as a way of bringing together critical social science theory and practice: 'Action research wanted to make theory practical in order to improve practice' (Altrichter & Gstettner 1993: 344; see also Moser 1975). The action research approach has been seen as a way to emancipate the people in organisations. In the field of personnel development, the idea is that the members of an organisation should be able to free themselves from domination and structural limitations by a process of (cooperative) self-reflection, which has to be organised according to the ideal of a discourse free of power and domination. Haag's (1972: 42) already classic formulation of the emancipatory interest of research suggests that:

> [critical social science] aims at co-operating with people in their practical everyday world through common working and learning processes and to communicate with them about these processes in order to reduce the sphere of power and control in these common processes of working, learning and self-reflection.

Accordingly, the role of the researcher is not that of an external and neutral expert who analyses qualification needs, derived from 'objective' characteristics of the job-structure. Characteristic is the idea of critical solidarity with the employees and an emancipatory interest that includes both the idea of 'substantial democratization' (Kappler 1980) of the organisation, and individual freedom. The central focus is not meeting the qualification demands to help the organisation achieve its output goals, but rather developing competencies that may lead to simultaneous learning by the individual and the organisation (Pieper 1988).

MID — re*ducing* or re*producing* the sphere of power?

In order to illustrate this kind of research and to point out some methodological implications, we want to discuss some of the experience we have gained in a research project in which we tried to use emancipatory

123

action research to initiate a *mutual* learning process between workers and scientists (see Laske & Schneider 1985; Schneider & Laske 1985). This experience should make clear that some of the *assumptions* of emancipatory action research are rather problematic.

The case

Originally a traditionally organised enterprise under a different name, MID (Möbel-und Industriedesign Genossenschaft, Imst, Tyrol) was founded in 1981 after the organisation suffered a severe economic crisis caused by managerial mistakes on the part of the owner. With the help of the Chamber of Labor, the Ministry of Labor and the union, the firm was newly founded as a cooperative by the former workers.

Our research project included several tasks:

- We wanted to analyse the conditions of survival for cooperative organisations in the economic and societal context of a capitalistic world.

- As 'research consultants' we wanted to contribute to a positive future of the newly founded cooperative. For us, this was a moral question, because the members of the firm had only minimal chances in the labour market of the region, and the supporting political institutions believed as we did that without help the experiment would fail very soon. 'Positive future' was conceptualised not only in terms of economic survival but also in terms of the 'communicative rationalization' (Habermas 1981) of the organisation.

Accordingly, we tried to combine both outside and inside views of the problem. Our research from the outside comprised looking at the labour market, the market conditions, the material and economic resources and the legal framework as structural conditions of the cooperative (which were implicitly conceptualised as limitations of cooperatives). Research from the inside consisted of reconstructing the history of the organisation in order to understand the rules guiding action in this context. In addition, we tried to initiate a *mutual* learning process between workers (the members of the cooperative) and the researchers. The basic principle of our research was to conduct research in the form of an emancipatory dialogue. The workers of the cooperative were to become *subjects* in the research process and in their 'life-world'. Practical action and scientific work were to result in a common process involving researchers and 'field subjects'.

Following the principles of emancipatory action research, we tried to replace the model of strategic action which reduces others to objects to be influenced and underlies technocratic training programs, and to conceptualise the research process according to the model of 'communicative action' (Habermas 1981). In contrast to 'success-oriented' or 'strategic' action, the framework of 'communicative action' implies *interac*ting partners who meet as subjects. The primary goal of communicative action is not the achievement of efficiency and successful outcomes, but reaching a mutual understanding concerning the shared situation and the common aim of development. In this model, language is the central communicative medium and central mechanism of coordinating actions. Communicative action, according to Habermas, can be seen on two different levels: the level of action and the level of discourse. On both levels, the participants or interaction partners retain a cooperative attitude. 'Action' refers to the everyday context of social interaction where experiences are gained and exchanged through ordinary language. On the rational or reflective level of 'discourse', the validity claims, which on the level of action are naively taken for granted, can be reflected upon. Thereby discourse becomes a central medium of individual and collective learning (Miller 1985).

In the research process, phases of communicative action were to alternate with those of the discourse. The discourse was, if possible, to be free of limitations and constraints, as well as to approximate the ideal speech situation as closely as possible. Of course, we were clear about the counterfactual character of the model of the ideal speech situation, which must not be confused with any real discourse. Nevertheless, this view strongly influenced our conceptualisation of the research process and our relationship to the 'researched': the idea of 'undistorted communication' (Habermas) and the goal of developing a *common* view of the problems served as a normative guideline. The 'Plurality of Voices' (Habermas 1988: 153) was expected to ensure the *unity* of the project.

Empirical reasons why this idealistic scenario cannot be put into practice are easy to find, and do not question the model in principle. But if we reconsider the research process and look at power and interests as an *integral* part of this process — rather than as something coming from outside which should be eliminated as far as possible — questions of theoretical principle arise. Is it possible that the emancipatory effort camouflages the establishment of new power relationships rather than frees the people concerned from arbitrary restrictions?

Power as an integral part of the process

The different phases of the project clearly show how the process itself constitutes asymmetrical power relationships that are reproduced in the course of the project in various forms.

Following the rules of critical empirical social science, we did, of course, ask for the consensus of the cooperative's members for our studies and clearly laid out our intentions at the beginning of the project. According to the nature of the project, neither we nor the members of the cooperative were able to know what this consensus would actually mean. The members of the cooperative got involved in a game in which the power to define the rules (and the context of action) was, despite all emancipatory efforts on the part of the researchers, hardly evenly distributed — something that does not seem possible anyway. Thus, from the very beginning, the project was not based on a consensus implying a free and rational agreement between equal communication partners. One can rather assume that the pressure of the economic conditions had a significant influence on how agreement was reached. In this respect, there was — as in every consultation process in which the client depends on outside help — an asymmetrical relationship, which also constituted a specific relationship of authority (see Schmitz et al. 1989: 122). This does not mean that the clients were dependent on the consultants in a one-sided relationship, but rather dependence existed on both sides. Nonetheless, because of the definitions of the roles of the researchers and participants as 'helpers' and 'those in need of help', there was a definite power relationship established. This power relationship is inherent in the consulting relationship and cannot be avoided, even if the attempt to achieve a definition of the situation is consensus-oriented.

The point of departure of the project was a common ideology of the 'midwives' (the Chamber of Labor, the Ministry of Labor and the union) and the researchers, namely that 'self-management is good'. To the people concerned this idea seemed strange, at least initially, and did not fit into their (rather conservative) world-view. The members of the cooperative accepted the idea mainly because it was made the precondition for the preservation of jobs — without this idea the new foundation of the company would not have been possible. Thus, the idea of a basic superiority, the fictitious lead of the expert, was characteristic of our model. Within the field of critical action research, various proponents have pointed out the necessity of creating a 'problem consciousness' on the part of the people concerned (cf. Moser 1975: 148). In principle, this seems possible only if the consultant is accepted as 'pedagogic authority' (Bourdieu & Passeron 1973: 21). In this case as well, one can say that such a pedagogic relationship always implies a power relationship, since the mediating authority is assigned the power to select methods and content. This paradoxical situation can be compensated only in part by the basic claim of action research, namely that 'research techniques may be used only with the consent of all those concerned' (Altrichter et al. 1993: 78). The reason for this is that essential preconditions for the formation of consensus, that is, at least an approximately equal information basis, do not exist at all. Additionally, it is difficult to clearly define the circle of those concerned. Consequently, the 'consent of all those concerned' does not overcome the authority problem.

In practice, language itself is not only a medium of communication, but always a medium of distinction as well. Our project, for instance, showed that managers with training in business administration understood our language more quickly. Despite all efforts, there was no symmetrical discourse, especially with the discourse of business administration itself not being an 'innocent discourse'. Thinking in terms of business administration categories already suggests certain solutions as realistic and others as unrealistic. For instance, no balance sheet, which is the instrument used in our society to measure the success of 'normal' and self-managed enterprises, can show the degree of quality of life. (Real) discourse is, therefore, not only a medium of learning and reflection, but also represents a powerful collection of tools for control and coercion: the determination of the topics, participants, discursive forms and external conditions of the discourse implies 'procedures of exclusion' (cf. Foucault 1991: 11). We certainly do not want to concur with some structuralist theories of discourse in underestimating the role of the subject in the discourse. Still, our experience has clearly shown that with regard to the possession of power:

> [the] reflexive elaboration of frames of meaning is characteristically imbalanced ... whether this be a result of the superior linguistic or dialectical skills of one person in conversation with another; the possession of relevant types of 'technical knowledge', the mobilization of authority of 'force', etc. 'What passes for social reality' stands in immediate relation to the distribution of power — not only on the most mundane levels of everyday interaction, but also on the level of global cultures and ideologies, whose influence indeed may be felt in every corner of everyday social life itself. (Giddens 1993a: 120)

The claim to make research an open, communicative process constitutes (emancipatory) action research. The individual phases of the process should remain open for corrections and changes, and it should be possible to adapt them to altered conditions by means of renewed negotiations with the participants. It is important in this respect to realise that this process is not always of the nature of a friendly talk or ordered discussion and that interest in reaching a 'rational consensus' cannot always be assumed to exist. This negotiation process rather has a political character, and the nature of the speech situation can be expected to be one of a political arena in which participants try to realise their own interests. Ideal communicative action or discourse requires that the discourse admits interest only in a future consensus. The only motive allowed should — according to the ideal — be 'a cooperate readiness to arrive at an understanding' (Habermas cit. in Thompson 1984: 259). This implies, however, that the participants would have to relinquish their basic existential interests. From our point of view, this relinquishment cannot be achieved in practice, since the interest of action research is never one of pure knowledge creation alone. Necessarily, on the parts of both the participants and the external researchers, additional interests play a role, interests that are anchored in the material conditions of life of all participants and which are not necessarily on the level of 'discursive consciousness' (Giddens 1992: 91). The prominence given to the idea of 'readiness to arrive at an understanding' does in our opinion not lead to a reduction of 'the sphere of power'. On the contrary, there is a tendency to suppress relevant differences in perspectives, problems and world-views that cannot be brought to a common understanding, but could themselves be resources for productive development.

In the research process, persons who are tied into different institutional contexts come together. This results in a number of advantages for research and for the processes of learning and change in the respective field. For instance, the researchers' institutional ties to and security offered by the university system facilitates the development of interpretative patterns, problem solutions and so on, in a situation which is relatively unburdened by the pressure of action contexts. These resources can also be used to support the endeavours of the people in practical business life to bring about change — for example, by means of publicity measures (Heinze 1987: 38). Conversely, the members of the cooperative (the research field) can contribute their expert knowledge and their experience to certain actions. One should, however, also take into consideration that the respective institutional background represents power resources as well — power resources that influence the research process and the relationship between external researchers and the researched. For instance, we as researchers were, to a substantial degree, endowed with 'symbolic capital' (Bourdieu 1994: 119). As a consequence, our words were attributed much more significance, which became obvious when, for example, one member of the project group assumed a more active role within the cooperative and was soon put into the position of an expert, although the members of the cooperative doubtless had considerably more practical experience.

In an action research project there is always a strong mutual dependence among the participants (researchers and researched). On the one hand, external researchers depend on the active participation of the researched and their acceptance of the main points of the planned course of the project. On the other hand, with regard to important points, the participants depend on the researchers (Moser 1975: 150). This mutual dependence creates, together with at least partially conflicting interests, an essential precondition for (micro)political processes (Neuberger 1990: 265). For instance, the refusal to answer certain questions in interviews that formed part of our project can be interpreted as micro-political strategies of interest realisation.

The basic ethical principle of critical action research is that '[r]esearch reports and case studies must not be published without giving the participants the opportunity to comment' (Altrichter et al. 1993: 78). In our research project we have certainly tried to comply with this principle. In this case, one must, however, consider that a presentation in written form is by no means a neutral medium. For instance, most members of the cooperative were not familiar with this presentation mode. The reluctance to read the reports that were presented regularly can also be interpreted as (latent) resistance against a culturally alien form of presentation of knowledge. Thus, formally the impression of a cooperative process is generated; in reality, however, considerable asymmetrical relationships seem to exist.

These points are meant to show that the conceptualisation of the research process according to the model of communicative action seems problematic. The actual discourse is always tied into a societal context so that the idea of a discourse free of power and domination must appear fictional. In our opinion, it is therefore not clear how this model *can* be implemented in the face of a reality characterised by different power structures and diverging interests, by scarce resources and conflicts. To the extent that this model is based on preconditions that cannot be found in actual discourses it runs the danger of becoming an ideological position (Thompson 1984). Consequently, and also because of underestimating the relevance of significant differences as productive force, we are also suspicious of consensus orientation as a normative ideal.

Action research as a powerful intervention in the political system of the organisation

Every active intervention in an organisation represents a political intervention with intended and unintended consequences. Every process of change, whether at the individual or collective level, influences the interests of the other actors and creates new political constellations and thus new lines of conflict and consensus. For example, our project, as mentioned above, was guided by the idea of initiating a mutual learning process. Yet, if we look critically at our own experiences, we have to realise that after a certain time there was a clear bias. Our direct partners in the process were the two managers of the cooperative. They were in a position to understand our language, which was clearly determined by our socialisation in the academic milieu and our definition of the situation in categories of social and administrative sciences. One of the unintended consequences of our facilitation was that we helped to create new elites and new hierarchies in the cooperative. The two managers were able to stabilise their position by using expert knowledge and 'symbolic capital' (Bourdieu 1994: 119). On the other hand, our own interpretation of the problems of the cooperative was clearly influenced by the view of these managers. We can say that we built a political coalition which served the managers' interests in stabilising and legitimising their positions and the interests of the research team in achieving visible success, thereby legitimising their work, and collecting material worth publishing. Another consequence with clearly political implications was the production of a new consensus in the cooperative: two members left the organisation because they felt totally overtaxed by the new organisational culture. These were concrete power effects of the creation of a new political *unity* based on consensus that emerged out of the process and which was secured by the exclusion of certain deviant voices.

The relationship between researchers and the researched

Against this background, the relationship between researchers and the researched should be critically considered. In our research project we defined ourselves as consultants and implicitly assumed the existence of common interests on the part of researchers and members of the cooperative. According to our experiences, however, we recognise that the idea of a common interest represents, at least in part, an ideological position. The interests of external researchers coincide only partially with those of the participants. In our case, for the people involved the research project was not primarily an experiment of learning (with learning never being an end in itself). Their overall interest was to secure their material basis of life. On the other hand, the research team was involved in a different institutional context with its specific rules of the game. Besides our 'emancipatory' interest we wanted to produce knowledge and to produce this knowledge according to the rules of the academic system. In addition to official aims and interests, unofficial aims and interests, such as career interests, also play important roles.

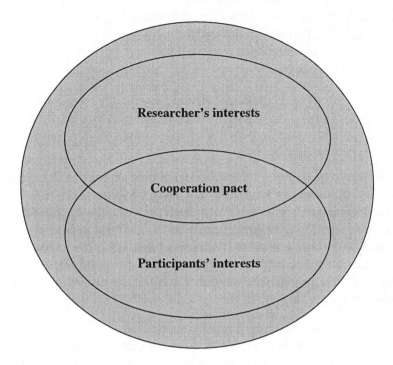

Figure 8.1 *Fusion model of emancipatory action research*

In principle one should, therefore, assume that the interests of research and practice and researchers and participants do not coincide, but exist in a relationship of tension and at least potential conflict with each other. In this respect, a clear separation of the roles adopted by researchers and people in practice makes sense. Thus cooperation cannot mean a fusion of the two parties.[1] Today we think it would be more fruitful to recognise the political character of the process and to see all participants as actors using specific power resources to realise interests. The basis of this relationship seems to be less a consensus regarding mutual interests than a kind of cooperation agreement or 'cooperation pact'[2] occurring from overlapping interests. This agreement or pact should not be seen as a stable one. Rather it is fragile and regularly has to be renegotiated as changes (in topics, problems, people concerned and so on) occur.

In a certain sense, emancipatory action research based on communicative action seems to represent a complementary misconception to the technical approaches. While the latter are correctly criticised for assuming the political neutrality of the expert and for the objectifying effect of the subject/object dualism, emancipatory action research seems to be built on the fiction of a common interest shared by both researchers and participants. We call this model the 'fusion model', which in our opinion leads to an overestimation of the possibility and value of consensus. As Moser (1989: 7) notes:

> in contrast to the principle of 'enlightening the people concerned' the common interests of researchers and people involved in many practical projects, which are conjured up in theory, frequently appeared on paper only.

To concentrate on the cooperation agreement or pact as the basis of cooperation means to recognise that there are common interests and different interests, conflict and consensus as well: it is the dialectics of 'the Same *and* the Different' (Burrell 1988: 234) that is held up in this cooperation pact and forms the productive basis. It implies a minimum of consensus rather than a maximum and sees resistance against an established 'truth' as more productive than the search for a better, more legitimate consensus.

> To say that consensus implies domination does not mean we should not make the best decisions we can together, but that we need to continue to look for domination and be ready to move on. To say that resistance lacks a clear politics does not mean that it is not doing something important and ultimately may be the only way we can see through domination that we like or that benefit and limit us. (Alvesson & Deetz 1994: 26)

Conclusion

As we have pointed out, emancipatory action research produces power effects that are easy to oversee when seeking consensual development. Nevertheless, we do not want to go as far as some (self-)critical action researchers and characterise action research or our project as 'just a new wave of "correction and patronizing"' (employees in our case) ... 'under the mask of co-operation' (Wünsche 1979: 23 cit. in Altrichter & Gstettner 1993: 344). Obviously, however, power cannot be excluded from the research process and is re*produced* in various forms rather than re*duced*: it is a constitutive feature of every social relationship.

Taking the resulting political character into account, the role of the researcher (or facilitator) could be described by three basic functions. First, the researcher facilitates actions in the research field, thus contributing to a politicisation of the organisation. The task in this respect might be to formulate the knowledge that guides the action of the members of the field in a discursive way and thus to trigger reflective processes. Second, researchers could reveal the consequences of actions that the members of the field are not aware of. Third, researchers could also have the task of bringing the structural conditions of actions to a conscious level and show that these structural conditions are not only restrictions to but also resources for action (see Giddens 1992). In providing *insight* into the arbitrary character of organisational order, existing orders, world-views, ways of being and research become 'a strategy toward recovering alternative practices and marginalized alternative meanings' (Deetz 1992b: 87). The basic idea and guiding principle is not so much to overcome differences in world-views and interpretations in individual and collective development, in researchers' and participants' interests: a politically informed research in processes of development and change should lead us to think of difference as a resource. If the claim of a critical science should be maintained, we must constantly ask which interest groups benefit from an established truth and who or which groups are marginalised and excluded by any established consensus.

> Practicing power in such a context thus becomes a case of listening acutely, to hear silences and ellipses, as well as what is evident; of seeking to draw others and oneself into discursive dissonance in order to find that which can be agreed as the basis for that which will be done that no one can deny the wisdom of doing' (Clegg 1994: 171).

References

Altrichter, H. and Gstettner, P. (1993) Action research: a closed chapter in the history of German social sciences. *Educational Action Research* 1(3), 329–60.

Altrichter, H., Posch, P. and Somekh, B. (1993) *Teachers Investigate Their Work. An Introduction to the Methods of Action Research.* Routledge, London and New York.

Alvesson, M. and Deetz, St (1994) Critical theory and postmodernism approaches to organisational studies. First draft for St Clegg et al. (eds) *Handbook of Organisation Studies.* Sage, London, Newbury Park, New Delhi, forthcoming.

Bourdieu, P. (1994) Social space and symbolic power. In A. Giddens et al. (eds) *The Polity Reader in Social Theory.* Polity Press, Cambridge, 111–20.

Bourdieu, P. and Passeron, P. (1973) *Grundlagen einer Theorie der symbolischen Gewalt.* Suhrkamp, Frankfurt.

Burawoy, M. (1979) *Manufacturing Consent: Changes in the Labor Process Under Monopoly Capitalism.* University of Chicago Press, Chicago.

Burrell, G. (1988) Modernism, postmodernism and organisational analysis 2: the contribution of Michel Foucault. *Organisation Studies* 9(2), 221–35.

Clegg, St (1994) Social theory for the study of organisation: Weber and Foucault. *Organisation* 1(1), 149–78.

Clegg, St (1992) Disciplinary power in the modern cooperation. In M. Alvesson and H. Willmott (eds) *Critical Management Studies.* Sage, London, Newbury Park, New Delhi, 21–45.

—— (1992b) *Democracy in an Age of Cooperate Colonization. Developments in Communication and the Politics of Everyday Life.* State University of New York Press, Albany.

Foucault, M. (1991) *Die Ordnung des Diskurses.* Fischer Wissenschaft, Frankfurt.

Giddens, A. (1992) *Die Konstitution der Gesellschaft.* Campus, Frankfurt and New York.

—— (1993a) *New Rules of Sociological Method.* 2nd edn. Polity Press, Cambridge.

—— (eds) (1994) Elements of the theory of structuration. In A. Giddens et al., *The Polity Reader in Social Theory.* Polity Press, Cambridge, 79–89.

Gorbach, St and Weiskopf, R. (1993) Personal-Entwicklung. Von der Disziplin des Handelns zur Disziplin des Seins. In St Laske and St Gorbach (eds) *Spannungsfeld Personalentwicklung. Konzeptionen — Analysen — Perspektiven,* Manz, Wien, 171–94.

Haag, F. (1972) *Aktionsforschung,* Kösel, München.

Habermas, J. (1981) *Theorie des Kommunikativen Handelns,* vol. 1. Suhrkamp, Frankfurt.

—— (1988) *Nachmetaphysisches Denken. Philosophische Aufsätze.* Suhrkamp, Frankfurt.

Heinze, Th. (1987) *Qualitative Sozialforschung.* Westdeutscher Verlag, Opladen.

Kappler, E. (1980) Aktionsforschung. In E. Frese (ed.) *Handwörterbuch der Organisation.* 2nd edn. Stuttgart, 52–64.

Keep, E. (1991) Corporate training strategies: the vital component? In J. Storey (ed.) *New Perspectives on Human Resource Management.* London and New York, 109–25.

Laske, St and Schneider, U. (1985): '... *und es funktioniert doch!'. Selbstverwaltung kann man lernen.* Bundesministerium für soziale Verwaltung, Wien.

Miller, M. (1985) *Kollektive Lernprozesse. Studien zur Grundlegung einer soziologischen Lerntheorie.* Suhrkamp, Frankfurt.

Moser, H. (1975) *Aktionsforschung als kritische Theorie der Sozialwissenschaften.* Kösel, München.

—— (1983) Zur methodischen Problematik der Aktionsforschung. In P. Zedler and H. Moser (eds) *Aspekte qualitativer Sozialforschung. Studien zu Aktionsforschung, empirischer Hermeneutik und reflexiver Sozialtechnologie.* Leske and Budrich, Opladen.

—— (1989) Aktionsforschung. In G. Endruweit (ed.) *Wörterbuch der Soziologie.* Enke, Stuttgart, 6–9.

Neuberger, O. (1990) *Führen und Geführt werden.* Enke, Stuttgart.

Pieper, R. (1988) *Diskursive Organisationsentwicklung.* De Gruyter, Berlin and New York.

Schmitz, E., Bude, H. and Otto, C. (1989) Beratung als Praxisform 'angewandter Aufklärung'. In U. Beck and W. Bonß (eds) *Weder Sozialtechnologie noch Aufklärung, Analysen zur Verwendung sozialwissenschaftlichen Wissens.* Suhrkamp, Frankfurt, 72–122.

Schneider, U. and Laske, St (1985) *Produktivgenossenschaften, Gesellschaften mit beschränkter Hoffnung?* Österreichischer Volksbankenverlag, Wien.

Storey, J. (1991) *New Perspectives on Human Resource Management.* Routledge, London and New York.

Thompson, J.P. (1984) *Studies in the Theory of Ideology.* University of California Press, Berkeley.

Townley, B. (1994) *Reframing Human Resource Management. Power, Ethics and the Subject at Work.* Sage, London.

Wünsche, K. (1979) Aufforderung an die Lehrer: Macht Eure eigene Unterrichtswissenschaft. *Paed. Extra* 7, 22–26.

Notes

1   It might be better to follow Giddens and talk about an 'immersion in a form of life'. However, 'immersion' does not and should not mean 'becoming a full member' of the researched community. 'To "get to know" an alien form of life is to know how to find one's way about in it, to be able to participate in it as an ensemble of practices.' (Giddens 1993a: 169)

2   In politically oriented organisational research, the term 'co-operation pact' is employed to designate a temporary 'consensus' resulting from partially complementary interests.

Chapter 9

Becoming Critical of Action Research for Development[1]

Graham Webb

Abstract

This chapter briefly traces the origins of critical theory and the interpretation
of the work of Habermas into educational contexts. Action research is
described and its links to critical theory discussed. A critique of action
research is then mounted which suggests: group privileging is a distortion
of critical theory; individual and group identity often blur; power is always
already present and cannot be dispersed by rationality; rationality often
serves the interests of the powerful, and so too does rational consensus;
solidarity can become a drive to conformity; false consciousness is
patronising and dangerous; the action research group assumes the aura of
the rational, autonomous individual; oppressor and oppressed roles are
complex and often combined; construction of difference and the Other is a
necessary consequence of action; and the need to contest and dispute an
attempted objectification of meanings associated with such terms as
emancipation, autonomy, democracy, consensus, rationality, solidarity,
social justice, community and so on. It is argued that a preferred stance is
that of postmodernity and a preferred practice one which is eclectic and
pragmatic.

Personal introduction

I am an educational and staff developer working in a university. Most of my life has been spent either teaching students, or teaching lecturers. Although I understand more about the processes involved in both of these than when I started, I am constantly surprised by my lack of understanding. I do not have a solid foundational rock upon which to base my practice. I find daily situations which I can interpret from different standpoints. I am never wholly convinced that the interpretive framework I use is correct. Early in my career I was attracted to the idea that rationality in the form of science could help me to determine how I should view the world and teach. Later, somewhat disillusioned with science, I turned to humanism and existentialism.

As a student I read Marx. I read him as a humanist and was impressed by his caring for the well-being of the individual. I was also impressed, however, by the need for systems change as a necessity for improving individual welfare. Making a better world by solidarity and common action became a pure and heartfelt passion. This translated into many forms, including putting an end to the limitations on life experienced by many of my peers, saving the world from oppressive classroom practices or seeking a redistribution of world resources. I saw all of these as essentially the same thing. Now I am less sure and far less trusting of totalising views. Now I tend to see the many fractures and inconsistencies in people and their motivations. My experience places me tantalisingly near to postmodernism, while at the same time retaining an attraction towards the spirit and instinct of the Enlightenment.

I have personally encountered the major movements in ontology, epistemology and methodology experienced by a generation. My experience persuades me towards a scepticism regarding any totalising theory or world view, and a charity towards others and their views. It tells me that I will never gain definitive answers concerning many of life's questions, or the questions which inhabit my professional practice. But it also tells me that those who claim differently should be challenged. In this chapter I will mount a critique of action research for development. I see this as simply an example of the will to challenge what has become an orthodox position. The more strident the claim to represent the good, the oppressed, the disempowered; the natural order of things; the divine, the keener the need for criticism.

Context introduction

Apart from phenomenography, action research is perhaps the most influential and almost certainly the fastest-growing orientation towards educational and staff development at present. Not surprisingly, the focus of action research is upon *action*. It is concerned with change, but change in a particular direction. It is argued that behind action research lies a philosophical tradition which legitimises and spurs change for the betterment of humanity. Educational and staff development is concerned with change too. If action research really can help us to decide what *is* better, then perhaps it can help us to resolve some of the suspicions and doubts which have been raised with respect to the view of education as a rational–scientific endeavour. Notions of development, evolution and progress all come with their own baggage and problems (Webb, in print). If action research can inform us about what is *meant* by better, then this would represent a major step forward. And if better educational and staff development means increasing the participation or giving voice to both teachers and students; collaboration on an equal footing; open-ended and progressive inquiry; and the emancipation of those involved, then we begin to see why the prospect of action research holds much hope.

Another area of considerable concern is the unequal power relationships which exist between human beings as they attempt to understand each other. Hermeneutics is the branch of knowledge which studies under-standing. It places humanity and understanding in the foreground, in that it is by gaining understanding of our shared humanity and of the position, concerns, thoughts and feelings of others, that we might help them learn and develop. But problems arise from the consequences of unequal power in the conversation between people as they strive for mutual understanding. What if the power of the person speaks more loudly than the power of the argument? What if we learn how another person sees the world, gain a deep and empathic understanding of their position, and still consider it to be wrong? In other words, is there a reliable compass mounted outside our conversations by which we may set direction and chart our educational or staff development activities? In this chapter I will consider claims that a critical theory of society can inform our direction and that progress in this preferred direction may be made through action research. The chapter begins by looking at the origins of the social and critical theory which has become associated with action research and then traces some of the consequences of this view of the world. This is followed by a critique of critical theory and action research in which the case is put that these positions are significantly flawed in their ability to clearly direct our efforts. There then follows a brief conclusion.

Origins: from Hegel to Marx

Plato's theory of forms took perceived reality to be but an imperfect reflection of timeless and absolute truths. Working in one direction, the French and English development of empiricism, science and the Enlightenment spirit of universal human progress suggested that these truths were open to discovery. Alternatively, as part of the German inclination towards metaphysics and disclosure, Hegel developed a universal method which he called the dialectic.[2] Essentially this involved the notion that a particular point of view (thesis) and its counter argument (antithesis) could both contain elements of truth. The dialectical method comprises bringing the truth from each side together in a new formulation called synthesis. He also believed that ultimate truth and reason was not given to individuals but was vested in social groups. The primary social group of Hegel's time was the nation and it was in the unfolding of social forces through national rivalry that Hegel saw the development of historical necessity. The Hegelian innovations of the (modern) dialectic and of the social group as arbiter of reason produced the seed bed for Marxism, critical theory and, ultimately, the emancipatory form of action research.

Marx replaced Hegel's insistence upon the nation as the unit of struggle in producing social history with the unit of class. History could be explained in terms of a class struggle, with each class representing a particular economic interest and relationship towards power. For both Hegel and Marx there was an inevitability in the way that history would unfold and this inevitability comprised both a causal explanation of what *would* happen together with a moral justification of what *should* happen. The dialectic of Marx had the struggle of classes as the means by which social progress and higher moral values would be realised. Marx saw power as the final arbiter of progress and he was sceptical of ameliorative measures or political progress through negotiation and accommodation. With hindsight, it is apparent that he offered little assurance that power in the hands of a new class interest (the proletariat) would be used in a less authoritarian or wiser way than it had in the hands of any previous ruling group.

Both Hegel and Marx saw history as a rational unfolding of progress towards a predetermined and higher goal. As products of their age, they were both essentially developmentalists. However, Hegel's vision was of Germany as the spiritual leader in the progress of European nations, whereas Marx's vision was of the proletariat as the leader of emancipation and social justice for all. Both have similar consequences for the action of individuals in that the appeal was:

> to loyalty rather than to self-interest, to duties rather than to rights, and it offered no reward except the hope that one's private life would gain meaning through service to a cause greater than oneself (Sabine 1963: 759).

There is a challenge to individualism in the vesting of legitimacy and moral aspiration in the group, and this is a constant theme in the development of this branch of social theory. It is important to note, however, that the 'necessity' or 'inevitability' which both Hegel and Marx saw in history should be viewed as a call to action and a moral obligation. It is individual action which spurs change and without action, progressive movements cannot eventuate. It is the duty of each one of us to join the march of progress towards an historically inevitable future, and in so doing to play our part in purging 'irrationalism' along the way.

Critical theory

Karl Marx died in 1883. The broad-based proletarian revolution he predicted for Germany and elsewhere in Western Europe had not eventuated and capitalism as a fundamentally flawed economic system was proving resilient to the inevitable march of history. On the other hand, in Russia — an agrarian and semi-feudal society that had barely experienced a bourgeois (democratic) revolution — Lenin led a successful revolt, spearheaded by a tiny Communist Party. Faced with changed circumstances, in 1923 German intellectuals founded the Institute for Social Research in Frankfurt which:

> ... became the first formally unaffiliated Marxist-oriented institute in Europe ... its members attempted to revise both the Marxian critique of capitalism and the theory of revolution in order to confront those new social and political conditions which had evolved since Marx's death. In the process a 'critical theory' of society emerged to deal with those aspects of social reality which Marx and his orthodox followers neglected or down played (Bronner & Kellner 1989: 1).

The 'Frankfurt School' of 'critical theory' has been one of the major instruments through which social reform, social theory and the message of socialism have been carried from their nineteenth century Marxian roots into current debate. This is all the more surprising as the term 'critical theory' was first used in 1937 when most of the Institute's members had already fled Hitler's Germany for the United States.³ 'Critical theory' was in fact a euphemism made necessary by the abhorrence with which any suggestion of Marxism was greeted in the United States. The first generation of critical theorists included Max Horkheimer, Theodor Adorno, Leo Lowenthal, Herbert Marcuse and Erich Fromm.⁴ Jürgen Habermas is the major figure of the second generation and it is Habermas' work which will be outlined in a little detail.

The early critical theorists were worried by the way science and its positivist view of the world had become accepted as the benchmark for any kind of thinking or acting and especially for thinking about society. Rationality had become defined according to science. Science was seen as being able to produce 'the facts' upon which social action could be based, but the values underlying these facts and the direction in which society *should* be travelling were outside its scope. Normative and critical questions of where society was going and why had been replaced by technical and instrumental questions. Science tended to consider whether a particular course of action was more efficient or effective than another, taking for granted that the end point was desirable. The task which Habermas took up was to show that 'scientific' or instrumental knowledge is but one way of thinking, and one which is not particularly valuable in giving direction to social action (including consideration of what should happen in educational or staff development).

His approach was to ask the basic question of why knowledge was produced at all. The answer he came up with was that knowledge is always produced for a purpose: it is produced because people want to know something. Knowledge is not produced from the 'disinterested' inquiry of minds, it is produced because of the basic needs or interests of humankind. These interests (which he refers to as 'knowledge-constitutive interests') he took as given or *a priori*. According to Habermas, there are three of them: the technical interest; the practical interest; and the emancipatory interest. The technical interest of people is to acquire technical control over the natural world and is the domain of science and technology. The practical interest (somewhat curiously named) refers to the interest of people in understanding each other and interpreting social practices. It is the domain of hermeneutics and the *verstehen* tradition.

According to Habermas, the problem with this standpoint is that there are 'objective' social, political, economic — *power* — relationships existing which distort people's subjective appreciation of the world. Coming to an hermeneutical understanding of a person or group is one thing, but that person or group may articulate a view of the world which is false or against their own 'true' interests. Only if they have autonomy and freedom can they give a 'true' account of their own interests. Also, only if there are equal, fair and democratic procedures in place will their voice be heard. For these reasons, the effective communication assumed by the hermeneutical tradition can only occur when appropriate and supportive social conditions apply. To put such conditions in place, which in the long term is in everyone's interest, is the basic human interest of emancipation, or the emancipatory interest. It is for a critical social science to show people how they are oppressed, how their interests have become repressed or distorted, and what life will look like when they have confronted their oppressions, changed their conditions and moved towards a more rational society.

What is a more rational society? To answer this Habermas turns to language and discourse. He claims that the point of speech is to communicate, to test counter positions and to gain understanding. In an 'ideal speech situation' each person is equally empowered to speak, there is no coercion from outside the conversation or between the discussants, and it is the power of the argument rather than the power of a particular person which carries the day. The very point of language in making it possible for communication to take place is underlaid by the idea of the 'ideal speech situation', which in turn is the model for a rational society and, interestingly, for science too. The ideal speech situation lies at the base of all communication and the conditions which come closest to the ideal at this microcosmic level provide the blueprint for a just and rational society. Again, the blueprint is of an open community with each person able to participate fully, and with the community being convinced by the force of the argument, rather than the power of the presenter. The same conditions apply similarly for scientific inquirers participating in an open, healthy and robust scientific community.[5]

Critical theory in education

It is hardly surprising that an attempt to provide such a foundational explanation and direction for communication, science and society has also attracted the attention of educators. If Habermas is right, then there are implications for our understanding of the place and process of education, not only with respect to knowledge and inquiry, but also in terms of social justice. It also follows that there are implications for the philosophy and practice of staff development.

Jack Mezirow (1981) was one of the first to bring the ideas of Habermas into the main stream of educational thinking. His 1981 paper opens with the words: 'This article presents the beginnings of a critical theory of adult learning and education' (p. 3). Critical theory is directly embraced and, according to Mezirow, the three 'knowledge constitutive interests' have direct corollaries in learning.

> ... each domain has its own learning goal (viz., learning for task-related competence, learning for interpersonal understanding and learning for perspective transformation), learning needs, approaches for facilitating learning, methods of research and program evaluation are implied or explicit (Mezirow 1981: 16).

Mezirow elaborates the three knowledge domains in terms of their relationship to learning. The 'technical' is task-orientated and can be associated with behavioural objectives, competency-based learning, skills training, criteria-referenced testing and empirical research and evaluation. The 'practical' domain emphasises empathy with others which can be developed as teachers encourage their students to:

> take the role of others ... develop empathy and ... confidence and competence in such aspects of human relations as resolving conflict, participating in discussion and dialogue, participating and leading in learning groups, listening, expressing oneself, asking questions, philosophizing ... (1981: 18).

But it is in the third domain that Mezirow has most to say. Here, Habermas' 'emancipatory' reason for knowledge becomes 'learning for perspective transformation' and is linked to other educational ideas. For example, 'meta-learning', the process by which learners become aware of and in control of their learning, is said to be common in many learning situations, including the technical and practical. It is a necessary but insufficient condition for perspective transformation. To undertake learning which is perspective transforming (or emancipatory), one must not only be aware of one's own thinking but also 'the cultural assumptions governing the rules, roles, conventions and social expectations which dictate the way we see, think, feel and act' (1981: 13). To achieve this appreciation we need 'critical awareness' or 'critical consciousness': we need to be aware of our own awareness and capable of critiquing it.

How is this to be accomplished? Here Mezirow turns to Paulo Freire (1970), the radical Brazilian educator, who suggests the need to start from the problems and perspectives of the learner and from these develop materials which pose dilemmas. Socratic dialogue may then be used in small group settings where experiences are shared, group solidarity and support developed, and a new perspective achieved. When people come together with a common problem, the early phase of pointing out the problem may be unnecessary and support groups, approximating the 'ideal speech situation', can take off from the beginning. Whatever the starting point, the main objective is clear and important:

> ... bringing psycho-cultural assumptions into critical consciousness to help a person understand how he or she has come into possession of conceptual categories, rules, tactics and criteria for judging ... perception, thought and behavior involves perhaps the most significant kind of learning. It increases a crucial sense of agency over ourselves and our lives (Mezirow 1981: 20).

So the knowledge which education may give us by this process of self-reflection in the context of ideology critique represents the most significant kind of learning we can achieve. What is more, it is the imperative of educators to ensure that such learning takes place.

> Learners *must* ... be led to an understanding of the reasons imbedded in these internalized cultural myths and concomitant feelings which account for ... the way they see themselves and their relations ... learners *must* be given access to alternative meaning perspectives for interpreting this reality so that critique of these psycho-cultural assumptions is possible (1981: 18, emphasis added).

We see here shades of the Marxist tendency to evangelise which results from an exaggerated confidence in a particular opinion. People must be saved, even from themselves. They may not want to face the truth of their exploitation and repression, they may even claim that they are not repressed, but they only say this because they cannot see through the ideology which surrounds and defines them. Just as it was the responsibility of the revolutionary class to ensure that in such conditions of 'false consciousness' people are saved from themselves, so too it is the responsibility of educators to ensure that people see the world 'properly'. And just as developmental theorists always place a mirror to themselves in representing the highest stage of development, so too critical theorists are the only ones to see clearly.

Educational and staff development from the stance of critical theory would ideally expect staff members to spontaneously come together as they realise that their common interests promote common purpose and solidarity, and that amelioration of the conditions which oppress them lies in their own hands. For example, it might be that the failure of students to take more than an instrumental or credentialling view of learning may be traced not to the individual student, nor to the type of instruction, nor to the departmental context. Instead, a wider critique of the nature of society in terms of its institutionalisation of competitive relationships could be mounted. Education might be viewed as but a part of the socialisation of the next generation's elite and this would help explain the difficulty 'non-traditional' groups have in gaining entrance. Education acts as the gate-keeper to privilege and as the supplier of labour to capitalist enterprise. The pathologies of society are also manifested in such diverse areas as sexism and racism in the curriculum, and the rationalist and managerialist orientation of the modern higher education institution. Such phenomena are to be resisted and it is important to recognise that resistance is played out in the curriculum. However, the confrontation of these issues in the curriculum is only one part of the story, as we should also be 'good citizens' by confronting them at the wider societal level. It is our duty to participate in making a better world.

The staff developer's role in all of this might be reminiscent of Lenin's view of the communist party. It is a role of leadership and facilitation. Staff developers are in the vanguard of the movement towards better educational methods; they mirror the values of a better institution and ultimately a better society. Staff developers may be catalysts of progressive transformation and of progressive pedagogy. The early socialists found that there was little use in waiting for a spontaneous uprising: it is the duty of those in the vanguard to lead the way. Even though they represent a small number of those involved, they are the ones with a clear view of the future. They must not shirk their responsibility. Thus the staff developer leads and facilitates 'action' projects to improve learning, guided by the precepts of group-based activity, equality, democracy and emancipation. We are talking here of the role of the staff developer in action research projects.

Action research

The term 'action research' was coined by Kurt Lewin (e.g. 1946), an American sociologist working on a range of community projects concerning integration and social justice in areas such as housing and employment.[6] Lewin's work in underprivileged communities was taken up by Stephen Corey (e.g. 1949), who was concerned that research into teaching should have a practical effect on classroom practices. His collaborative research projects for teachers were further developed by John Elliot (e.g. Elliot & Adelman 1973) in the Ford teaching project and generalised in later writings (e.g. Elliot 1978). Essentially practical endeavours such as these later became explicitly linked to critical theory and in particular the work of Habermas in Carr and Kemmis' important book *Becoming Critical: Education, Knowledge and Action Research* (1986).

The method of action research also became somewhat codified into the moments of planning, acting, observing and reflecting. Having completed one such cycle, action researchers may then spiral into a further cycle, or into offshoot spirals (see McNiff 1988). What has become perhaps the standard definition of action research is given by Kemmis and McTaggart (1988a) as follows:

> Action research is a form of *collective* self-reflective enquiry undertaken by participants in social situations in order to improve the rationality and justice of their own social or educational practices, as well as their understanding of these practices and the situations in which these practices are carried out ... The approach is only action research when it is *collaborative*, though it is important to realise that the action research of the group is achieved through the *critically examined action* of individual group members (5–6).

We see here the collective (group) emphasis which reaches back to Hegel and Marx. Although there is an Enlightenment-like assurance that 'rationality and justice' can be improved, this is not, of course, a natural process of development and evolution, so much as a moral imperative and obligation to become involved.

So how should staff developers be involved in action research projects? In theory, emancipatory action research follows from the spontaneous coming together of people with a common problem. It is unlikely in this case that the staff developer will be involved at all. Being largely outside of the context, the staff developer may not have the same motivation and view of the problem as those more intimately concerned. In fact it is far more likely that staff developers will either be called in for 'expert' advice on how to tackle a particular issue, or may themselves attempt to interest people and initiate projects (the catalytic role). The question of 'equality' then becomes interesting as the staff developer brings to the problem an expertise which the originators cannot provide themselves. Often the staff developer has greater general experience of pedagogy and a far better sense of the epistemology and methodology of educational research projects. The staff developer will be able to interpret a project more generally than other participants, to explain where it fits, point to useful literature and use previous experience to guide the development of the project. Inevitably the staff developer may become a central and crucial element in the project and take an active role in suggesting future directions, spin-offs or similar projects in different contexts. In short, the staff developer may find it hard to play the part of 'just another member' of a project team.

Should this cause us concern? I would argue that it is a point of which staff developers need to be acutely aware. In a 'pure' view of action research the inequality generated by the staff developer's expertise and different stance must certainly be construed as a cause for concern. However, it has always been a fiction that those with common interests start with common abilities or a common desire to contribute to a project group. 'Equality' as a starting point is a myth despite any number of declarations of intent and attempts to set ground rules. The ground rules are there *because* inequality exists in the opportunities for all to contribute to the group. It is important for group members to talk about their hopes and expectations concerning levels of participation and for the development of the group process to be monitored.

But it is a pity if participants enter the project with unrealistic expectations about working relationships. Often there is a binding together of an action research group as individuals come to discover their commonalities and find solace in each other against the doubts and criticisms of those outside. Structural inequalities and human frailties may appear later as group members get to know each other better, find interests in the others to which they cannot relate, or aspects of them which they do not particularly like. Jealousy and friction are not easily banished, even for the common good.

Of course much of this also applies equally to students learning in groups. The moral we may draw is that the adoption of a group-based approach, whether in learning or in professional development, does not constitute an assurance of virtue. Virtue needs to be earned and demonstrated, and it is worthwhile to urge some caution concerning a non-critical adoption of action research for the purpose of staff development.

Action research is presently gaining widespread acceptance in educational and staff development practice. Its claim to the moral high ground makes for difficulty if one chooses to criticise it, especially as some of its advocates display an evangelical faith. But as Gibson (1985) points out in his engaging critique of Carr and Kemmis' *Becoming Critical* (after apologising for the alarmingly long sentence):

> What's very worrying about his book is that it is intensely uncritical (i.e. it doesn't practice what it preaches); its prescriptions are likely to result in increased conformity, (i.e. it would produce its own rigid orthodoxy); it is naive about group processes; it prefers the group over the individual, and the in-group over the out-group; it is bedazzled by the notion of 'science'; it rejects objectivity, yet privileges its own view of reality; it is characterised by hubris (i.e. it lacks modesty in its claims and perceptions); it is highly

contradictory (actually not a bad thing in the human condition but the book doesn't recognise its own contradictions); it has far too much respect for the authority of critical theory; it is an elitist text masquerading as an egalitarian one; it insufficiently acknowledges that action research at the three levels of the interpersonal (e.g. classroom), institutional (e.g. school or LEA), or structural (e.g. economic, political, ideological) involve different activities and levels of difficulty for would-be action researchers; and in its seeming preference for the institutional and structural levels, it is attempting to set action research off on a course very different from its present practice (1985: 60).

Gibson goes on to show how problematic and contestable can be many of the core notions of an action research based in critical theory. Both Hegel and Marx were clear that the greater good would be served by the hegemony of one entity (the German state and the working class respectively). Action researchers can easily be led into denying their own partisan positions and claiming that their actions are for the good of all. The excesses of communitarian politics are played out in miniature if groups become carried away with building their own 'solidarity', manifestly or subtly encouraging their own conformity or, in short, becoming intolerant of alternative views to their own. The idea that a 'rational' position may be reached when all 'distortions' (to the correct view) have been eliminated is dangerous and so too is the recreation of 'false consciousness.'

The falsely conscious are those who believe and act against their own 'true' interests. An early example would be working class supporters of conservative politics, but in the educational sphere we could imagine students who do not want to work in groups, or lecturers who resist such things as problem-based learning, or other examples of 'good practice.' The trouble with false consciousness is that it is patronising and gives one group the power to ignore the views of another. This is not to say that the views of any group must necessarily be viewed as equal. For example, it is not necessary to believe that creationists or supporters of a flat earth theory should be afforded equal time in the curriculum with geological explanation. But it does make incumbent upon a particular group, in rejecting the views of others, that they explain their own partisan position and seek legitimacy and continual reassurance in their use of power. After all, an action research group may be accused of false consciousness and self-delusion as readily as anyone else.

A similar point also applies to tensions between an individual and the group. It may be claimed that just as groups can be deluded, so too might an individual who does not submit to the critique of the collective. But there is always the potential for tension between the aspirations and interests of individuals within a group. This applies in so-called 'communal' or tribal societies just as it does in societies which emphasise individual rights. The privileging of the group, solidarity and conformity over the individual bring their own dangers.

Gibson (1985) points out that the vesting of power in a 'professional' group is highly questionable. Much though teachers might wish for the power to determine what will be taught, how it will be taught and by whom, it is not transparently clear that such an arrangement will serve the best interests of all. The current word for those with interests in education (such as students, parents, employers, professional bodies, government and so on) is 'stakeholder'. Teachers are certainly 'stakeholders' themselves, but why should they as professionals, or a particular action research group of professionals, lay claim to the only legitimate view of what is good for education? The same point can also be put to staff developers as they contemplate the foundation of a national association. To be an interest group is one thing; to claim to be the only legitimate voice of educational and staff development is quite another.

In fact all the words which tend to appear on the side of the 'good and holy' in action research and critical theory are problematic and contestable. These include: emancipation, autonomy, democracy, consensus, rationality, solidarity, social justice and community. In the philosophy of education literature, articles abound testing and contesting what each of these words might mean and suggest for educational practice. As staff developers, we should maintain a healthy scepticism for the idealised turn taken in the coupling of action research and critical theory. As I have suggested elsewhere:

> We should not be too depressed ... by the fact that critical theory may give us little more than the suggestion of a direction in which we wish to travel. Glimpses of ideals such as the good, the beautiful, the just, have perhaps always provided inspiration for the material practicality of and existential responsibility for, the decision making of everyday life (Webb 1991: 41).

When it comes down to involvement in an action research project, the hermeneutical nature of the group process is often all-important. Claims to ownership of rationality and a 'true' or 'undistorted' view of reality are likely to be unhelpful, to say the least.

How then are differences of opinion or interpretation within the group to be resolved? How is the happy consensus necessarily arrived at — are there no grounds for clear and honest disagreement about what the emancipatory course of action should be? And in such cases how is the 'right' course (the emancipatory interest) decided? Democracy means many different things to different people and often poses problems for minorities. Even agreeing upon a system for seeking agreement (making decisions) is problematic. Foucault's formulation of 'the truth of power' as opposed to 'the power of truth' has not been overcome despite the best efforts of Habermas, or educational action researchers.

What of action research without its critical theory grounding? Can lecturers in higher education undertake practical ('technical') action research without regard to ideology critique or changing the world? Of course they can, and indeed it is quite likely that useful 'local' projects of this nature represent the majority of action research undertakings.[7] These projects should not escape critique in terms of the values and ideologies within which they are located and very often they display the instrumental values of efficiency and effectiveness associated with the 'improvement' and 'rationality' of the Enlightenment. The point is that what constitutes improvement in teaching and learning, and whether or not this leads into a discussion of what should constitute a better community or a better world, is contestable, and should be protected from capture and the drive to conformity of a particular world view.

Contestability and a refusal to curtail criticism should be hallmarks of our staff development endeavours in the face of reassurances that a particular position or approach leads to better education, better staff development, or a better world. The social theory which reached its zenith in Marxism has always attracted a crusading zeal and the current form of this sees action research as panacea and best practice for academic staff development. In a recent book entitled *Professional Development in Higher Education*, Ortrun Zuber-Skerritt (1992) suggests that:

> Through systematic, controlled action research, higher education teachers can become more professional, more interested in pedagogical aspects of higher education, and more motivated to integrate their research and teaching interests in a holistic way. This would in turn lead to greater job satisfaction, better academic programmes, improvement of student learning, and practitioners' insights and contributions to the advancement of knowledge in higher education (1992: 122).

While this might be true for some, it needs to be balanced against the legitimate concerns which others might have concerning the ontology, epistemology, methodology and lineage of action research based upon critical theory. It is when the clarion call sounds that our (truly) critical sensibilities should be alerted.

> Action research in higher education *must* consist of a *group* process of *rational* reflection generating a critique of the social and educational milieu in which the members operate. For the aim of action research is not only the improvement of learning, teaching and professional development, but also the improvement of the social context in which this personal and professional development takes place (Zuber-Skerritt 1992: 122, italicised emphasis added).

But why *must* action research consist of a *group* process and what does *rational* reflection mean? Is there no possibility that we might agree to disagree about local politics, national politics or social policy, and still work together to improve teaching? And even if we do broadly agree on matters of social policy, is it not possible for us to argue legitimately for the emancipatory value of quite different approaches to teaching and learning?

The example provided by Jack Whitehead (1991) may be argued as a challenge to the privileging of group over individual. He has shown how an action research approach may be applied to an individual — in fact, to oneself.

> I believe that the incorporation of 'I' as a living contradiction in explanations for the educational development of individuals, has distinguished an original contribution to the action research movement ... I experience problems or concerns when some of my values are denied in my practice; I imagine ways of improving my practice and choose a course of action; I act and gather evidence which will enable me to make a judgement on the effectiveness of my actions; I evaluate the outcomes of my actions; I modify my concerns, ideas and action in the light of my evaluation (1991: 94).

The point should also be made that early members of the Frankfurt School were intensely interested in psychoanalytical (intra-individual) analysis. Indeed, the link between this level of analysis and group-based action may be clearly seen:

> ... critical theory was strongly influenced by psychoanalysis; the analyst assisting in the emancipation of the individual from seemingly unknowable complexes being mirrored at the social level by the critical theorist facilitating the emancipation of groups from

oppressive but unknown or poorly understood ideologies (Webb 1991: 40).

It would be perfectly feasible to take action research along a number of paths, including the psychoanalytical or the aesthetic, both of which were of interest to early Frankfurt School writers. The point here is not that this would in some way 'correct' the 'errant' ways of group-based critical theorists, but to demonstrate that the issue is contestable. However, some alternative approaches would help to counter a tendency to identify those on the side of the 'good' with those who follow a particular and somewhat narrow interpretation.

There are yet more interpretations. For example, it is possible to 'deconstruct' what is meant by individuals and groups in learning situations as the categories have a habit of escaping the limits which define them (see Webb 1992). While some may argue that a group is something more than the individuals it includes, each individual is unique, special and can change the nature of the group by their participation. It is hard to think 'group' other than abstractly. For example, in thinking of a particular group of students or staff, one sees individuals and remembers specific exchanges with one's self and with others. A group is always a group of something (for example, students) and it is these 'somethings' which we remember. On the other hand, it is also a mistake to regard the individual as the essential unit — in terms of learning, for example. Students talk about what they are doing (learning) to the person sitting next to them in class, to their flatmates, to their friends, spouses, grown-up sons and daughters, and so on. In collaborative projects they share and discuss ideas and talk these over with the teacher. Their identities are formed in the flow of history and society. In what sense is their learning individual?

Apart from the privileging of the group over the individual in action research, the meaning of *rationality* may also be questioned. At one level this repeats the questions already raised concerning whether legitimate differences of opinion on what constitutes progress can be allowed, and how one moves forward in the face of disagreement. At another level, however, the concept of rationality itself has been argued as being disempowering and anti-emancipatory.

In what has proved to be an influential paper on 'the repressive myths of critical pedagogy' Elizabeth Ellsworth (1989: 297) suggests that 'critical pedagogy ... has developed along a highly abstract and utopian line which does not necessarily sustain the daily workings of the education its supporters advocate'.

In attempting to teach a course following the tenets of critical pedagogy (including such things as 'classroom analysis and rejection of oppression, injustice, inequality, silencing of marginalized voices, and ... authoritarian social structures') she took the position of a '"radical" educator who recognizes and helps students to recognize and name injustice, who empowers students to act against their own and others' oppressions ... who criticizes and transforms her or his own understanding in response to the understandings of students' (1989: 300). This approach to the theory and practice of critical pedagogy came from her reading of leading writers in the field.

But the very admonition that critical pedagogy should encourage rational debate of educational and social issues ignores the fact that the teacher and students enter a course 'with investments of privilege and struggle already made in favor of some ethical and political positions ... and against other positions' (1989: 301). The idea that, through rational debate, the structured differences which inhabit society may be brought to consensus is in line with Habermasian thought but antithetical to what has come to be called 'poststructuralism.' Poststructuralism has now

> amassed overwhelming evidence of the extent to which the myths of the ideal rational person and the 'universality' of propositions have been oppressive to those who are not European, White, male, middle class, Christian, able-bodied, thin, and heterosexual. (1989: 304)

To some extent, the idea of the rational, voluntary individual so despised by critical action researchers has simply been recycled in the idea of the rational, voluntary group. Rational argument serves the interests of those who have the power to form and define rationality, and power imbalances permeate society. For example, the power imbalance between teacher and student (or between staff developer and staff member) has never been satisfactorily addressed.

> ... theorists of critical pedagogy have failed to launch any meaningful analysis of or program for reformulating the institutionalized power imbalances between themselves and their students, or of the essentially paternalistic project of education itself. In the absence of such an analysis and program, their efforts are limited to trying to transform negative effects of power imbalances within the classroom into positive ones. Strategies such as student empowerment and dialogue give the illusion of equality while in fact leaving the authoritarian nature of the teacher/student relationship intact. (1989: 306)

Ellsworth looks at the notion of 'voice' in allowing students to express their experiences and understandings. Feminism has used this strategy as a means for allowing women to formulate language and concepts in terms of their own understandings or self-definitions and oppositional to the constructions of others. It has been argued, similarly, that teachers may encourage their students to find their authentic voices. But the structural problems remain. How does the well-educated, middle class, white teacher contribute to the emancipation of her working class, black female or male students?

Attempting to teach according to critical pedagogy (or forming an action research group) assumes that by a rational process of dialogue and sharing of experiences a unity of purpose will be forged and a common understanding of oppression gained. Counter to this, Ellsworth argues that a unified understanding is an undesirable fiction and that each one of us has the ability to be both oppressor and oppressed. She quotes Minh-ha: 'There are no social positions exempt from becoming oppressive to others ... any group — any position — can move into the oppressor role' and Mary Gentile: 'everyone is someone else's "Other"' (1989: 322).

We have thus moved a long way from the Marxist formulation of economically based oppression of the proletariat by the bourgeoisie; from the essentialist feminist position that to be male is to be oppressor of female; and from similar formulations according to disability, race or sexual orientation. As Lynne Chisholm (1990: 255) points out:

> Whilst some of us, as feminists ... can legitimately claim membership of (a) relevant oppressed group, we are, at the same time, class-privileged — and where young people are involved, we have the privilege of adulthood. Therefore, our identities are multiple and contradictory; and we are inevitably bound up in power relationships which we should not be able to afford to deny (253) ... I propose that we begin by not kidding ourselves: about what is achievable in action research; that we know and understand what emancipatory action is; about the elusive character of symmetrical research relations.

Even those representing the standard of privilege (according to Ellsworth the young, white, heterosexual, Christian, able-bodied, thin, middle-class, English-speaking male) may be oppressed by the expectations which their families and society hold of them — they may strive to resist such expectations and attempts to inscribe them with 'essential' characteristics.

There are implications in all of this for staff development informed by critical theory and pursued by action research. If critical theory has failed to take sufficient account of the imbalance *which must always* persist in educational encounters, then it is unrealistic to base classroom practice on the utopian concept that by equally empowered, rational debate, a way will be found through to the empowerment of all. Put simply, there can never be an assurance that the interests of all are in common, or will remain in common. There is thus every chance of 'the interests of all' becoming, in fact, the interests of the most powerful. In an action research setting, the interests of the most powerful may easily be recast as the interests of the best informed ('knowledge is power'), those with a wider and more generalisable knowledge of educational matters or of the action research process itself. This is exactly the position of power which the staff developer can occupy. Chisholm (1990) also predicts that the interests of 'action' and 'research' may work in parallel rather than in collaboration or synthesis. We should not be too surprised, then, if staff developers rather than discipline-based academics are seen as the 'seeders' of action research projects and the main publishers of action research reports.

Conclusion

There is no doubt at all that action research projects can effect good educational developments. Participation in action research groups can also be stimulating for those involved, including developers. However, this chapter has argued that a healthy scepticism and retention of our critical facility needs to be maintained against the ebullient claims and drive to conformity of critical theorists and action researchers. It has also opened the area of multiple claims to understanding which is indicative of postmodernism.

A major criticism of postmodernism has come from social theorists and philosophers of the left. If 'anything goes', if there are no solid foundations upon which to stand, how can social improvement and social justice be affirmed? Postmodernism has thus been argued as an aberration of late capitalism or as a conservative reaction to progressive politics. (Much has also been made of links between some deconstructive writers and fascism.) Put simply, the argument is that there is truth — it is the truth of exploitation and suffering; the truth of the historical struggle for emancipation. This represents an interesting return to words as objective signifiers of reality, and Strohmayer and Hannah (1992: 41) comment on this as follows:

> Contrary to popular belief, paying heed to the problem of representation does not require one to deny non-textual determination, just to treat with extreme scepticism any claim to have established an 'objective' understanding of 'how it works'.

In other words, we should not let ourselves be duped into accepting an 'objective' account of oppression, exploitation or emancipation. And although we do not accept someone's 'objective' account of the 'reality' of oppression, exploitation or emancipation, this does not mean that we are powerless to act.

> ... we still would much prefer to have founding principles present themselves to us. We chafe at having to make difficult (because at some level arbitrary) choices on our own. *But, this lack of external guidance does not suddenly transform concern into indifference.* If anything, it makes the unavoidable choices more painful. (Strohmayer & Hannah 1992: 49, original emphasis)

This is the message of postmodernism generally. It challenges us to move out of our particular comfort zones (reflective practice, action research, phenomenography, and so on). As we articulate our version of what is 'good' as an educational practice, as we espouse our values for education and for staff development, we do so in the knowledge that we are party to the *construction* of difference, the Other, the alternative case. Our horizons and our knowledge are tied to our interests. We are not indisputably on the side of the good and the holy. We should therefore perhaps be more wary and critical of the educational and staff development discourse into which we have been inducted. We should be interested in the use of language within the discourse and the way that discourse and practice inform each other. We should not lose our values or abrogate responsibility, but these become less anchored, more contingent. This does not excuse us from action: postmodernism will not imprison us and prevent us from acting. Indeed, it could help us to see for the first time the imprisoning characteristics of our most cherished standpoints.

Developers need to make contingent and strategic judgments as a result of their participation in a postmodern world. Hopefully, as part of this participation, they will be actively critical within the discourse. They will be critical from the stance of their various experiences (for example, feminist, class, ethnic, sexuality) and increasingly they will be critical from the perspective of their multiple identities (post-feminist, post-Marxist and so on). They will assume a critical orientation to narratives claiming foundational status, such as critical theory or phenomenography. In mounting such critiques they will inevitably look for the reduced form of 'solidarity' which postmodernism suggests: always in construction, subject to re-negotiation, pragmatic, contingent and transitory.

In 1981, David Boud and Rod McDonald suggested three models which 'educational consultants' (that is, developers) might adopt. These were professional service, counselling and colleagual. The professional service model casts the consultant as a provider of specialised services such as audiovisual aids; the counselling model sees the consultant providing conditions 'under which academics can explore the nature of their teaching problems, and ... help teachers reach an understanding of how they might be able to deal with problems which they have identified' (1981: 5). The colleagual model occurs when developers and teachers collaborate on a joint research project to improve practice (for example, an action research project). They suggest that the best approach for educational and staff development is 'an eclectic approach' because 'in practice the educational consultant needs to draw from each of these models' (1981: 5). In an astonishingly perceptive passage, they provide an outline which remains relevant today.

> It is necessary to work flexibly and eclectically in order to respond to the unique demands of each situation. The skills which need to be developed are those of each of the practitioners we have described: both technical competence and interpersonal skill are necessary, and the consultant's presentation to the rest of the educational community needs to be that of a colleague and fellow academic. At particular times and for particular teachers the consultant may need to adopt one or other of these roles exclusively, but if one approach takes over completely then effective development is likely to be hampered.

The three dimensions which Boud and McDonald identify find corollaries in the areas of positive knowledge for technical expertise, human understanding, and collaboration for practical and social improvement. Educational and staff development will always continue to reflect such broad areas in the theory of knowledge and the world of ideas. Especially in the partial and fractured postmodern world of educational and staff development, the eclectic approach advocated by Boud and McDonald still has much to recommend it.[8]

References

Boud, D. and McDonald, R. (1981) *Educational Development Through Consultancy*. Society for Research into Higher Education, Guildford.

Bronner, S.E. and Kellner, D. M. (eds) (1989) *Critical Theory and Society. A Reader*. Routledge, London.

Carr, W. and Kemmis, S. (1986) *Becoming Critical. Education, Knowledge and Action Research*. Falmer Press, London.

Chisholm, L. (1990) Action research: some methodological and political considerations. *British Educational Research Journal* 16 (3), 249–57.

Corey, S.M. (1949) Action research, fundamental research and educational practices. *Teachers College Record* 50, 509–14.

Elliot, J. (1978) What is action-research in schools? *Journal of Curriculum Studies* 10 (4), 355–57.

Elliot, J. and Adelman, C. (1973) Reflecting where the action is: the design of the Ford teaching project. *Education for Teaching* 92, 8–20.

Ellsworth, E. (1989) Why doesn't this feel empowering? Working through the repressive myths of critical pedagogy. *Harvard Educational Review* 59 (3), 297–324.

Freire, P. (1970) *Pedagogy of the Oppressed.* Herter and Herter, New York.

Gibson, R. (1985) Critical times for action research. *Cambridge Journal of Education* 15 (1), 59–64.

Habermas, J. (1971) *Knowledge and Human Interests.* Beacon Press, Boston.

—— (1984) *The Theory of Communicative Action. Volume One. Reason and the Rationalization of Society.* Beacon Press, Boston.

—— (1987) *The Theory of Communicative Action. Volume Two. Lifeworld and System: A Critique of Functionalist Reason.* Beacon Press, Boston.

Kember, D. and Kelly, M. (1994) *Improving Teaching Through Action Research.* HERDSA, Campbelltown, NSW.

Kemmis, S. and McTaggart, R. (eds) (1988a) *The Action Research Planner.* Deakin University Press, Geelong, Victoria.

—— (eds) (1988b) *The Action Research Reader.* Deakin University Press, Geelong, Victoria.

Lewin, K. (1946) Action research and minority problems. *Journal of Social Issues* 2 (4), 34–46.

McCarthy, T. (1978) *The Critical Theory of Jürgen Habermas.* MIT Press, Cambridge, Massachusetts.

McNiff, J. (1988) *Action Research: Principles and Practice.* Macmillan Education, Basingstoke.

Mezirow, J. (1981) A critical theory of adult learning and education. *Adult Education* 32 (1), 3–24.

Roderick, R. (1986) *Habermas and the Foundations of Critical Theory.* St Martin's Press, New York.

Sabine, G.H. (1963) *A History of Political Theory.* George G. Harrap & Co., London.

Strohmayer, U. and Hannah, M. (1992) Domesticating postmodernism. *Antipode. A Radical Journal of Geography* 24 (1), 29–55.

Webb, G. (1991) Putting praxis into practice. In C.J. Collins and P.J. Chippendale (eds) *Proceedings of the First World Congress on Action Research and Process Management. Volume 1: Theory and Praxis Frameworks.* Acorn Publications, Sunnybank Hills, Queensland, Australia, 33–42.

—— (1992) Groups and individuals in action learning. In C.S. Bruce and A.L. Russell (eds) *Transforming Tomorrow Today. Proceedings of the Second World Congress on Action Learning.* Action Learning, Action Research and Process Management Association Inc., Griffith University, Brisbane, Australia, 229–32.

—— (in press) *Understanding Staff Development.* SRHE and Open University Press, Buckingham.

Weeks, P. and Scott, D. (eds) (1992) *Exploring Tertiary Teaching.* Queensland University of Technology, Brisbane.

Whitehead, J. (1991) How do I improve my professional practice as an academic and educational manager? A dialectical analysis of an individual's educational development and a basis for socially orientated action research. In C. Collins and P. Chippendale (eds) *Proceedings of the First World Congress on Action Research and Process Management. Volume 1: Theory and Praxis Frameworks.* Acorn Publications, Sunnybank Hills, Queensland, 93–107.

Zuber-Skerritt, O. (1992) *Professional Development in Higher Education. A Theoretical Framework for Action Research.* Kogan Page, London.

Notes

1   This chapter is based upon material from *Understanding Staff Development*, Open University Press (in press). In that book, arguments for the conception of educational and staff development

as rational–progressive, humanistic, critical and postmodern are explored in greater depth. The author wishes to gratefully acknowledge Open University Press for granting permission for this material to be used in the present chapter.

2   Hegel adopted the word dialectic from Plato's dialogues, which he saw as epitomising the process of taking what is right from each side of a discussion (thesis, antithesis) in order to form a new position (synthesis) containing the truth of both.

3   The headquarters of the Institute moved to Columbia University in New York in 1934 although some of its original members joined other institutions in the United States.

4   For a compilation of readings by these and other leading first generation critical theorists see Bronner and Kellner (1989).

5   An outline of the theory of knowledge in terms of human interests is given in the appendix of Habermas (1971). The theory of communicative action is presented in Habermas (1984) and Habermas (1987). Good commentaries on Habermas are McCarthy (1978) and Roderick (1986). A good and accessible introduction to Habermas can be found in Carr and Kemmis (1986).

6   Accounts of the history of action research are given in Kemmis and McTaggart (1988a) and Zuber-Skerritt (1992). A collection of papers representing this history is to be found in Kemmis and McTaggart (1988b).

7   Kember and Kelly (1994) and Weeks and Scott (1992) give accounts which illustrate many such action research projects in higher education.

8   Further implications of educational and staff development practice in postmodernity are presented in Webb (in press).

Part IV

Postmodernism
and Critical
Action Research

Chapter 10

Exposing Discourses Through Action Research

Leonie E. Jennings and Anne P. Graham

Abstract

This chapter examines some ways in which action research may be reconceptualised to incorporate aspects of the postmodern 'moment' in the reflection phase of the cycle. It raises the possibility of opening up subject positions which allow the modern and postmodern to 'speak'. It provides an opportunity to look at the world from a number of different and possibly incompatible points of view, providing an opportunity for personal challenge, an acknowledgment and acceptance of difference, and a chance to experience professional growth.

Positioning the writers in the postmodern 'moment'

It is appropriate at the outset for the writers to make a provisional attempt at declaring their own position. It is a provisional attempt because we do not claim to be fully aware of our own position as 'authors'. In a chapter which explores the possibility of establishing a dialogue between postmodernism and action research, we are mindful that this interpretation (typical of any in the postmodern) is open to reinterpretation by the reader. The point of this chapter is not to 'prove' or 'hypothesise' the possibilities of dialogue between the modern and postmodern but to communicate our interest in both modernist action research and postmodernism and to attempt to illuminate the strengths of both. Our commitment to both necessarily influences the discussion and positions us in particular ways within the text. Hopefully this chapter will heighten awareness of the potential of postmodernism to provide fresh and radical ways of invigorating the process of action research.

This chapter grows out of a practical interest in the relationship between action research, change and empowerment on the one hand, and a theoretical interest in postmodernism on the other. To some degree it represents a personal struggle — possibly shared by many others. As researchers who have engaged in modernist action research and research projects which draw upon postmodern perspectives and concepts, we are conscious of the need to reflect upon the veiled and subtle ways in which 'modernist' thinking (of the kind underpinning emancipatory action research) manages to influence our current attempts to research in the 'postmodern'.

In attempting to work within postmodern political discourse, researchers are threatened by what could be interpreted as a new dogmatism: that is, one dare not speak (as one does in the action research 'cycle') for fear of 'essentialising', 'excluding', 'marginalising' or 'oppressing'. However, most researchers would acknowledge the difficulty of trying to pursue a postmodern view from everywhere. It seems that a methodological pursuit of postmodern political correctness would only lead to an extreme relativism which would render any research project self-destructive. Researching in such a domain puts one on an intellectual see-saw, struggling on the one hand not to be 'essentialist' in the research process, while at the same time trying to avoid relativistic paralysis. It appears that the challenge may lay in finding ways, if not to bridge the modernist–postmodernist perspectives, then at least to allow them to 'speak' to each other and to critically utilise the tools used in each. The purpose of this chapter is to investigate such possibilities.

Modernist action research

In the reflection stage of its process, action research does not necessarily dictate a prescriptive theoretical stance. Grundy (1982) and Carr and Kemmis (1986) provide a very useful theoretical typology in undertaking action research by challenging the 'intents' behind the research. They clearly argue the case for distinguishing between technical, practical and emancipatory action research. Grundy names the latter form 'critical' action research. Grundy's paper, along with the Kemmis and McTaggart (1988) and McTaggart (1991) manuals, have provided countless action researchers with a *raison d'etre* for critical action research. But two concerns emerge in the 1990s as we continue to use these frameworks.

First, most of these works have provided exhaustive discussion on procedures and methods but have not grounded the approach to data analysis within a social perspective. For example, how does a feminist action researcher differ from the phenomenological action researcher? Are they mutually exclusive? How do groups of participants reach agreement on a particular theoretical perspective from which to discuss their data? These concerns lead to questions about perspectives. How does the action researcher interrogate the data in the reflection stage? Because action research has been grounded in practitioner-oriented terms, many of these theoretical perspectives have not been adequately explored.

Second, much of action research has been grounded in Habermasian thought. The propositions operational in the practical reasoning of action theories are considered to be valid or 'true' if they lead to the realisation of the state of affairs that is desired. There is, however, a complexity to be noted. Greenwood (1994), for example, suggests that practical reasoning must be responsive to situational idiosyncrasy because practice is characteristically ambiguous, uncertain and worthy of interrogation. It may be possible, then, to reconcile poststructuralist and Habermasian thought (as argued by Bernstein 1993). The question inevitably arises as to how this might change the nature of action research in the 1990s and beyond.

The modern/postmodern debate

Whether we have entered the postmodern age is still a matter of heated conjecture. Nevertheless, it is hard to deny, or avoid, the influence that postmodern thought has had on almost every field of human practice. As Shapiro (1991) notes, it has cut a swathe through everything from architecture and art to dance, television, philosophy, politics, literary theory and cultural critique. Extending even beyond confines of the academy there is growing recognition that something of a new era is afoot. A postmodern vocabulary with its attendant consciousness seems to be situating itself in popular as well as intellectual discourse.

Postmodernism is an approach which requires that we look at things in new ways. It also suggests that we look at new things, given the changing nature of the world in which we live. The sociocultural complex known as the 'postmodern condition' (Coombe 1991) refers to a diversity of processes brought about by the breakdown of boundaries and an implosion of difference in cultural contexts. These developments are part of a global restructuring of capitalism involving new media, information and communications technologies.

Writers such as Habermas (1987), Giddens (1990) and Jameson (1991) assert that the 'modern' is still with us, while others such as Lyotard (1984) and Baudrillard (1988) recognise a move toward the 'postmodern'. In postmodern thought there are no universal criteria of truth; claims to knowledge are always contextual. The postmodern image of contemporary social institutions is based on the emergence of a consumer society, replacing the old productivism. The consumer society has no fixed roots, and everyday experience within it is influenced by a diversity of sources of communication; it is an inherently pluralistic order. Power (1990) suggests there is no absolute line to distinguish between modernity and postmodernity, as the latter comes to signify both the termination of the former and a differentiated continuation of it. Other writers such as Bernstein (1993) see the 'modernity/postmodernity' couplet as being inextricably interrelated and entwined with each other — seeing them as a constellation, not as an *either–or* but rather as *both–and*. It is important to note that the signifiers, modernity and postmodernity, are unstable and have been used in shifting and conflicting ways. Ambiguity helps to sustain the debates while also creating spaces for dialogue.

The question of whether the term 'postmodern' reflects a 'period' or an 'epistemology' underpins current debates and remains problematic. The former view makes ontological claims about the changing nature of society whilst the latter view makes claims about the nature of knowledge itself. A useful discussion of these views is that provided by Hassard (1993). Perhaps as Smart (1992) astutely points out, the assumption that the millennium is upon us is a common theme in human thought. We always think our time is like no other. Acceptance of Smart's view is not to reject the periodising ontology inherent in postmodernism, but rather to suggest a healthy climate of debate.

It is important to highlight that there are problems confronting those who wish to relate postmodernism to such fields as education and training. As Usher and Edwards (1994) highlight, education is particularly resistant to the postmodern 'message' discussed in this chapter. Educational theory and practice is founded on discourses of modernity and its self-understandings have been forged by the assumptions implicit in that discourse. Postmodernism's emphasis on the inscribed subject, the decentred subject constructed by language, discourses, desire and the unconscious seems to contradict the very purpose of education which was founded on modernity's self-motivated, self-directing, rational subject, capable of exercising individual agency. This then becomes one of the major 'cutting edges' in attempting to relate postmodernism to action research in education.

'Critical' action research and the modern/postmodern

What is the significance of the modern/postmodern couplet for action researchers? Can reflection on action be sustained in the midst of such postmodern pluralism? 'Critical' action researchers have become adept at exposing 'meta-narratives' through the processes of 'critical reflection'. What postmodernism can provide is a new way of accepting that there are multiple representations of events. In fact postmodernists argue that the overarching 'meta-narratives' of the modern period have given way to the 'little stories' of the postmodern condition. Language, metaphor and discourse, the central elements of postmodern epistemology, can provide new ways of exposing competing meta-narratives. There are no 'final' stories but each story reflects our own way of organising and understanding the social world.

In the postmodernist view, truth is relative and human action is reduced in its importance. Postmodernists seek to avoid totalisation or closure which results in a disavowal of any meta-theoretical or political claims. Many commentators regard postmodernism as a position of 'anything goes', partly because of the difficulty in delineating and defining its meaning. The postmodernist leaves the question of values as a matter of choice for others to make.

The modernist view, on the other hand, makes an assumption about unity which is implicit in the Enlightenment notion of reason. Hassard (1993) distinguishes between 'systematic' modernism which reflects 'instrumental' reason and 'critical' modernism which confronts instrumental reason and provides for the emancipation of social action. Much of action research in the 1980s has been based on critical modernism. The best known advocate of this critical modernist position, Habermas (1987), has stressed that discourse is the medium of analysis because language is the medium of reason. However, Habermas' 'communicative rationality' has been repressed by the discourse of 'systematic' modernism. Habermas argued that it is through the 'language of community' that critical modernism can prevail.

Hassard (1993) suggests that in 'systematic' modernism the rational subject is the system itself, while in 'critical' modernism it is the knowing subject that reaches the consensus of human understanding. Hence in both forms of modernism, 'systematic' and 'critical', there is an assumption of an underlying unity that provides legitimacy and an authoritative logic. Postmodernism rejects this meta-position of unity.

Thus, in postmodern theory the subject is no longer seen as a unitary, rational ego. Rather it is seen as occupying different subject-positions within discursive practices; positions which are produced by the power/knowledge relations of particular discourses. As such, the subject exists in-process, only as partial, and sometimes non-rational 'voices' occupying sites or positions which might themselves be contradictory.

In the critical/modernist view, truth is the attempt to sustain agreement — not the end of enquiry but a temporal consensus on what is important in a particular situation at a particular time. This does not mean any account of truth will suffice, because certain narratives do not correspond with the way the subjects perceive their world. The problem with this view is that the 'final' consensus view is only ever 'temporal'. It would seem, as Cooper and Burrell (1988) argue, that what we find at the so-called origin of things is not a reassuring state of perfection, now lost but still reclaimable. Instead there is disparity, difference and indeterminacy. For this reason, Habermas criticises Foucault (and the postmodernists in general) for being 'irrational'.

Habermas considers reason to be conditional on a concept of the perfect origin; his 'communicative rationality' presupposes just such an ideal state. But the thrust of postmodern thought starts from a different understanding of reason — a rationality that is based not on finding answers to problems but of 'problematising' answers. Foucault can only see answers as ways of short-circuiting problems. The complex process of how thoughts are structured so as to give a solution is always subject to the work of power. Power precedes the answer through its subtle and covert prior structuring of the problem. Cooper and Burrell (1988) suggest that this is why Foucault is so concerned with 'problematising', since the proper understanding of a solution can only be attained from seeing how the problem was structured in the first place.

Habermas claims that thinkers like Foucault and Lyotard are 'neoconservative', in that they offer us no 'theoretical' reason to move in one social direction rather than another. They take away the dynamic which liberal thought has traditionally relied upon — namely the need to be in touch with a reality obscured by 'ideology' and disclosed by 'theory' which then precipitates action.

It would seem that the significance of the modern/postmodern debate in the present context lies in the counterpointing of issues and concepts that are at the heart of the action research process. The proponents of each stance deal with similar themes such as differentiation, power, authority and discipline, but produce radically different interpretations of them. Yet it may be that such rivalry will highlight the relevance of the modernist/ postmodernist debate in the reinvigoration of action research.

The disjuncture of action research with postmodernism

Many critical action researchers would argue that the incorporation of a postmodern epistemology would be a way of avoiding making choices in the action research process, while at the same time reducing human agency. So what is the significance of postmodernist thinking for action researchers?

Postmodernist thinking can provoke us to reconceive the concept of 'action' research in terms that integrate it into a study of power. It requires us to consider meaning in terms of relations of struggle embodied in everyday practice, and it demands that we view our actions in local contexts, related in specific ways to historical conjectures.

Through the lens of the postmodernist, action researchers may come to the realisation that their actions could have multiple meanings. Every action can imply its contradiction. To affirm something by action is to set in motion a chain of signification that simultaneously confirms its negation. Actors do not 'control' the fate of their expressions. The actor signifies, but a supplement is required to determine its meaning; it is the listener/observer who supplies the supplement.

Intersecting postmodernist thinking with action research: exposing discourses

One of the most useful devices that action researchers could utilise in the reflection stage of the process includes the postmodernist tool of discourse analysis. It is often difficult in the reflection stage to change taken-for-granted assumptions that become obscured in our observational data. Foucault's work shows how we can deconstruct what we take for granted and regard as self-evident. His work also shows how objects of knowledge are not natural, but are ordered or constructed by discourses which determine what is 'seeable and sayable'. In his work, *The Archaeology of Knowledge*, Foucault (1972) shows the 'conditions of possibility' which help to perpetuate a certain way of thinking (a discourse). Discourse refers to the underlying rules, the *a priori*, assumed parts of knowledge which limit the forms of the 'sayable'. Discourse or discursive practices determine what is taken as known and how this is established.

Gee (1991: xix) explains discourses in this way:

> Discourses are ways of behaving, interacting, valuing, thinking, believing, speaking, and often reading and writing that are accepted as instantiations of particular roles by specific *groups of people*, whether families of a certain sort, lawyers of a certain sort, bikers of a certain sort, business people of a certain sort, churches of a certain sort, and so on through a very long list.

171

Hence in the reflection stage of action research, as we begin to uncover the ideological underpinnings of belief systems inherent in the data we are closely examining, we ourselves are likely to be engaging in some form of discourse. It is language that 'makes sense' to us as a community of action researchers. If the process has been truly participatory, it is likely that we share a common use of languages. But what 'makes sense' to us who are engaged in the action research process may not make sense to others. Consider the discourse of basketball. It makes little sense to those who play bridge. Not only is discourse determined by community, it is also embedded in the larger framework of social relationships and social institutions.

Gee (1991: 144) further explains discourses by suggesting five key features:

- Discourses are ideological in that they involve a set of values and viewpoints about people in their relationship to the distribution of social goods (money, power, status) in society.

- Discourses are resistant to self-analysis and define what counts as acceptable criticism, which of course is constituted by another discourse.

- Discourses are defined positions in relation to other, ultimately opposing discourses.

- Discourses value concepts and viewpoints at the expense of others, hence marginalising viewpoints and values central to other discourses.

- Discourses are related to power relations and hierarchical structure in society; that is control and exercise of certain discourses can lead to the acquisition of social goods in society.

Over the last few decades, teachers, practitioners and researchers who have engaged in critical action research projects, often in collaboration, have helped to reproduce their own discourse about their practices. That is, they have engaged in a dialogue about education and workplaces that has been driven by a perceived need for emancipatory educational interventions within organisations such as schools. Through the social practices in which action researchers are enmeshed, dominant discourses have emerged about how change can take place.

Hence 'action research' itself is constituted by instances of discursive practice. Action research constitutes its own discourse. This means it has its own particular narrative or story, with its own rules and metaphors. Its narrative is underpinned by certain political and ideological assumptions.

Thus the concepts of 'action', 'problematising', 'cycles', 'being reflective' and so forth have to be understood as 'discourse' rather than descriptions of 'what is'. These concepts (along with many others) constitute the discursive practices of action research. It is important to note that they are not direct representations of the practices of action research — but are merely the constituted discourse. Hence in the process of 'action research', discursive practices emerge which determine how 'objects' become spoken of in a certain manner.

The value of discourse for the action researcher

If the action researcher is prepared to accept that the process itself is constituted through its own discourse then the 'objects' of study themselves are so constituted. That is, the boundaries of the action research 'problem' or 'question' are not given but are constructed and constituted through discourse. This raises the interesting question of what is the effect of constructing the 'problem' in a particular way? What are the limits within the constructed discourse? As the action researcher uses categories that are familiar within the discourse, other possibilities are 'silenced'. Foucault's work shows that what counts as 'truth' depends on the conceptual system in operation, thereby forming a discourse and limiting our analysis.

One way of disrupting the discourse is to use Foucault's power/ knowledge couplet. Foucault uses the idea of 'relationships of power', rather than the singular term 'power'. He suggests that when one speaks of 'power' one thinks immediately of a political structure or a dominant hegemonic class. Rather, the analysis of power cannot be reduced to institutions, class or the state, but rather the power relations within them. For Foucault, power is associated with practices, techniques and procedures. Power is relational, not a possession, exercised rather than held, and is not limited to a central point.

For Foucault, the rise of modern society is bound up with the intensifying of surveillance. 'Surveillance' means the use of direct supervision and the control of information to create what Foucault calls a 'disciplinary society' (Foucault 1980). The way we structure our social life through institutional arrangements or technologies helps to create 'docile bodies in corporate control'. Power and knowledge are dimensions of the same practices and social relations. Power informs knowledge and produces discourse. It unintentionally achieves strategic effects through methods of discipline and surveillance. These methods of discipline and surveillance are a form of knowledge constituted not only in texts but also in definite institutional and organisational practices. Hence disciplinary practices are 'discursive practices'. Knowledge constitutes discipline, and discipline is an effective constitution of power. As a result, knowledge yields obedient bodies, regulated minds and ordered emotions.

What does this mean for the action researcher? It suggests that in the reflection stage, power can no longer be portrayed as 'external', something which operates on something or someone. As Foucault (1977: 194) suggests:

> ... we must cease once and for all to describe the effects of power in negative terms: it 'excludes', it 'represses', it 'censors', it 'abstracts', it 'masks', it 'conceals'. In fact power produces; it produces reality; it produces domains of objects and rituals of truth.

The value of this reconceptualisation of power disrupts the modernist view of the critical action researcher by expanding our understanding of the political and, in doing so, opens up the possibilities of countering and changing it. For the critical action researcher, understanding power as a relational activity widens the scope from the 'who' and 'why' questions endemic to action research, to questions of 'how'. This creates spaces for new dialogue and contestation. As Dreyfus and Rabinow (1983: 185) argue:

> [if] ... power is not a thing or the control of a set of institutions ... then the task for the analyst is to identify how it operates.

This approach shifts the action researcher from critically reflective concerns such as 'who has the power?' or 'where, or in what, does power reside?' to questions which focus on the 'how' of power — the practices, techniques and procedures by which it operates. It involves the tracking of knowledge production (webs of power) and its power effects. Knowledge is integral to the operation of power. Hence we can appreciate Foucault's concept of power/knowledge.

In a later work, Foucault (1988) develops the concept of the 'individual as subject'; that is, how individuals come to see and understand themselves in a particular way and, through this, become tied to a particular conception of their identity and subjectivity. The individual is continuously constituted and constructed through social relationships, discourses and practices. As well, individuals are constructed and known through being made an 'object' of knowledge and a target of power. This ambiguity of how human beings constitute themselves as subjects and how they treat one another as objects is the main focus of Foucault's later works. This emphasis on the constituted nature of self is a strong theme in postmodernist thinking and can provide new ways for the critical action researcher to interrogate subjectivities that form in the observation phase of the action research cycle.

The main advantage to the critical action researcher who is prepared to embrace this analysis is its political potential. By adopting this framework, the critical action researcher can focus on those practices and discourses which establish objects and power relations. This focus on practices, the 'how' of power, is not without its critics. Modernist proponents demand to know the 'who' and the 'why' of power. An argument can be advanced that to concentrate on 'how' as opposed to 'who' or 'why' denies the role of the subject and hence presents the critical action researcher without an adequate base for change. But this is questionable. The 'how' question is part of the political process.

An analysis of the nature and limits of practices through which experience is constituted undermines their 'naturalness', and with this comes the possibility of change through critique. For Foucault, critique is the questioning of the 'politics of truth', that is, questioning which knowledge becomes an instrument of policies and practices, and forming the basis of a political position. The formation and implementation of relations of power depend upon the production, circulation and functioning of discourses of truth. However, truth is linked in a circular relation to the systems of power which promote it, and to the effects of power which truth itself generates. For the postmodernist, truth is not perceived as a universal concept which traverses all human societies. Rather it is local and politically constituted through practices which define what is false and what is true.

Postmodern ideas and insights provide some cautions to critical action researchers that perhaps should not easily be dismissed. Power, it is asserted, differs from being identified only with the forces of repression and exploitation. It is omnipresent and exists even among the forces of liberation trying to overthrow domination. Concepts such as equality, freedom and justice are merely tokens in a game, in an interplay of forces. This position is very much like that of Nietzsche, who claimed that when the oppressed want justice, it is just a pretext for the fact that they want power for themselves. The danger, it seems, is that the dialogue can become very one-sided if liberation is 'done' for others, even if it is done in the name of a universal concept of freedom.

For the action researcher, the resolution of problems is often given priority over the desire to question, even though resolutions only result in new questions. Certainty is valued over doubt (Usher & Edwards 1994). Rather than tight solutions, then, action researchers might reflect upon the need to struggle without end or resolution, indeed to deconstruct, construct and reconstruct meanings in 'making sense' of the world. A postmodern perspective suggests that there is no single definition to be tied down with which everyone involved in the action research process will agree, irrespective of the historical moment or space they inhabit. Indeed, postmodernism allows for the fact that even though at a surface level people may appear to be agreeing, there may well be conflicting values, strategies, meanings or assumptions at work underneath the critical action research process.

Dialogue with other postmodernists

If the critical action researcher is prepared to take on this challenge of dialogue with postmodernists, then a willingness to explore the writings of other key theorists becomes essential. Probably the most notable writers in the postmodernist field are Jean-Francois Lyotard, Jacques Derrida and Jean Baudrillard, whilst Michel Foucault is classified more as a poststructuralist, but still postmodern. It is important to note that these writers do not negate social action — the idea central to action research. Each of these writers has important, yet varying things to say about the postmodern. Although none of these writers, with the exception of Lyotard, writes specifically about education, they each contribute to a re-examination of educational theory and practice in the context of a developing postmodern society.

Lyotard has defined postmodern discourse as 'the search for instabilities' (Lyotard 1984: 53). He elaborates a considerable argument against the 'grand narratives' that legitimate modernity. The drive towards determinancy is also a drive towards consensus, and as Lyotard argues, the more one reaches for it, the farther away it seems. Instead of consensus being the powerhouse of social action, it is 'dissensus' which continually compels our attention (Cooper & Burrell 1988). For Lyotard, then, postmodernism rejects the grand narratives such as the emancipation of the subject — a key pillar in the 'critical' action research agenda. Rather, knowledge is based on nothing more than a number of diverse discourses, each with its own rules and structures, with no discourse being privileged. The actor in the postmodern is one who struggles with an infinite number of language games within an environment characterised by diversity and conflict. The challenge for the action researcher is to embrace this notion of language games, which can give rise to further social action. That is, making a 'space' for social action is possible only if there is continuous struggle through language games. When struggle goes out of the game it loses its potential to motivate social action.

Derrida's (1978) postmodernism is founded on the deconstructive approach which, on inverting the notion of construction, illustrates how artificial are the ordinary, taken-for-granted structures of our social world. Derrida's work shows how processes of rationality (used in critical action research) serve to obscure the logical undecidability which resides at the core of social action. Derrida moves beyond the idea of the social actor and locates his theory in the concept of the 'text'. The text refers both to the interplay of discourses — political, social and so forth — and the stage upon which the process of deconstruction is enacted. Basically his deconstructive method exposes the inherent contradictions which reside in any text.

Baudrillard (1988) argues that in postmodern society, simulations structure and control social affairs. In modern society, production provides the key. In Baudrillard's approach, the opposition between what things look like and what is really going on dissolve in the 'hyper-reality' of the media age. He argues that the mass media symbolise a new era in which the old forms of production and consumption have given way to a new universe of communication. Models and codes precede reality and are reproduced unceasingly in a society where the contrast between the real and the unreal is no longer valid. 'Simulacra' — that is, copies or representations of objects or events — constitute the 'real'. Rational critique and the will to change the world are characterised by what Baudrillard calls the 'ecstasy of communication' — a state characterised by 'banal education' and 'mindless' fascinations when any kind of judgment, not just artistic but moral and political, becomes impossible (Shapiro 1991). Hence in the postmodern world there is a universe of nihilism where concepts float in a void, whereas in the modern world we found meaning in the laws of production. For the action researcher, social action is caught up in the play of images (simulacra) which have less and less relationship to an outside reality.

Reframing dialogue

There is thus a possibility of dialogue between those who advocate a human agency approach to change, such as critical action research, and those who advocate a postmodern reading of the human state. Action researchers need to find intersections that will enhance their knowledge. As Usher and Edwards (1994) suggest, the postmodern moment does not signify a failure to engage in issues of oppression and emancipation but a reconfiguring of the way such issues are conceptualised. Perhaps what needs to be incorporated into the understanding of critical action research is that oppression and emancipation are co-implicated in ever-shifting patterns arising from ongoing struggles. It is for this reason that *resistance* rather than *emancipation* has become integral to much postmodern discourse. Notwithstanding, the following are offered as new ways for the critical action researcher to start a dialogue with postmodernists, despite major differences.

First, both the postmodern and critical approaches share a common message about the nature of society. That message is one of knowledge and power, conflict and contradiction, as well as the irreconcilability of social goals, aims and values. Conflict, contradiction and lack of consensus primarily exist because of power relations which produce subordination, and consequently assign some voices to silence and marginalisation. The value of poststructuralist approaches (a subset of postmodernism) can provide a very useful tool to the action researcher in exposing dominant forms of discourse which silence non-dominant voices by power and power relations. By dictating the terms of the discourse, one is able to dictate the relations of power. Critical action research should be concerned with deconstructing authoritative voices — those who speak for and on behalf of others. The difficulty, of course, is to reconcile the tension between the espoused goals of democracy and emancipation on the one hand, and the complex workings of power and oppression on the other.

Second, postmodernism disrupts the concept of continuity. This discontinuity might have a place in the reflection stage of action research as part of the 'reconstruction' process. Through the use of postmodernist concepts such as 'representation', 'reflexivity', 'writing' and 'de-centring' the subject, derived from the works of Baudrillard, Lyotard and Derrida, the action researcher has a wider set of tools with which to reflect upon the actions taken.

Third, both the critical action researcher and the postmodernist often share and examine 'narrative' as a useful form of discourse. These narratives help to communicate meanings, project a voice, provide multiple perspectives and can provide future possibilities. Jameson (1991) argues that narratives are not specifically a literary form but rather abstract coordinates with which we come to know the world. Postmodernism suggests that the world is constituted by our shared language and that we can only 'know the world' through a particular discourse.

Fourth, by applying some of the tools developed by Derrida's deconstruction method (1978) and the concept of *difference* (which refers to the deferral of meaning), action research can examine the data/text from the observation phase in the reflection moment by seeing that text as a contested terrain. Because meaning constantly slips beyond our grasp, what the text appears to say on the surface cannot be understood without reference to the concealments and contextualisations of meaning going on simultaneously to mark the text's significance. Deconstructionism provides a useful tool to the action researcher for disrupting theory and opening up conflict for reconstruction.

Finally, an examination of Foucault's (1980) analysis helps the critical action researcher to understand how power is located in the body rather than the mind. For example, in schools and workplaces bodies are distributed in a grid of time and space to optimise their visibility. Surveillance measures are put in place to ensure this domesticity. However surveillance is not the only form of control. In Foucault's later works he developed the epistemological concerns of the specialist disciplines such as psychology and pedagogy, which attempt to control the administration of disciplinary power. Indeed, the insights provided by Foucault (cited in Gore 1992: 287) provide some necessary inspiration for the critical action researcher attempting to take the postmodern into account:

> ... I would say that the analysis, elaboration, and bringing into question of power relations ... is a permanent political task inherent in all social existence.

Creating spaces

To date there has been a concern among educators to define action research in more precise terms. Perhaps a static definition is neither feasible nor appropriate in a postmodern world. Unless action researchers are willing to investigate and incorporate new directions then we will become prisoners of our own perspectives, which, as Foucault suggests, is a subtle form of social control. As far as critical action research is concerned, it might be as Peters and Marshall (1991: 133) suggest:

> ... that empowerment may depend upon a recognition of 'community-in-process', that 'in-process' means an historical projection which, working through the differences of gender, race and class in collective self-reflection, can also provisionally re-establish an unforced unity of community — a unity which is not a transcendental synthesis of sociality and individuality, but one which openly and critically appraises difference and heterogeneity — as a basis for collective self-consciousness and community action.

Such a process (influenced as it is by postmodern theorising) may shift the understanding of democratic research methodologies such as critical action research but may still involve 'empowerment'.

It may be argued that there is considerable satisfaction in the opportunity to examine the gaps, silences, conflicts and contradictions in the understanding of taken-for-granted 'truths' or 'answers' which (to use postmodern-'speak') may provide a 'space' for much needed change. Thus the use of such postmodern theorising may provide an important contribution to the critical action research process.

References

Baudrillard, J. (1988) *Selected Writings*. Polity, Oxford.

Bernstein, R., Jones, J.P., Natter, W. and Schatzki, T.R. (1993) Postmodernism, dialogue, and democracy: questions to Richard J. Bernstein. In J.P. Jones, W. Natter and T.R. Schatzki (eds) *Postmodern Contentions: Epochs, Politics, Space*. The Guildford Press, New York.

Carr, W. and Kemmis, S. (1986) *Becoming Critical: Knowing Through Action Research*. 2nd edn. Deakin University Press, Geelong.

Coombe, R.J. (1991) Encountering the postmodern: new directions in cultural anthropology. *Canadian Review of Sociology and Anthropology* 28, 187–205.

Cooper, R. and Burrell, G. (1988) Modernism, postmodernism and organisational analysis: an introduction. *Organisation Studies* 9, 91–112.

Derrida, J. (1978) *Writing and Difference*. Routledge and Kegan Paul, London.

Dreyfus, H. and Rabinow, P. (1983) *Michel Foucault — Beyond Structuralism and Hermeneutics*. Harvester, Brighton.

Foucault, M. (1972) *The Archaeology of Knowledge*. Routledge, London.

—— (1977) *Discipline and Punish: The Birth of the Prison*. Allen Lane, London.

—— (1980) *Power/Knowledge*. Harvester, Brighton.

—— (1989) Technologies of the self. In L. Martin, H. Gutman and P.H. Hutton (eds) *Technologies of the Self*. Tavistock, London.

Gee, J. (1991) *Social Linguistics and Literacies: Ideologies in Discourses*. Falmer Press, London.

Giddens, A. (1990) *The Consequences of Modernity*. Polity, Cambridge.

Gore, J. (1992) Foucault and educational discourses. In T. Lovat (ed.) *Sociology for Teachers*. Social Science Press, Wentworth Falls, 281–88.

Greenwood, J. (1994) Action research: a few details, a caution and something new. *Journal of Advanced Nursing* 20, 13–18.

Grundy, S. (1982) Three modes of action research. *Curriculum Perspectives* 2, 23–34.

Habermas, J. (1987) *Lectures on the Philosophical Discourse of Modernity.* MIT Press, Cambridge MA.

Hassard, J. (1993) Postmodernism and organisational analysis: an overview. In J. Hassard and M. Parker (eds) *Postmodernism and Organisation.* Sage, London.

Jameson, F. (1991) *Postmodernism, or, the Cultural Logic of Late Capitalism.* Verso, London.

Kemmis, S. and McTaggart, R. (1988) *The Action Research Planner.* 3rd edn. Deakin University Press, Geelong.

Lash, S. and Urry, J. (1987) *The End of Organised Capitalism.* Polity, Cambridge.

Lincoln, Y. (1989) Critical requisites for transformational leadership: needed research and discourse. *Peabody Journal of Education* 66, 176–81.

Lyotard, J.F. (1984) *The Postmodern Condition: A Report on Knowledge.* Manchester University Press, Manchester.

McTaggart, R. (1991) *Action Research: A Short Modern History.* Deakin University Press, Geelong.

Peters, M. and Marshall, J. (1991) Education and empowerment: postmodernism and the critique of humanism. *Education and Society* 9, 123–34.

Power, M. (1990) Modernism, postmodernism and organization. In J. Hassard and D. Pym (eds) *The Theory of Philosophy of Organization.* Routledge, London.

Shapiro, S. (1991) The end of radical hope? Postmodernism and the challenge to critical pedagogy. *Education and Society* 9, 112–22.

Smart, B. (1992) *Modern Conditions, Postmodern Controversies.* Routledge London.

Usher, R. and Edwards, R. (1994) *Postmodernism and Education.* Routledge, London.

Chapter 11

Managing Change Through Action Research: A Postmodern Perspective on Appraisal[1]

Jack Sanger

Abstract

The aspiration of collaborative, self-critical enquiry on the part of practitioners is constantly eroded by the need to be credentialled or otherwise supported by academic centres whose own agendas often lead to hegemonies in research approaches and relationships. Terms such as 'empowerment', 'emancipation' and 'ownership' signal external agency. This chapter seeks to clarify practitioner control over the entire action research process by exploring the term 'authorship' in the context of an appraisal project involving nearly four hundred individuals. Using action research as the basis of a radical approach to appraisal, the cycle of planning a focus, gathering evidence, self-evaluation, modification and further planning was introduced by an action research project team into all staff's professional work in a large, mixed economy college. The appraiser, as critical friend, would seek to develop a discourse with the appraisee which would explore the relationships between professional practice and evidence (research methods) and between evidence and self-evaluation (analysis). Finally, the pairing would produce a statement of the outcomes of their engagement (reporting).

Introduction

I take, as the starting point of this chapter, some thoughts of Paulo Freire (1973) in *Education: the Practice of Freedom.* He explores the notion of 'extension' in agrarian reform and shows how the term actually denotes a form of imperialism on the part of the agents who seek change in, say, Third World cultures.

> Thus, in its 'field of association' the term extension has a significant relation to transmission, handing over, giving, messianism, mechanical transfer, cultural invasion, manipulation, etc. (1973: 93)

What concerns Freire is how agents of change, representing the Central Bank, governments, universities and so on, embody within their role forms of cultural exchange which negate recipients' rights as *'beings who transform the world'.* If we subject some of the current terminology of action research to this kind of analysis, would we learn something about the problematics of support to practitioners? I feel strongly that this is the case. The three terms which are currently in vogue are 'empowerment', 'emancipation' and, to a lesser and more general extent, 'ownership'. Each has an essential ingredient which calls into question the power relations between practitioner researchers and external support agents. This ingredient is a subject–object relationship. Each term involves some agency having a privileged position, a meta-view, or superordinate vantage point over others. In most circumstances in the field of professional development, we do not think of people emancipating themselves or empowering themselves. The terms become hyperbole once used outside despotic regimes. Professional development within the central educational structures of most Western societies does not involve freeing from bondage (emancipation), nor does it involve acts of authorisation or the licensing of individuals to act (empowerment). Yet the terms are used liberally in action research literature and, in their use, mask the inherent violation of practitioners' rights as beings who might transform their worlds. If ever there was a trilogy of double-headed terms in action research, empowerment, emancipation and ownership are the three. I have added ownership because it is the term used by managers or project researchers to indicate that certain acceptable ideas should take root in those they manage or support in action research. For this to happen, Freire's notion of transmission must be mediated by *translation into context.* The subject–object relationship still inheres. I offer — you own. But what is owned? Usually, concepts, speculations, ideals and methods originated by those who have implicit or explicit superiority. The fact of their common usage is significant and contains its own thread of duplicity. What the terms speak of is a hidden paternalism within the support agency in action research to 'free' the practitioner into a state of consciousness possibly enjoyed by the support agents, to 'license' the practitioner (with accreditation from centres of higher education) and to transfer ownership of suitable understanding. In other words, we are in the Freirian territory of cultural invasion.

In what circumstances does the practitioner from the university have the right to offer support to teachers in classrooms? What ought to be the guiding principles of such a relationship? How do we offend less and achieve forms of parity that enable us to learn and change alongside fellow practitioners in schools?

The first question we, as prospective support agents, might ask concerns our own commitment to pedagogical change. Do we higher educationalists, as fellow practitioners, ask serious questions concerning our pedagogical practices in universities? Are we 'at risk' in the same way that teachers in schools are? Do we introduce challenging appraisal systems that contain observations of our teaching practice, student feedback, feedback from those we manage? Do we actively engage in innovations in our own classroom management? Do we regularly write new materials and explore new approaches to teaching and learning in our own classrooms? Do we, in fact, engage in action research? Do we use it to have impact on our own institutions?

There are some laudable cases in the literature which suggest that this may happen in isolation (Walker 1993; Schratz 1993; Zuber-Skerritt 1992) but the world of action research is not one commonly thought to embrace university practice. Nor have university departments of education generally been seen to seek to change the understanding of colleagues in fellow departments, concerning students' learning styles and their own pedagogical responsibilities. The prevailing view tends to be that staff are subject experts, full stop.

As is the case in this chapter, some of the above issues have been addressed in a large-scale action research project involving the introduction of an appraisal system to a college of further and higher education staff of about 370 individuals. As project facilitator, there was an opportunity to introduce an action research approach to appraisal which did not fall into the trap of paternalism, and which sought a complete parity in the principles and procedures of the appraisal process for all participants, managers, teaching staff and project team.

Since empowerment and emancipation were not terms which conceptualised our intended approach, what were? And how did the project team operate?

An integral element of the college appraisal project involved support agents (appraisers) becoming readers who learned from the authorship of practitioners. Authorship is the means by which we claim respect from our colleagues. It may be via words on paper. It may be via the spoken language. It may be via videotape or drawing. The appraisers could then ask questions about the processes of authorship. What were these?

In our appraisal system, each member of staff constructs a portfolio of evidence concerning professional practice over a two-year period. Each is asked to collect evidence about his or her practice; to elicit student, parent, industrialist, colleague and manager perceptions. Each is asked to focus on an area of practice and illuminate it with this detailed evidence. The ensuing picture or case study is then self-evaluated and decisions are made by the individual as to what should ensue in the next appraisal cycle. The appraiser's role is that of a critical friend, whose purpose is to facilitate discussion on the interfaces between professional profile (job description) and the evidence collected, and between the evidence and the self-evaluation. Staff choose their appraisers. Staff define focus. Staff define what evidence to collect and how to collect it. We, as a project team, offer training in ways of collecting evidence. We try to demystify research and suggest it is all common sense, problem solving. We say that staff can develop their own evidence-gathering approaches. The result, we hope, is authorship. Individuals are free to construct their professional selves for joint critical discussion. Our overriding aim is to improve the quality of discourse about teaching and learning, about curriculum development, about managing staff, about every aspect of institutional life. We want to move the culture towards openness. If every individual conducts his or her appraisal on a basis of evidence collected, then, by resonance or isomorphism, the same may eventually be true on the grand scale.

Unlike the more normal appraisal systems, we feel that the texts of people's professional lives provide a cathartic element to appraisal which is more influential in enabling them to make decisions for change. They gain a distance on themselves by examining evidence, rather than speaking rhetorically — action research rather than hearsay-based evaluations.

I conclude this introduction by listing the values made explicit by the project team, as they have worked alongside their fellow staff:

- *parity* (everyone goes through the same process);
- *difference* (recognition of individual biography);

- *resonance* (structural similarities should be seen at all levels. For example, lecturers should be evaluated by their students and managers by those they line manage);

- *autonomy* (each member of staff 'authors' his or her own appraisal, by choosing appraiser, deciding focus, choosing data collection methods);

- *challenge* (there should be no cosiness, complacency or lip-service);

- *evidence* (reviews are based on evidence collected over time);

- *targets* (objective and subjective targets are set for each cycle's completion);

- *support* (the system is independently supported by monitoring panels to ensure its principles and procedures are adhered to);

- *flexibility* (monitoring, reviewing and evaluation by these panels constantly modify the system); and

- *impact* (no secret has been made of the panel's intention to open up the institutional culture to critique at all levels.

It is these values which go some way towards combatting power imbalance within appraisal through action research. However, no one should assume that all staff are happy with the prospect of having authorship and control over their professional destinies. Dependency is an inexorable conditioning factor in all hierarchies. Staff, both managers used to wielding authority and subordinates used to receiving it, can find this turn of democracy very unappealing.

Context

Central to issues of management in the 1990s is the relationship between management and action. The effects of the free market philosophies and attendant uncontrolled expansion into uncharted and irresponsible organisational growth in the 1980s are still leading many organisations to continue with administrative and bureaucratic superstructures which could dog potential development until the end of the decade. Despite the search for economy and efficiency through the innovative approaches of de-layering or flattening organisations, re-formed hierarchies often still retain vestigial habits which hark back to the status, territorialism, personal aggrandisement and attendant loyalty of a past ideology.

Because of the grip that principles such as order, efficiency, predictability, goal achievement, role definition, planning, differential status, differential responsibility and differential reward have on our daily lives, in both personal and institutional contexts, and in ordinary or extraordinary situations, we find it almost impossible to think about difference without reducing it to variations upon that one original theme of which we, ourselves, are but a variation (Boyne 1990: 122).

Attempts to skin graft over the stretch marks of organisational resistance to change can be seen in quality circles, project-led development and staff consultation. Nevertheless, many organisations still maintain a lopsided equation between top-heavy management and production. In effect this means that decision making is still the prerogative of those beyond or distant from the essential products or core activities of the organisation, whether they come from the shop floor, the classroom, the ward or the office. Not only might all decisions be made by non-participative managers, but the numbers of these non-participants may be grossly out of proportion to the work required of them. Delegating responsibility to productive personnel and tolerance of their partial autonomy in sub-sectors remains an illusory hope for many capable staff in organisations.

What we have here are the lingering remains of a modernist style of organisational culture. Through it, there is management's attempt to provide unification of purpose via mission statements, policy papers, strategic development plans; and unification of practice via communication systems, appraisal systems and organisational structures. Though no one yet doubts the need for overviews and consequent strategic planning, the shift in this period was towards making each of these an end in itself. The energies of staff taken up in the overall bureaucratisation of the organisation was to the detriment of productive action.

So why use the term 'postmodern' to signal some of the changes that are needed? There is, after all, no absolute cleavage between what is beginning to happen now in organisational cultures and what was happening before, no real Foucauldian 'rupture' (1991). Cultural outlooks which belong to former and latter styles of management also blur and interpenetrate. Nevertheless, a typological comparison between postmodernist and modernist assumptions about organisational culture would include those listed in Table 11.1.

What modernism adds up to — and it is not difficult to extend the list — is the central metaphor of the organisation as a mechanism, an entity which has a clearly dedicated purpose and intent and, provided sub-elements are kept tuned, their combined effects will ensure a totalisation of endeavour amongst those who work within it. Applying a postmodern cultural critique such as that originating in literature, Barthes (1982) would say that what

Table 11.1 *Postmodernist and modernist assumptions*

Postmodernist	Modernist
Decentred, flexible clusters, semi-autonomous	Core authority and top-down hierarchical relationships
Interpretative understandings of mission and purpose	Assumptions about the understood focus or mission of the organisation
Permeable boundaries, synthesis, transitory states and flexible roles	Rigid boundaries protecting sub-cultures relating to organisational roles
Decentralisation	Centralisation
Semi-autonomous agencies utilising organisational support systems	Powerful regulatory systems controlling all sectors
Emphasis on units of excellence	An emphasis on corporate identity

we see is an attempt to provide an unambiguous narrative for the total workforce. A story for the organisation where everyone is a partof it, and all read it the same way. However, the critique goes on, such texts can be decoded by their readers in many ways.

No matter how draconian the attempts to produce uniformity and a single narrative, the organisation will betray its diversity, its politics, its conflicts and its plurality of mission, whether its senior managers or other staff want it to or not. The next stage in the progressive focus of such a critique is to suggest that if lessons are to be learned from this analysis, then we need to explore ways of utilising inevitable plurality of understanding and purpose in search of more dynamic organisational structures.

The simpler the organisation's intent (product range), the clearer the relationship between single narrative and organisational outcome. The more complex the organisation's intent, the more unanticipated are the consequences and the more pluralist the narratives. For example, a factory which produces a range of washing machines can unify organisational understanding of the entire process of innovation, development, production and sales. Hence, the organisation is dealing with a relatively unitary (and linear) narrative. That is, the organisation's text has an implied 'reading' which all in the organisation tend to share. However, if the organisation's intent is to produce a range of less tangible products (such as learning, better services, healthier patients and so forth) then there is an exponential increase in ways in which its text is read by its staff.

When charged with the responsibility of developing an appraisal system for the 370 academic staff of a mixed economy college of further education/ higher education, the project team was faced with the issues raised above. The college's structures are top-heavy in the way described. The post-Fordian flattening process is just under way. Too many decision-makers do too little teaching. Power has become vested in timetablers, curriculum and staff developers, budget-handlers and general administration. Within the one college, there are seven schools, and each school has a noticeably different culture. There are examples of dependency cultures with top-down management and little delegation. There is a quasi-cellular culture with semi-autonomous sections, still, nevertheless, managed by a powerful executive. There is a paternalistic culture. There is a mechanistic bureaucracy. There is autocracy. Placed above these schools is a senior management group of a principal and assistant principals with responsibility for particular aspects of institutional work: curriculum, staff, administration, external affairs, marketing, resources and so on. The work of the college is to provide education and training for all who have the desire, whether they be objectified as customers, clients or students(!). Because of a historical, adversarial competition for resources, the boundaries between schools never become more porous than politely semi-permeable.

If past precedent had ruled the day, an appraisal system for the college would have been bought off the peg. Induction would have been via external consultants and a named individual within. Yet another bolt-on, so-called quality measure would have been added for shop window display (in its BS5750 format) and, probably, would quickly have become another unbought item, a hostage to the bureaucratisation of teaching. In other words, there would have been little in either the content of the system or the process of its implementation which would have challenged subcultural norms or overall gloss. The individual teacher would not be stimulated to think about his or her teaching, nor would the manager be exhorted to examine his or her management effectiveness. Worse, each might well collude with the other to reduce the appraisal's impact. However, to return to the main theme of this chapter, such approaches to change depend upon modernist assumptions about unity of purpose, unitary themes, the single narrative and the non-arbitrary intentions of the author(s) — in this case, the progenitors of the appraisal system. In what ways did the appraisal system at the college diverge from traditional development and implementation?

Appraisal project philosophy, structure and style

In an effort to recognise salient issues in its organisational culture(s), the following decisions were made. Pluralism would be recognised at the outset. Each school culture and that of the senior management grouping would have an equal voice in the development of the appraisal system through representation on the action research (action science) project team. An expectation was that during the development and implementation phases, these voices would change because of acculturation. The ratio of teachers to senior managers was fairly represented in the team. What had been learned from other pilot appraisal projects was not regarded as significant, merely useful background information. The team members were given the role of joint authors of appraisal. Whatever products they devised would apply to all academic staff in the college, whether teacher or manager. Each team member was charged with the responsibility of introducing appraisal in his or her own school culture. It was agreed that loyalty to the appraisal project and to the college had precedence over loyalty to the school.

I will try to summarise quickly the system as the team devised it. Then this chapter will return to the issue of management of change and postmodernity. The system was created as a consequence of explicitly shared values among team members. Together they comprise an action research approach to professional development although this was never made explicit. These values were embedded in its operations and they have been listed at the outset of this chapter. They include:

- *parity* (everyone goes through the same process);
- *difference* (recognition of individual biography);
- *resonance* (structural similarities should be seen at all levels. For example, lecturers should be appraised by their students and managers by those they line manage);
- *autonomy* (each member of staff 'authors' his or her own appraisal process by, for example, choosing an appraiser, deciding on focus and choosing data collection methods — an anti-authoritarian system);
- *challenge* (there should be no cosiness, lip-service or complacency);
- *evidence* (reviewing would be based on evidence of professional practice, collected over time);
- *targets* (objective and subjective targets would be set for the next cycle, based on the analysis of evidence collected during the previous cycle);

- *support* (the context for appraisal would be evaluated to monitor its facilitation of the process and support for its outcomes);
- *flexibility* (the system would be modified and developed through constant monitoring, reviewing and evaluation); and
- *impact* (no secret was made of the intention to use appraisal to open up the institutional culture(s) to critique at all levels).

The values delineated in the introduction led the team to develop a portfolio system of appraisal. The portfolio is a one-step appraisal system applicable to all staff. The coverage of professional practice is intended to be so comprehensive that staff can pick and mix within its requests for evidence to meet the idiosyncratic nature of their individual job and role descriptions.

The portfolio is divided into the three broad areas of teaching, managing and professional development: these activities are in turn subdivided into the activities that comprise them. Suggestions are included as to methods by which evidence can be collected to illuminate how the individual is handling different kinds of activity, whether it be chairing meetings, managing small group discussion or offering pastoral care support to staff or students. The portfolio also contains the necessary forms for self-evaluation prior to the appraisal review meeting and the one public outcome — the shared statement between appraisee and appraiser (or reviewer). This is the only part of the process which is kept on file. All else is confidential to the appraisee.

The system, as described, fits into the organisational culture in the following way. Every school has a monitoring, review and evaluation panel to oversee its adherence to the principles or values outlined above. These panels also report to the College Staff Development Committee and, as a consequence, feed into college policy and strategic planning, as well as policy and planning in their own schools.

To illustrate how this might work in practice, here are two concrete examples.

Lecturer

He teaches twenty-two hours per week. His subject is accountancy. He is on a course team which develops new courses in his specialist area. His focus for the two-year cycle is on the range of strategies he employs in moving from a didactic approach to teaching towards flexible teaching and learning. He collects student evaluations (by open-ended survey) of the range of methods he employs. He is observed by a member of the course team. He includes documentation of course team meetings which contain staff feedback and student representative feedback. He analyses his teaching and fills in the self-evaluation form in his portfolio. Portfolio and form go to his chosen appraiser–reviewer two weeks before his review. His reviewer prepares to discuss with him the relationship between his job/role descriptions (at the beginning of the portfolio) and the evidence he has collected. The reviewer also prepares to discuss with him the relationship between the evidence that has been amassed and the self-evaluation document, which asks the individual to determine strengths and weaknesses, together with the support required in future to improve in particular areas. This dialogue becomes summarised in a joint document which outlines his target for the next appraisal cycle.

Manager

She does no teaching. She handles staff issues, timetabling, external relations with the school, including marketing, and maintains a large budget. Her focus for this appraisal cycle is leadership. She collects data from those she line manages and other colleagues, by anonymous survey, one-to-one interviews and 'shadowing', concerning the effectiveness and style of her interpersonal communications with staff. She has chosen an appraiser outside her school, another woman, because she wants to explore the issue of gender in her appraisal. All her immediate colleagues are men. She evaluates the collected evidence and then follows the procedures outlined in the example above.

As you see, the appraisal system is a large-scale action research project. It meets the objectives laid down by Lewin (1946) in the 1940s, in that it is a concerted attempt to grasp the politics of cultural change. It is flexible, responsive and thrusts responsibility for professional development back upon the individual. It attempts to enrich conceptual understanding by improving the quality of dialogue and reflection in the professional milieu. It raises the status of critical discourse in the institution by formalising it in every member of staff's practice. At the centre of this process is the notion of appraisal as a narrative text. Professional biographies are inscribed in the text that individuals include in their portfolios. They can then reflect upon the writing that they have chosen to constitute the picture of their professional experience. A form of collaborative deconstruction becomes possible.

This is significant when dealing with Althusser's (1971) exploration of the way in which individuals imbibe ideology and then assume it is their own. The capacity to change direction (adopting new ways of teaching and managing) is fundamental to successful appraisal. Thus the rhetoric.

What are the main practical and theoretical reservations being raised by staff as they navigate and negotiate their first appraisal cycle? I will leave aside, though not discount, the problem of 'time'. 'There is no time' would be the cry whatever the system — unless we were to adopt the cosy, hearsay-based, end-of-year chat about how we are getting along. A productive appraisal system may well produce, as a by-product, staff who use their time better and are more fulfilled in their use of it. What is proposed by this appraisal process is that appraisees gain in the long run from a more fulfilling engagement with their working milieu. Deep-seated staff reservations which arose during the implementation of the appraisal system may be grouped under four metaphoric assumptions about how the process might work: assumptions about the appraisal system as a court of law, a physical science, a conspiracy and as a chimera.

A court of law

A major issue, born of a fundamental disposition with regard to how life is experienced and understood, relates to gathering supportive evidence. Unable to shake free of past constructions of appraisal as a mixture of surveillance and judgment, staff attack the validity of evidence-gathering and evidence, itself. They do this in much the same way defence counsels argue for acquittal because of some technical oversight in the prosecution's case. Caught up in an everyday, commonsensical notion of truth, objectivity and justice, the appraisal system represents for them a court of law. Here, evidence is presented to a review trial and contested by opposing advocacies; that of defamation versus affirmation. Appraisal equals punishment for failure and reward for the strong. In our staff training, the aim is to present them with an alternative model, something more therapeutic, facilitative and enabling. The aim is also to help them transpose the adversarial nature of disputation into the processes of personal critical reflection. The reviewer becomes witness to this process, rather than a prosecuting counsel.

A physical science

For some, there can be no objective setting or target setting without measurement. Therefore an appraisal system which has outcomes which include objectives or targets for the next cycle must, perforce, require a scientific methodology. Such staff question the validity of a sample, the rigour of the questionnaire or the arbitrary and subjective nature of the interview. For them, training is needed in the two aspects of handling appraisal evidence: the use of measurement for student numbers, exam marks, budgeting, teaching hours and so on, and the use of qualitative indicators in exploring teaching or management effectiveness and style. Only by placing them in a review simulation or management role play do they begin to acknowledge that many aspects of their work are not amenable to direct measurement. Often, we discover that they have never had feedback concerning their personal approaches to professional work. Over time they have withdrawn into the autism of a systems approach and those mechanisms which involve measurement.

A conspiracy

An appraisal system which devolves so much responsibility to the individual is, for some, tantamount to giving individuals licence to print whatever they like, select whatever they like for their portfolios and evaluate however they like, pointing up strengths and playing down weaknesses. Staff will, they argue, choose friends to appraise and they will do all they can to diminish the challenge in the system whilst using it to promote their own interests. Since training for appraisal in this college does not discriminate between appraiser and appraisee, manager and lecturer, the focus for training is on the interface between evidence and self-evaluation. The capacity to evaluate critically and analyse what needs to be developed, professionally, become new yardsticks of quality among teaching staff. Already, there is evidence of staff having misgivings about whom they have selected as their appraiser. Will the appraiser give them the fulfilment demanded by the system's philosophy? How will their capacity to reflect upon practice be augmented within the review? Critical friendship is an issue.

A chimera

This metaphor could equally well have been entitled 'A Fools' Paradise'. The problem, these staff would have it, is that the appraisal system runs counter to the culture of management and organisational ethos. Government and governing body are demanding that managers make harsh decisions. Harsh decisions become translated into mechanistic systems, denying the humane and, therefore, why adopt a system which is in conflict with the times? Training here is of a less practical and more theoretical nature. By admitting at the outset, and ever since, that appraisal can be a change agency in cultural terms, that it can act as the Trojan Horse in bringing about a more open, participative culture, the project team is seen to have a vision and a mission. They need to be applauded for their strength of purpose, rather than denigrated for their other-worldliness. Appraisal should seek the moral high ground, then all criticisms are reduced to matters of procedure only — a major tactical strategy in successful implementation.

Appraisal and causality

What the objections above have in common is a pervasive underpinning of that age-old conundrum, causality. It is an issue which constantly erodes the morale of the action researcher (appraisee) who at some level of understanding assumes that he or she should be able to show that some particular action or intervention in the workplace will lead to some particular conclusion or outcome. It is as seductive to think so as it is unreal.

The love affair with causality has been inbred in the logocentric West despite the apparent decrease in passion for its major vehicle, science. Whereas the latter, according to university entrance statistics, examination results and the growing *fin de siecle* alternatives, appears to face a declining public interest, the former remains rooted as the basic premise of much of practitioner thinking. Why an action research-based appraisal system must deal with it at the outset of the process is revealed in what follows. In brief, mistaken conceptions of impact, outcome and eventual change may restrict the process of critical awakening, entrap proponents in coils of pseudo-scientific objectivity and eventually lead to lowering professional morale.

David Hume (Noxon 1978) demonstrated that causality, as a guiding principle to human action, was in fact based on dubious premises. For example, people may well say that the nail went into the wood *because* it had been hammered. Hume suggested that the two events are not causally linked in this way. He showed that observation of the relationship merely indicates that the nail enters the wood *following* it being hammered. In strict terms, no one can predict that events are caused by other events, merely that they may succeed them with regularity. There are so many circumstances surrounding even this simple act: the force of the blow, the accuracy, the strength of the nail, the quality of the hammer face, the condition and type of wood, the physical condition of the hammerer, gravity, and so on. No matter how many times we witness successful hammering, we are still wrong in attributing causal relationships to hammer and nail. Such causal relations can only occur in a world of absolute uniformity. So what of events in the social world, where uniformity can only ever be a statistician's dream? When we talk of managers bringing about change or teachers introducing successful strategies into the classroom, where is our truth and where is our error?

Action research suffers from the confusion emanating from a blurring of causality and contingency. Since it has become housed as the orthodoxy underpinning much Masters degree teaching in universities, in education, nursing, management and so on, it has fallen into a causality trap. In order to satisfy the demands of university course assessment requirements, students are encouraged to produce dissertation outcomes and show the logical relationship between strategic interventions and changes to the working environment. Thus, hypothetico-deductive reasoning creeps into the camp of inductive reasoning, unannounced.

Conclusion

It is probably time that we begin to focus upon the action in action research. Perhaps the academic stamp of approval for research is beginning to impede the possible progress that individuals might make, if they were not weighed down by a false consciousness about the validity and consequences of their actions. Better to act and then use text of that action as a point of departure for reflection via textual analysis. The question of how the author (appraisee) is revealed in the text becomes the central issue. Thus author and reader become alternating roles for the appraisee. The reviewer/appraiser acts as a critical interlocutor, constantly helping the appraisee to focus on what his or her text is saying. Thus there is the possibility that individuals will begin to disengage themselves from dependency upon unquestioned, tacit ideologies as they see what aspects of themselves and their dominant ideologies are inscribed in their texts.

Just as causality has a logical link with the notion of objectivity, so contingency may have affiliation with subjectivity. By concentrating appraisees' focus on their own text, there can follow a gradual interrogation of the subjective qualities of such a text, how and why it has been constructed and what kind of imperative drives that construction.

> It is to the detailed examination of *subjectivity* that we turn to try to understand how old patterns are held in place and how they might be let go. (Davis & Banks 1992: 4)

Within our appraisal system this detailed examination occurs during the review meeting, through focusing upon not only the biographic details of professional life but also the reasoning that led the individual to choose such evidence. As the college moved towards the final phase of its first appraisal cycle, training took place to provide reviewers with an understanding of their role. In summary, this role is to enable the appraisee to engage with his or her own constructed narrative, to see what that says about personal and professional understanding of practice and to help individuals construct new possibilities for their future practice, with or without staff development.

References

Adelman, C. and Lewin, Kurt (1993) The origins of action research. *Educational Action Research* 1 (1), 7–24.

Althusser, L. (1971) *Lenin and Philosophy and other Essays*. New Left Books, London.

Argyris, C. and Schön, D. (1989) Participatory action research and action science compared. *American Behavioural Science* 32, 612–23.

Barthes, R. (1982) *Image Music Text*. Fontana, London.

Beare, H., Caldwell, B. and Milligan, R. (1989) *Creating an Excellent School*. Routledge, London.

Boyne, R. (1990) *Foucault and Derrida*. Unwin Hyman, London.

Carr, W. and Kemmis, S. (1986) *Becoming Critical: Education, Knowledge and Action Research*. Falmer Press, London.

Davis, B. and Banks, C. (1992) The gender trap: a feminist post-structuralist analysis of primary school children's talk about gender. *Journal of Curriculum Studies* 14 (1).

Deal, T.E. and Kennedy, A.A. (1982) *Corporate Cultures: The Rites and Rituals of Corporate Life*. Addison-Wesley, Reading, Mass.

Elliott, J. (1994) Research on teachers' knowledge and action research. *Educational Action Research* 2 (1), 133–37.

Foucalt, M. (1991) (trans. A.M. Sheridan Smith) *The Archaeology of Knowledge*. Routledge, London.

Freire, P. (1973) *Education: The Practice of Freedom*. Writers and Readers Publishing Co-operative, London.

Gummesson, E. (1991) *Qualitative Methods in Management Research*. Sage, London.

Lewin, K. (1946) Action research and minority problems. In G.W. Lewin (ed.) (1948) *Resolving Social Conflicts*. Harper and Row, New York.

Naisbitt, J. and Aburdene, P. (1986) *Re-inventing the Corporation: Transforming Your Job and Your Company for the New Information Society*. MacDonald and Co., London.

Noxon, J. (1978) *Hume's Philosophical Development.* Claredon Press, Oxford.

Peters, T. and Waterman, R. (1982) *In Search of Excellence.* Harper and Row, New York.

Sanger, J. (1986) Classroom observation workshops, ethics and perception. *Cambridge Journal of Education* 18 (3).

—— (1989) *Teaching, Handling Information and Learning.* R&D Publications, British Library, Boston Spa.

—— (1990) Awakening a stream of consciousness: the role of the critical group in action research. *Theory into Practice* 29 (3), Ohio University Press.

Schön, D. (1983) *The Reflective Practitioner: How Professionals Think in Action.* Basic Books, New York.

Schratz, M. (1993) Researching while teaching: promoting reflective professionality in higher education. *Educational Action Research* 1 (1),111–36.

Walker, M. (1993) Developing the theory and practice of action research: a South African case. *Educational Action Research* 1 (1), pp. 95–111.

Zuber-Skerritt, O. (1992) *Action Research in Higher Education.* Kogan Page, London.

Note

1   This chapter is an extension of a paper published through *Educational Action Research* 3 (1), an international journal in association with CARN.

Chapter 12

Emancipatory Aspirations in a Postmodern Era[1]

Stephen Kemmis

Abstract

This chapter presents an argument against the criticisms of critical theory advanced by certain poststructuralists, that critical perspectives in education have continuing relevance in education, and offers an approach by which educational researchers and practitioners may engage as active participants in the process of educational change, and ways of responding to the challenges of the present 'postmodern' era. The chapter begins by describing the postmodern condition and postmodernisms, then examines broad views of the task of education (functionalist, interpretivist, poststructuralist and critical) to open the question of the continuing relevance of the critical perspective in the light of poststructuralist criticisms of the critical view. Instrumental, practical and critical (or emancipatory) perspectives on change are outlined, as a basis for an argument that a 'first-person' (participatory), critical approach is needed for the task of finding solidarity with others in the regulated world of education systems. Here, the discussion draws upon MacIntyre's distinction between practices and institutions, Habermas' distinction between system and lifeworld, and Giddens' views about the institutional reflexivity characteristic of late modernity. The focus then turns to an examination of emancipation as a contemporary aim for a critical theory of education, responding to poststructuralist critics of critical theory, and referring particularly to the forms of reasoning their criticisms employ or imply. It is argued, against the views of these critics of critical theory, that the task of emancipation remains manifestly necessary in a vast range of political struggles in the contemporary world, and concludes that the quietism or conservatism of some poststructuralist perspectives must be rejected in favour of a continuing commitment to emancipatory–critical perspectives. Drawing on a variety of commentators on postmodernity, or 'late modernity' (as some prefer to call it), it is argued that resources for resisting the incursions of system-shaped relationships into our lifeworlds and consciousness are to be found in communicative action, collaborative endeavour and engagement in the politics of social movements.

Introduction

There is no doubt that we are living in 'interesting times'. Major social changes are underway in every aspect of our society — knowledge, social practices, social structures and the very social media in which we connect with one another.[2] What do we do as curriculum workers — the people whose work it is to give life and form to curricula — when confronted by so many, so rapid, and such profound and subtle changes? The demands of a new era impose themselves upon us, and education and our curricula must respond. But we should do so not with the narrowness of vision that threat and uncertainty often provoke; to the extent that we are able, we should respond by trying to put the changes — those underway and those yet to come — into critical perspective.

In this chapter, I will describe three perspectives on change — technical, interpretive/poststructuralist and critical. I want to make an argument for the continuing relevance of critical perspectives in education, which engage all of us as active participants in the process of educational change, and which may still offer us ways of responding to the challenges of the present 'postmodern' era.

The 'postmodern condition' and postmodernisms

In the view of many commentators, we are now in an age of postmodernity and postmodernisms and, though there may be differences in the degree to which these transformations and ruptures are to be regarded as 'epochal', it seems reasonable to conclude that world societies do confront new challenges as a consequence of the 'postmodern condition' in which we find ourselves.

Frederic Jameson (1983) describes the concept of postmodernity as:

> ... a periodizing concept whose function is to correlate the emergence

of new formal features in culture with the emergence of a new type of social life and a new economic order — what is often euphemistically called modernization, postindustrial or consumer society, the society of the media or the spectacle, or multinational capitalism. This new moment of capitalism can be dated from the postwar boom in the United States in the late 1940s and early '50s or, in France, from the establishment of the Fifth Republic in 1958. The 1960s are in many ways the key transitional period, a period in which the new international order (neocolonialism, the Green Revolution, computerization and electronic information) is at one and the same time set in place and is swept and shaken by its own internal contradictions and by external resistance. (1983: 112–13)

A little later, he writes that:

... at some point following World War II a new kind of society began to emerge (variously described as postindustrial society, multinational capitalism, consumer society, media society and so forth). New types of consumption; planned obsolescence; an ever more rapid rhythm of fashion and styling changes; the penetration of advertising, television and the media generally to a hitherto unparalleled degree throughout society; the replacement of the old tension between city and country, center and province by the suburb and by universal standardization; the growth of the great networks of superhighways and the arrival of automobile culture — these are some of the features which would seem to mark a radical break with that older prewar society in which modernism was still an underground force. (1983: 124–25)

On the basis of such features, Jameson concludes that a new kind of social formation has emerged. Arguably, this new social formation is characterised by changed social structures and functions, but this is not its only significance. At the level of the individual and the social group, it is argued, this new period has produced substantial shifts in the way people experience the world.

If our societies have changed so dramatically, and if our ways of experiencing the world have changed with them, then these shifts must have very significant implications for the conduct of social life and education. Arguably, they demand the development of new forms of analysis and new social practices in philosophy, the arts, natural and social science, and education. For some, however, these changes are so significant that they may be regarded as decisive — they have called into question the very possibility of doing philosophy, art, science and education in the ways these activities have been understood over the last century — and perhaps the last four centuries or more.

A number of key transformations is said to signal the new 'postmodern' era, including transformations of the content and forms of contemporary *culture* (transformations even of our notions of 'culture' — for example, high versus low or popular culture), including dramatic changes in the nature of the media and in the content and forms of presentation of media images (the 'television generation', the 'electronic age', the 'information age', the 'society of the spectacle' and so on); increased awareness of the plurality of national, ethnic and linguistic viewpoints with international-isation of communications and global interaction and so forth; a radical shift from colonialist to postcolonialist perspectives on modernisation, North–South relations, and questions of 'Third World' and community development, which produces problems of coping with the plurality of perspectives on the world without any credible source of authoritative readings of societies and their interrelationships; 'depthlessness' in perspectives on history and society as historically and regionally distinct perspectives appear in the daily montage of media presentations; the loss of the relative autonomy of the cultural sphere (as distinct from the economic and political spheres) with the recognition that culture and communications are an industry and that they are politicised, not 'objective', 'neutral' or necessarily critical; and the apparent loss of a critical space for intellectuals and avant-garde movements.

A second group of transformations is said to have occurred in the nature, content and form of *economic structures and interrelationships,* for example through the shifts which have made a large proportion of the world's production cultural production and the production of information rather than the production of goods and services as these were understood before World War II (and in earlier phases of capitalism); the development of 'late capitalism'; the global unification of control of the means of production and a complementary diffusion, fragmentation and privatisation (individualisation) of consumption; and new conflicts over the imperatives of development, modernisation and exploitation versus the imperatives of the ecology movement, conservation and the preservation of natural diversity.

A third group of transformations concerns the nature, content and forms of *political life,* for example, through internationalisation; the decline of the nation-state with the rise of transnational economic structures; the restructuring of politics by the media; the emergence of social movements which have restructured previously taken-for-granted relationships between classes, rich and poor, men and women, ethnic groups, and between regional and subnational groupings; and the decline in authority (and legitimation crises) of the state and of cultural institutions (like churches and universities), with the attendant loss of a clear role for critical voices and perspectives (which seem to be swallowed up by, and assimilated into, the 'information industry' and the media industry).

On the basis of such transformations, all of which are highly interrelated, it seems reasonable to conclude that there is some basis for saying that we are entering a new era — though, arguably, it is a new phase of the 'modern' era, rather than something entirely new. Moreover, our (reflexive) *self-consciousness* of the condition of postmodernity means that we must take seriously the view that the new era we have now entered requires a substantial critical re-evaluation not only of those 'modern' forms of thought and the theoretical categories conventionally employed in social science, but also the theoretical categories employed in understanding education.

Some have argued that most of our previous, 'modern' modes of analysis must now be abandoned — most especially Jean Baudrillard (1983), though others like Jean-François Lyotard (1984) seem to share his view in more modulated tones. Others believe that existing or revised 'modern' forms of analysis can and do meet our needs — among them, in their different ways, are Alasdair MacIntyre (1990), Stephen Toulmin (1990) and Anthony Giddens (1990; 1991). Jürgen Habermas (1981; 1983; 1984; 1987a; 1987b; 1990; 1992), by contrast, believes that the theoretical resources that modernity itself has produced can still provide the basis for substantially new ways of approaching the theoretical work required. And still others believe that our modes of analysis need considerable supplementation and modification — people like Frederic Jameson (1983; 1984; 1991), Douglas Kellner (1988; 1989), Steven Connor (1989), Stuart Hall (1986a; 1986b) and Edward Said (1978; 1983; 1993), together with a range of feminist theorists who have taken very different views of the postmodernity debates — from those like Jane Flax (1990) who believe that postmodern theorising provides resources for recasting patriarchal science and philosophy, through to those like Seyla Benhabib (1992) who believe that it provides new points of departure for understanding our world and ourselves though these show clear affinities with 'modern' theorising of recent decades.

Clearly, these transformations in society and in ways of thinking about society — the transformations of postmodernity and postmodernisms — have very substantial implications for education and schooling. Clearly, not only educational theory and research, but also education itself must take into account the social changes which have produced 'postmodernity' or 'the postmodern condition'. That said, it is less obvious how our thinking about and practices of curriculum, educational administration, teacher education, and educational research and evaluation should be reconsidered in the light of various postmodernisms. This is a task I cannot hope to undertake here, but in what follows, I will try to identify a few ways in which some of our traditions of educational theorising may need reformulation.

A functionalist view of the task of education

Representation

The very possibility of education depends on arriving at some view about how people and societies can and should be *represented*. This involves taking some stand on the nature of knowledge, on the question of what can be known, and on the question of what is worth knowing — questions which are thrown into considerable doubt by advocates of some postmodernisms (notably the poststructuralist postmodernists like Lyotard and Baudrillard).

Education requires that educators attempt to represent a society to its rising generations in ways which make representations accessible as forms of knowledge about a society, or some aspect of its activities. It thus involves deliberately *reading* a society, developing *texts* which organise and express these 'readings' in particular forms (some written, some oral, and some just enacted in the forms and rituals of the work of education; some more 'literal' and some more 'symbolic'), and making these texts available to specific groups of *readers* who may be able to learn about the society from the texts. To have such 'readings' and 'texts' requires having some way of representing things, having people who are 'literate' (in whatever sense) as 'authors' and 'readers' of these representations, and having ways of passing on the different kinds of 'literacies' involved (whether by teaching and learning in schools or other formal or informal or non-formal settings, or by participation in rituals and ceremonies, or by whatever other means). What the texts should contain, how they should be organised so that specific groups of learners can learn from them, and how they should be transmitted (and how learning from them should be evaluated) are some of the abiding concerns of *curriculum*. According to the Swedish educational theorist Ulf Lundgren (1983; 1991), the *'representation problem'* is the central problem of curriculum — a central concern not only for curriculum development, but also for curriculum theory.

Some traditions of curriculum theorising, notably the functionalist tradition, see the question of representation in a relatively straightforward way. On the question of the nature of knowledge, advocates of this tradition may incline towards the view that language can in some sense correspond to reality; on the question of what can be known, they may take an objectivist (or foundational) view of knowledge; and on the question of what is worth knowing, they may take a utilitarian view about what serves the greatest good.

Since education always involves inducting individuals into some particular aspect or other of the life of a society, it always involves working out practical ways to relate the realm of the individual to the realm of the social. In relation to the specification of curricula, advocates of the functionalist tradition may set about defining what should be in the curriculum by considering relationships between the realm of the individual and the realm of the social by considering, on the one hand, *knowledge,* defined in terms of *understandings, skills* and *values* (cf. Benjamin Bloom's [1956] cognitive, psychomotor and affective domains of knowledge) and, on the other hand, the *social structures* of *culture,* the *economy* and *political life.*

Without doing too much violence to this tradition, I hope, it may be that such a view sees the essential problem of defining curricula in terms of theoretical categories like those in Table 12.1.

Table 12.1 *Some key theoretical categories characteristic of a functionalist perspective on curriculum*

	KNOWLEDGE		
	Understandings	Skills	Values
INDIVIDUAL (subjectivity)			
	SOCIAL STRUCTURES		
	Culture	Economy	Political life
SOCIAL (structure, ideology)			

In the functionalist tradition, the curriculum theorist and curriculum developer aim to 'read' the social realm and to represent it in the curricula in the form of knowledge which can, in turn, be 'read' by students. On this view, characteristic perhaps of Ralph Tyler's (1949) view of curriculum, 'reading' society was problematic — of course — but the means for representing what had been read was less problematic (though one needed to be careful to specify it adequately for teaching, with a preference for stating educational objectives in measurable ways), and the problem of representing it for students could be resolved by the pragmatic approach of trialling and revising curricula until students could perform the tasks in which the objectives had been operationalised.

The technical view of curriculum, of which Tyler was one of the most sophisticated advocates, assumes that debates over the proper aims of education and objectives of a particular curriculum can be more or less satisfactorily resolved, at least to the extent that they can provide a basis for specifying a particular piece of curriculum, and that the main task of curriculum development is refining curricula so student performances match the curriculum developers' views of what counts as mastery of the content of the curriculum. This view has been the subject of extended critique over four decades (see, for example, Kemmis & Fitzclarence 1986; Lundgren 1983; Schwab 1969; Stenhouse 1975).

Opponents of the technical view of curriculum: interpretivists and poststructuralists

A first wave of criticism of the technical view of curriculum came from thinkers who drew on pre-technical perspectives on education — that is, views of education which regarded education as a practical activity in which not only the means but also the ends of education are regarded as highly problematic (Reid 1978; Schwab 1969; Stenhouse 1975). In such a view, education requires that teachers interpret the situations in which they find themselves in the everyday world of teaching and learning and decide on the basis of their judgment what educational means and ends are appropriate in that particular situation. Teachers must make such judgments in a highly responsive way, and in making their judgments they must take into account that education is always a moral and practical activity (as well as a technical one). The technical view of curriculum was regarded by these critics as too narrow and inflexible to permit the wise and prudent exercise of professional judgment about what might be appropriate on any given day with any given groups of students in any given social and historical situation.

This old line of argument against the technical view of curriculum has been overtaken by a new and more recent wave of criticism associated with various streams of postmodernist and poststructuralist thought (see, for example, Cherryholmes 1988). This second wave takes a more radical perspective. The interpretivists took the view that what can be represented is a matter of interpretation of the world, and that interpretations might change with the perspectives of those involved (teachers, students, curriculum developers, for example), so that what might be 'read' from the social world would differ from time to time and place to place, and what it might be appropriate to 'read' from the social world might also be different at different times. The poststructuralists, by contrast, take the view that representation can never be innocent or value-neutral, that representation can never be more than the fabrication of simulacra which distort (as well as shape) our perceptions (representations can never 'correspond' to reality), and that interpretation changes radically depending on who is doing the interpretation, when, where, and from what perspective. On this more radical view, the reader of a text always reads a very different text from the one written by its author — for example, because the readings (interpretations) each makes of the text are shaped by different webs of intertextual cross-reference.

Given this radical doubt about what can be represented and interpreted from the social world, the second wave of critics of the technical view of curriculum reject the possibility of representing key features of social life (the structures of culture, economy, political life) in forms of knowledge (understandings, skills and values). Instead, they focus on the *social media* in terms of which social life is constructed: *language (discourses), work* and *power.* These social media shape, and are shaped by, different kinds of *social practices: communication, production* and *social organisation.* Instead of focusing on the knowing subject (whether teacher or student) as a subject of *knowledge,* they regard the subject as the bearer of social media (language, work and the social relations of power) whose very *subjectivity* is shaped by these media, and as an agent is able in some small way to reshape them through the particular way the agent participates in social practices of communication, production and social organisation.

Again, without wanting to do too much violence to the variety of poststructuralist perspectives at play here, it is perhaps possible to summarise some aspects of these views of curriculum in terms of broad theoretical categories like those in Table 12.2.

On such a view of curriculum, specific curricula do not simply represent the world for students; the authors of curriculum texts (whether curriculum writers or the authors of the 'live' performance of curriculum in the classroom) actually fabricate the world they write of by constructing narratives about it; and it can never be entirely clear what students will read from them. Hence, for example, Michel Foucault (1970; 1977; 1978; 1980) writes of 'discursive practices' which are shaped by institutions and 'regimes of truth'; hence, also, some contemporary writers (for example, Bill Green 1992; 1993) focus on 'textual practices' involved in different kinds of contemporary literacies (including computer literacies).

Table 12.2 *Some theoretical categories characteristic of a poststructuralist perspective on curriculum*

INDIVIDUAL (subjectivity)	SOCIAL PRACTICES		
	Communication	Production	Social Organisation
SOCIAL (structure, ideology)	SOCIAL MEDIA		
	Language (discourses)	Work	Power

There is not time or space here for an adequate analysis of the competing claims of these approaches to curriculum, curriculum theorising and curriculum development. For my purposes, I can do little more than juxtapose these perspectives as one way of exploring the possibility that there may be a perspective which can at least engage some of the problems raised by technical and poststructuralist theorists of curriculum.

A critical perspective on curriculum

Some social theorists take the view that postmodernity and the 'postmodern condition', if it exists as a new epoch at all, are not a rupture or radical break with modernity but, rather, the contemporary social condition is actually a new phase of modernity. For Toulmin (1990), for example, the current era is very much a product of the debates and traditions which, in the sixteenth and seventeenth centuries, gave rise to the period we know as modernity (especially through the innovative philosophical ideas of René Descartes). Similarly, for Giddens (1990; 1991), the current period might better be characterised as 'high' or 'late modernity'. For several theorists, like Jameson (1984; 1991) and Kellner (1988; 1989), the new era is marked by changed world conditions of capitalism brought about by the globalisation of markets and communications, especially through the emergence of new technologies; and this new phase of 'late capitalism' has engendered new social forms and new social problems, and it requires new modes of theoretical analysis, which have some continuities with 'modern' modes of analysis even if they must also involve some new modes of conceptualising our societies and our social condition. For still other theorists, notably Jürgen Habermas (1981; 1984; 1987a; 1987b; 1990b; 1992), however, the analysis of the new social conditions and new social problems may require new philosophical and theoretical perspectives, but these perspectives can be developed from within the rich philosophical and theoretical traditions of 'modernism' — just as the social changes of former times have, in the past, permitted theoretical innovations which have been part of the development of 'modern' social theory and philosophy as we know it today.

I cannot do justice to the diversity of these perspectives here. Perhaps, however, taking a lead from those who take the view that the 'postmodern' condition is a new phase of modernity, and from those who take the view that new developments in 'modernist' theorising can help us to address some of the philosophical and theoretical problems outlined by the postmodernists and poststructuralists, it is possible to juxtapose the functionalist and poststructuralist perspectives on curriculum previously outlined to describe the field of curriculum in general terms. By doing so, I hope to introduce some aspects of a critical perspective on curriculum. Table 12.3 outlines a more general set of relations which might be considered in developing a critical theory of curriculum.

If thinking about curriculum requires considering this whole web of relationships, then the idea that a curriculum can provide a 'map' of social life for students begins to fall into tatters. There can be no simple correspondence between knowledge to be taught and learned, on the one hand, and the structures of cultural, economic and political life, on the other. Similarly, it seems to me, the complexity of this web of relationships suggests that it may be insufficient to regard a curriculum as consisting merely of the engagement of learners in social practices of communication, production and social organisation as a way of inducting them into the patterns of language and discourse, work and power which constitute the social media of a society — since this view occludes consideration of knowledge and the learner, on the one side, and the evident structures of social life, on the other. A critical perspective on curriculum will use a table of categories like those presented in Table 12.3 to explore the relationships between these categories as they come to bear in considering any particular educational situation, and any particular curriculum. How we relate to such a table of categories will tell us a good deal about the politics of change, however, and also tell us something about where we stand in those politics.

Table 12.3 *A more general set of relations to be considered in a critical theory of curriculum*

	KNOWLEDGE		
INDIVIDUAL (subjectivity)	Understandings	Skills	Values
	SOCIAL PRACTICES		
	Communication	Production	Social organisation
SOCIAL (structure, ideology)	SOCIAL STRUCTURES		
	Culture	Economy	Political life
	SOCIAL MEDIA		
	Language (discourses)	Work	Power

Perspectives on change

To caricature a little, a relatively powerful system administrator may read the set of relationships outlined in Table 12.3 as a description of the dynamics of the social world, capable of suggesting ways of re-ordering an education system as a means to established ends. By contrast, a teacher or learner may read Table 12.3 as presenting a way of thinking about what to do (and what to take into account) when confronted by practical decisions in the lifeworld of their educational settings. Or again, a critical educational theorist (who might well be a teacher or a learner) might use Table 12.3 to explore contradictions in the structures and processes of education as it occurs in some practical setting, as a basis for generating shared understandings which could lead toward collaborative action to reconstruct educational policies or practices in the setting. The first way of viewing Table 12.3 is an example of 'instrumental' or 'technical' reason; the second is an example of 'practical' reason; and the third, 'critical' or 'emancipatory' reason (Habermas 1974; Carr and Kemmis 1986).

These different forms of reasoning also imply different patterns of social relationship between the person (subject) doing the reasoning, on the one hand, and, on the other, the people — or social or educational systems — which are the object of this reasoning. While there is no smooth one-to-one correspondence about this, it seems to me that (in the context of social and educational change) instrumental (technical) approaches to change presuppose what might be described as a 'third-person' relationship between the person thinking about the change and those inhabiting the systems or settings to be changed; practical approaches presuppose a 'second-person' relationship between them; and critical (and especially emancipatory) approaches presuppose a 'first-person' relationship (in which people are thinking about such issues together, and making changes to their own practices together).

In *instrumental or technical reasoning* about social and educational change, one adopts an objectifying stance towards the others involved in the setting to be changed, treating them as elements of a 'system'. One is therefore predisposed to regard these others, in a sense, as objects — as 'them' — that is, in the third person.

In *practical reasoning* about social and educational change, one adopts a more 'subjective' stance toward the setting in which change is to occur, treating the others involved as members of a shared lifeworld — as persons who, like oneself, deserve the respect due to knowing subjects who are not only 'others' but also autonomous and responsible agents. One is therefore predisposed to regard these others, in a sense, as people to be addressed as 'you' — that is, in the second person.

In *critical (or emancipatory) reasoning* about social and educational change, one adopts a more dialectical stance with respect to the (mutually constitutive, dialectically related) 'objective' and 'subjective' aspects of the setting (seeing it as socially, historically and materially constructed); and it is to be understood in terms of both its 'system' and 'lifeworld' aspects. In such a view, one treats the others involved in the setting as co-participants who, through their participation in the practices which daily constitute and reconstitute the setting both as system and as lifeworld, can work together collaboratively to change the ways in which they constitute it, and thus change both system and lifeworld. One is therefore predisposed to regard such people as members of the group that is 'us' — that is, in the first person.

These forms of reasoning (which I have loosely correlated with 'third-person', 'second-person' and 'first-person' social relationships inasmuch as they imply different moral and political stances towards the people in the social–educational systems and lifeworlds involved) manifest themselves in quite different ways as we address questions of *stabilisation and change* in education and in social life more generally. These three modes of reasoning, and the social relationships correlating with them, will orient people in rather different ways towards the relationships between the categories depicted in Table 12.3.

In general, instrumental (technical) reasoning manifests itself in attitudes of *systematisation, regulation and control* — focusing on the 'system' aspects of the social settings involved (which are regarded in a rather abstract, generalised and disembedded way). By contrast, practical reason manifests itself in attitudes which value *wise and prudent judgment about what to do in shared social contexts* — focusing on the 'lifeworld' aspects of particular settings (understood in a more localised, concrete and historically specific way). And emancipatory–critical reasoning manifests itself in attitudes of *collaborative reflection, theorising and political action directed towards emancipatory reconstruction* of the setting (understood more dialectically as both constituting and constituted by the personal as well as the political, the local as well as the global, and from the interrelated aspects of both system and lifeworld).

Arguably, the first two approaches, the instrumental and the practical, were more intertwined and interrelated in educational theory, policy and practice in the West at the end of the nineteenth century, and they have diverged in sharply opposed theories, policies and practices in the twentieth (for example, in debates between educational 'conservatives' and 'progressives'). The third, the critical approach, emerged early in this century (in response to emerging problems of Marxist theory), in a self-conscious attempt to overcome the increasing polarisation between instrumental and practical tendencies in social and political theory and practice; in education, it has been employed in the attempt to overcome similar tendencies in educational theory and practice — evident, for example, in the polarisation between vocationalism and progressivism. It would be wrong to conclude, however, that critical approaches have actually been successful, in any practical sense, in overcoming such polarisations — far from it. In the last quarter of this century, all three approaches have had their advocates, many apparently implacably opposed to one another, so that contemporary debates over the nature and objectives of educational reform in the late twentieth century are consistently confused and politicised (in the narrow sense) as advocates of the different approaches contest the ground in educational theory, policy and practice.

How then might we approach the demands of a new era in education, in the light of the theoretical relationships outlined in Table 12.3?

Finding solidarity with others in the regulated world of education systems

If we wish to take a 'first-person' stance on changing education and education systems, we must find ways of connecting with others who share our tasks and our concerns. In times when education systems increasingly oblige us to act as employees, and as operatives required to implement a barrage of new curriculum policies and packages, rather than as professional educators who share a commitment to the educational development of our students and our world, it may be up to us to make the necessary connections with one another if we are to share the critical and self-critical task of improving education. This means forming new kinds of solidarity (Rorty 1989) with others in the face of the hyperrationalised mass systems by which education is meant to be 'delivered' to students today. A variety of conceptual categories may help us in these tasks: the distinction between practices and institutions, the distinction between lifeworld and system and between social order and social movement (Touraine 1981), and the concept of institutional reflexivity.

In the real, practical world of educational policy and practice, little is guaranteed. What individuals will actually learn, and what social consequences will actually flow from the work of educators is always uncertain. Educational plans are not just instrumental means to individual and social ends, though questions of means and ends arise in education as in other fields of human endeavour. Nor are educational practices merely the expressions of wise and prudent practical judgment by those involved in educational processes, though these judgments are always relevant in deciding what to do in the practice of education. Educational plans, policies and practices are always framed by contexts which stretch from the intimacy and immediacy of local circumstances to reach and intersect with broader social frames, nationally and internationally, communally and globally. They are the products of struggle, and they give rise to still further struggles for better education for a better world.

Practices and institutions

Education is a social practice.[3] Alasdair MacIntyre (1983: 175) defines a practice as:

> ... any coherent and complex form of social activity through which goods internal to that activity are realized, in the course of trying to achieve those standards of excellence which are appropriate to, and partially definitive of, that form of activity, with the result that human powers to achieve excellence, and human conceptions of the goods involved, are systematically extended.

To say that education is a practice, however, is not to say that it is *sui generis* — something existing independently, in its own terms. On the contrary, as Alasdair MacIntyre (1983: 181) argues:

> no practices can survive any length of time unsustained by institutions. Indeed, so intimate is the relationship of practices to institutions ... that institutions and practices characteristically form a single causal order.[4]

As he goes on to show, however, there are also deep tensions between the internal 'goods' which characterise practices (like the values which characterise good history, or good chess-playing, or good teaching) and the external 'goods' (like money, power and status) required for the operation of institutions. So it is in education: in Australia today — and I am sure it is also true elsewhere — educators at every level are aware of the increasing sharpness of the tension between educational values and institutional imperatives as educational institutions are 'rationalised' in a climate of financial stringency and increasing bureaucratic surveillance of educational work. The dialectic of *practices and institutions* is an important fifth dialectic constituting contemporary education.

In the institutionalised forms in which we know it today, education is constituted through a constellation of practices which operate at at least four institutional 'levels':

- First, and at the most immediate 'level', education is constituted by *curriculum practices* (or, more familiarly, practices of teaching and learning), which necessarily interrelate curriculum content, forms of pedagogy and (especially in institutionalised education) patterns of authority and evaluation which govern the relationships between teachers and learners.

- Second, in Europe at least, as education systems became formalised (especially as they were formalised in mediæval times by the church and then the guilds, followed, in the eighteenth. and nineteenth centuries, by the state), another 'level' was added above this one, so that the practice of education was framed by practices of *educational administration,* necessarily interrelating educational policy, administrative practices and patterns of authority and evaluation between teachers and administrators and between different levels of system administrators.

- Third, as the education of teachers became more specialised, a further 'level' emerged, so that the practice of education was still further framed by practices of (initial and continuing) *teacher education,* necessarily interrelating the content of the teacher education curriculum, the pedagogy of teacher education, and patterns of authority and evaluation between teacher educators and their students.

- Finally, as the continuing development of education came under the reflexive control of these 'framing' institutions (especially state education systems and teacher education institutions), still another 'level' of framing arose, as the practice of education came to be shaped and re-shaped through practices of *educational research and evaluation,* necessarily interrelating educational theory, policy and practice, research and evaluation practices, and the social–political relations of educational research and evaluation.

System and lifeworld

These four sets of practices together constitute some of the major elements of contemporary education *systems.* To some extent, they also define some of the major workplaces of education. Where people actually get together to *do* education, their relationships with one another are not defined solely in 'system' terms, however (for example, in terms of their role relationships) — their relationships are simultaneously constructed in terms of the human and social interaction of the *lifeworld* (which includes not only formal but informal relationships, not only role relationships but also such matters as friendships and the sense of commitment a person may feel to the group). Though there may seem to be a great distance between the educational researcher in the university and the parent of the child in school, or between the curriculum developer in the state curriculum development agency and the adult learner in the part-time course, in the institutional world of education, they live in worlds created by and for one another (though the influences between them are rarely equal). Within the real-world settings of education, however, the co-participants in these settings (whether the classroom or the home or the office of the curriculum developer or the fieldwork site of the educational researcher) have personal relationships with one another which, though always modulated by the institutional frameworks in which they meet, are nevertheless direct, immediate and human. In the real-life settings of contemporary education, as in other arenas of contemporary life, there is a powerful tension in the relationship between the values of the system and the values of the lifeworld — a tension which Habermas (1987b) characterises as the 'colonisation of the lifeworld' by the values of the system. In contemporary times, this tension seems to me to be fundamental in the constitution of education: *the dialectic of system and lifeworld* seems to me to be a sixth key dialectical relationship constituting education as a process of social formation.[5]

The dialectic of system and lifeworld makes itself evident not only within the settings of curriculum practice, educational administration, teacher education and educational research, as people bring to bear their different perspectives and histories, forged in the narratives of their own lives (tensions among teachers and learners, curriculum developers, educational administrators and the rest); it is also evident in the contradictions and conflicts people experience as they 'cross the boundaries' between these different frames and the institutional roles associated with them.

These relationships between practices and institutions, and between systems and lifeworlds, may be summarised in the following proposition: education mediates between the knowledge of the individual and the structures of society through specific social practices of curriculum, educational administration, teacher education and educational research and evaluation, which constitute educational institutions, as well as educational systems and lifeworlds. As educational institutions, systems and lifeworlds change, these practices themselves, reflexively, become objects of further contestation and institutionalisation.

Institutional reflexivity

In the view of Anthony Giddens (1990; 1991), a variety of new tensions about risk and uncertainty are characteristic of life in our age — what he describes as 'the late modern age'. He identifies three key features of 'the dynamism of modernity' in the present era:

- *Separation of time and space:* the condition for the articulation of social relations across wide spans of time-space, up to and including global systems.

- *Disembedding mechanisms:* consist[ing] of symbolic tokens and expert systems (these together = abstract systems). Disembedding mechanisms separate interactions from the particularities of locales.

- *Institutional reflexivity:* the regularised use of knowledge about circumstances of social life as a constitutive element in its organisation and transformation. (1991: 20)

According to Giddens, the first of these dynamics consists in the regularisation of space and time (for example, through maps and the coordination of activities across increasingly distant settings, and the use of clocks, the standardisation of world time zones and so on, which together permit the ordering of activities in time and space in ways which transcend the more 'local' and 'immediate' boundaries within which activities were formerly coordinated in space and time, especially in pre-modern or 'traditional' societies). The second dynamic, disembedding mechanisms, consists in the use of symbol systems with relatively standard value across time and space (for example, money), and expert systems, which allow the technical application of expertise relatively independently of particular locations, practitioners and clients; taken together (as abstract systems), symbolic tokens and expert systems evoke new and increasingly diverse possibilities for ordering social life, independently of the particularities of time and space. The third dynamic, institutional reflexivity,

> refers to the susceptibility of most aspects of social activity, and material relations with nature, to *chronic revision* in the light of new information or knowledge. Such information or knowledge is not incidental to modern institutions, but constitutive of them — a complicated phenomenon, because many possibilities of reflection about reflexivity exist in modern social conditions. (1991: 20, emphasis added)

Each of the four 'levels' of educational 'framing' I referred to earlier (social practices of curriculum, educational administration, teacher education and educational research and evaluation) is the subject of institutional reflexivity, not only in its own terms, but also in relation to every one of the others. To take just one case, curriculum practices change not only in relation to changing ideas about what content, pedagogy and authority relations are appropriate for given settings, but also in relation to changes in educational administration, teacher education and educational research and evaluation. Each, reflexively, is open to reconstruction in the light of changes in the others.

Given this institutional reflexivity, contemporary education has a new fluidity — it is characteristically unstable over time. It follows from this that every framing 'level' is constantly re-opened as a realm for fresh assaults of contestation and increasingly impermanent institutionalisation. Paradoxically, it seems that the very 'success' of the institutionalisation of education systems in our era is to be read in the extreme transience of the institutional forms taken by curriculum, educational administration, teacher education and educational research and evaluation.[6]

I think it is only in recent times that it has become apparent that in contemporary society institutions will be subject to rapid change as they are iteratively reformed (subject to 'chronic revision', as Giddens puts it) in the light of new knowledge and techniques for system regulation. Is it merely nostalgic to think that educational institutions can be relatively stable? That the rationalisation of education systems would express itself in 'chronic revision' seems unexpected. The surprise is that the resilience of postmodern institutional forms is evident not in their stability, but in their capacity for reflexive change. The observation gives new piquancy to the memorable phrase coined by Alphonse Karr in 1849: *'Plus ça change, plus ça même chose'* — 'the more things change, the more they are the same'.

This chronic revision of highly rationalised contemporary institutions might be regarded as a new and difficult pathology characteristic of late modernity, which Giddens describes as like 'riding a juggernaut' of modernity. But perhaps our sense that somehow things are out of control can generate not only critical responses but also new forms of action to address the problem. For Giddens, one practical response is in the development of what he calls 'life politics' — a 'politics of self-actualisation, in the context of the dialectic of the local and global and the emergence of the internally referential systems of modernity' (1991: 243).

Habermas (for example, 1987b: 391–96; 1990; Holub 1991) also comments on the potentials for protest in various contemporary social movements (the women's movement, peace movement, the greens, and others), but his response to the fundamental social problem he diagnoses — the colonisation of the lifeworld by the institutionalised social forms which constitute social systems — both in his public commentary and in his philosophical and social–theoretical work,[7] is nevertheless guardedly optimistic. I say 'guardedly optimistic' because Habermas is suggesting that, precisely in becoming aware of the enclosing imperatives of the institutionalised forms of interaction of systems, we are enabled to recover the modes of thought and interaction which constitute the lifeworld as such (in particular, communicative action) — that is, *as opposed to* the forms of interaction characteristic of institutionalised systems.[8]

It seems to me that the values of communication and solidarity I have been advocating as part of the 'first-person' critical perspective have a new pointedness in postmodern times: while perhaps they were articulated long ago in a context in which people envisaged that modern science would lead to the development of a new *and stable* social order which could overcome the pathologies of existing social and educational systems, maybe these communicative values are also relevant even in the context of new and *inherently unstable* systems. Perhaps communicative values can provide a critical perspective from which solidarity can be sustained and developed among people who live and work together in shared lifeworlds, even within increasingly regulated and hyperrationalised social and educational systems. On this view, what Freire (1970) described as 'cultural action for freedom' is to be understood not just as emancipation *from* existing forms of unfreedom, but also as emancipation *for* the continuing task of overcoming the as-yet-unrecognised forms of dependency, oppression, suffering and irrationality which emerge with the new forms of structuring of chronically changing institutional systems.

Emancipation as a contemporary aim for a critical theory of education

When, earlier, I discussed 'third-person', 'second-person' and 'first-person' perspectives on social and educational change, I did so in order to draw attention to the possibility of maintaining a critical and emancipatory perspective on education despite the challenges of postmodernity and, more particularly, postmodernisms. And there is considerable debate today about whether the emancipatory aspirations of 'modern' and critical theories of education can be sustained in the face of the challenges of postmodernisms.

There have been intense methodological debates in social and educational theory which have made the question of emancipation much more problematic than my earlier account suggested — debates provoked by the rise of poststructuralist perspectives in social and literary theory, by the development of various 'postmodernisms' which lead from them, and by various kinds of reconstructions of 'the incomplete project of modernity' in the light of these challenges to 'modernity'.

The postmodernity debates have created a new sense of unease about how social life and social change are to be understood, and there has been a substantial critical attack on the emancipatory aspirations of critical theory and critical social science — an attack which some believe has undermined the basis for the very notion of emancipation. Jean-François Lyotard (1984), for example, in his famous postscript 'What is postmodernism?' to his book *The Postmodern Condition,* defines postmodernism in terms of an increasing incredulity towards the 'grand narratives' of progress and emancipation — it is even the case, he says, that 'Most people have lost the nostalgia for [this] lost narrative' (1984: 41). Representatives of other positions in the postmodernity debates share similar suspicions, especially about the claims of positive science, agreeing with Lyotard that the Enlightenment hope for emancipation through science cannot be fulfilled.

The difficulty then arises, 'From what perspective is it possible to formulate theories *for,* rather than *of,* social transformation?' For a number of poststructuralists and postmodernists, it seems, theories *for* social transformation are little more than the manifestations of a now-debunked ideology, and so we are left with little but the possibility of constructing theories *of* social transformation — perhaps 'genealogical' or 'archæological' theories of the kind Foucault (1970; 1972) advocates, or perhaps literary deconstructions of texts of the kind advocated by Derrida (1978). But from what standpoint can even these theories be created? If the standpoint is not to be that of emancipatory–critical theory, are they driven 'back' to instrumental–technical or practical standpoints?

The answers to these questions are by no means clear. While at one point Foucault describes the genealogical approach in terms of 'felicitous positivism', it hardly seems likely that this is a serious description, though there is a clear sense in which the historical materials with which he works, and the 'cynical gaze' with which he views the texts he analyses, put him in a third-person relation to the objects of his investigations (characteristic, I suggested earlier, of an instrumental–technical approach to social change). Elsewhere (for example, in Gordon 1972, and in Rabinow 1984), however, it is clear that Foucault engages contemporary problems of social transformation in a spirited way which suggests that, at the very least, he adopts a practical standpoint with respect to these issues — as a commentator and as a contributor to public debate. But his position may be more 'connected' even than this. In his essay 'Taking aim at the heart of the present: on Foucault's lecture on Kant's *What is Enlightenment?'* Habermas (1990b) goes so far as to say that 'Perhaps ... in this last of his texts, [Foucault is drawn] back into a sphere of influence he had tried to blast open, that of the philosophical discourse of modernity' (179) — which may mean that Foucault is himself drawn back into the emancipatory–critical approach of reconstruction (for example, the critical task of reconstruction of our contemporary discourses about discourse).

To put the issue as pointedly as I can, then, it seems to me that various poststructuralists and postmodernists have wanted to repudiate all three of the forms of reasoning I outlined: instrumental–technical, practical and emancipatory–critical. In doing so, some seem to seek forms of analysis which either retreat from their objects to a standpoint of 'cynicism' or cold objectivity (in a new sense), or to an endlessly reflexive engagement with texts which, in 'interpreting' them, simply adds to or rewrites them. As Foucault noticed, the former response is reminiscent of positivism; the latter seems to me to be a repudiation of the dialectic of theory and practice which, in very different ways, animates each of the three forms of reasoning (instrumental, practical, critical) I outlined.

But the story does not end there. The particular poststructuralists and postmodernists I have mentioned here *do* seem to want to distance their work from the realm of human and social affairs — and to disengage it from the political tasks of social transformation. In a way, they seem to want to deny a sense of responsibility for taking a role in the reconstruction of society that has become burdensome because — as they see it — emancipatory perspectives no longer seem justifiable. A number of commentators have remarked that this position involves 'a self-referential inconsistency'[9] or a 'performative contradiction'[10]: such poststructuralists and postmodernists seem to want to assert the critical (and, one might say, emancipatory) potency of their insights while denying that the emancipatory–critical project is justifiable.

The rather simple characterisation of the standpoint of each of the three forms of reason I outlined earlier may offer clues to what is going on here. Clearly, these poststructuralist and postmodernist theorists do stand in a particular form of social relationship to (a) those *about whom* they theorise, and (b) those *for whom* they theorise. While they take a decidedly third-person stance towards those *about whom* they theorise (the dead and distant authors of historical texts, or the living but distant authors of contemporary texts), their stance towards those *for whom* they theorise is more ambiguous. While Lyotard seems to write in a highly objectivising way about contemporary science and scientists, *The Postmodern Condition* was written for a Canadian government agency, hence its subtitle *A Report on Knowledge*. Insofar as he adopts this stance, he writes for the agency as 'you' (in the second person), but despite the view he espouses of the uncontrollability of science and meaning in the contemporary world, he seems to be giving the government agency views about how science can (or cannot) be regulated. To this extent, I take him to be writing for a technical, instrumental purpose, primarily 'about them' (that is, about those involved in the production and dissemination of narrative knowledge).

Foucault, by contrast, is clearly writing about texts as 'things' (note the irony in the title of his book *The Order of Things* 1970), but he is clearly writing for a public he hopes to galvanise by his ideas ('you', in the second person). Perhaps, in the forms of solidarity he shows with his contemporaries and fellow-intellectuals who, like him, are imprisoned by the discursive practices of a highly-institutionalised era, he can reasonably be said to be adopting a 'first-person' standpoint — 'this is *our* situation', 'this is happening to *us*', '*we* must find ways to deal with this'. If this is so, it suggests that he is, in a more layered and complex sense, adopting a critical standpoint (though I am inclined to think that it is more the conventional, practical standpoint of the liberal intellectual — 'please take this into account as *you* address the issues we are confronting today').

In each case, the material social relationships of the research — *about whom, for whom* — give clues to the forms of reasoning being employed. On the argument so far, I am inclined to concede that there *may* be a standpoint in some versions of poststructuralist and postmodernist social theory which differs from the standpoints implied in earlier forms of reasoning about social change and transformation (the standpoint which sees itself as simply extending or rewriting the texts of other theorists or social agents — that is, at the same level as those texts, not a commentary from 'beyond' or 'above' them), but the material social relations of their texts seem to me to betray these announced purposes and to fall back towards one or other of the three general forms of reasoning I have described. There is a performative contradiction in what the texts of these authors announce: they seek to repudiate the possibility of writing *about* and *for* the people they engage in their writings, but their work creates the very relationships they seek to repudiate.[11]

Reflections on 'emancipation' in relation to a critical view of education

In practice — the practice of political struggle in the contemporary world — the growing fashionability of various postmodernisms is undermining the philosophical and theoretical conditions necessary for any emancipatory project. This is to be feared — not because there is nothing to learn from these perspectives, but because the task of emancipation remains manifestly necessary in a vast range of political struggles in the contemporary world. These struggles continue to be necessary not just in Third World settings, but also in the new, sometimes desperate, conditions of First World social life — especially as First World social life becomes increasingly disfigured by new forms of division between the employed and the unemployed, by new levels of alienation, new forms of anomie, and new forms of suffering and pathology as the lifeworld relationships of key institutions (the family, the church, the school and the state, for example) are attenuated to the point of crisis by demands like those Giddens (1990; 1991) described in terms of disembedding, chronic revision and escalating risk.

I believe that Habermas is right to describe the opponents of modernity in terms of three forms of conservatism,[12] distinguishing between the *anti-modernism* of the 'young conservatives' who 'recapitulate the basic experience of aesthetic modernity' (he traces this line of thought as leading 'from Georges Bataille via Michel Foucault to Jacques Derrida'); the *premodernism* of the 'old conservatives' who reluctantly give up the unfulfilled promises of modernity and advocate a return to Aristotelianism (here, Habermas cites Leo Strauss, Hans Jonas and Robert Spaemann — though on some points he might perhaps also include some of the recent works of Alasdair MacIntyre); and the *postmodernism* of the 'neo-conservatives' who celebrate (if that is the word) the technical advances made possible through late modernity, while recommending 'a politics of defusing the cultural content of cultural modernity', and keeping 'politics as far aloof as possible from the demands of moral–practical justification' (here, Habermas names, among others, the early Wittgenstein, though he does not cite Lyotard or Baudrillard).

To focus just on the last of these: the postmodernism of the 'neo-conservatives' is particularly troubling in terms of practical politics, since it suggests that it is beyond the *scientific* or *theoretical* or *philosophical* competence of social theory to provide rational foundations for the emancipatory project. It seems to me that this position stands and falls by its presupposition that the problem is one of finding 'rational foundations'. The anti-rationalism of Lyotard and Baudrillard defines itself in opposition to debunked ('straw man'?) notions of rationality and foundationalism (especially Cartesian rationalism), rather than the very different successors to those notions within the modern tradition which diverge from, as well as sustain, aspects of the Enlightenment project. Post-Wittgensteinians like Toulmin and MacIntyre advocate views of rationality which do not depend on foundationalist perspectives, for example, and Habermas' theory of communicative action, while agreeing with some arguments of the postmodernists on the unsustainability of 'the philosophy of the subject', nevertheless finds an alternative to it in communicative rationality. What is more, in both of these positions one finds a recourse to ordinary language as a basis for addressing contemporary problems of social theory and practice — in the post-Wittgensteinians; in forms of practical reason nurtured by historical self-awareness of the illuminating potential of traditions; and in Habermas, through the notion that everyday communicative practice (ordinary discourse about practical questions) exhibits, though often in pale and unsung forms, the qualities of communicative rationality.

It would be extravagant to claim that an emancipatory–critical view of education like that of Paulo Freire (1970; 1972) was vindicated by Habermas' theory of communicative action, since they are, in a sense, responses to different questions posed in different contexts at different times. Freire's views of education are a critical response to problems of literacy in circumstances where institutionalised forms of education denied access to, and success in, education for large numbers of people in the particular cultural, economic and political circumstances of particular places in the world; Habermas' theory of communicative action is a response to more general trends and tendencies in the social formations of advanced capitalism, and to trends and tendencies in philosophy and social theory as it relates to such social formations. Nevertheless, it seems to me that a Freirean view of education can take some sustenance from Habermas' theory of communicative action, and that there are opportunities for some illuminating theses and tracts and texts to be written criticising and reconstructing Freirean views from this perspective.

Such critical and emancipatory aspirations find no place in contemporary poststructuralist postmodernist views of education and curriculum. Rejecting not only the aspirations of critical theorising, some contemporary theorising about education inspired by Foucault's writings (for example, Cherryholmes 1988; Popkewitz 1991) is marked, in addition, by a curious absence of awareness of the nature and necessities of practical reasoning in the world of affairs which those involved in education (and social life more generally) necessarily inhabit — whether as learners, parents, teachers, administrators or policy-makers (to name just a few of the relevant roles). Deprived by postmodernist theorising of the 'innocence' which characterised the positivist educational research of the middle of the century, and 'suspicious of the grand narratives' of modernity and the emancipatory project, some of these poststructuralists have opted for a Foucauldian cynicism and aloofness from the world of educational affairs. It is too harsh to say their world-weariness is a retreat from the struggles of educational change itself to a position from which one writes (from the sidelines, as Joseph Schwab [1969] once described it) about the nature of the struggles of the others who remain within them; rather, they argue, it is the role of the intellectual to uncover the nature of the politicisation at work in such struggles and to avoid falling back into existing political positions which only seem to justify particular ends-in-view. Thus, for example, Tom Popkewitz (1991: 244) argues that 'theory or theorists entail no prescriptive tasks', quoting Foucault (Gordon 1972: 190) in support of this 'critical pragmatic stance':

> Political analysis and criticism have in a large measure still to be invented — so too have the strategies which will make it possible to modify the relations of force, to coordinate them in such a way that such a modification is possible and can be inscribed in reality. That is to say, the problem is not so much that of defining a political 'position' (which is to choose from a pre-existing set of possibilities) but to imagine and to bring into being new schemes of politicisation. If 'politicisation' means falling back on ready-made choices and institutions, then the efforts of analysis involved in uncovering the relations of force and mechanisms of power are not worthwhile.

It seems to me that this 'choice' between existing political institutions and possibilities, on the one hand, and the critical task of political analysis, on the other, involves a sleight of hand. It opposes the practice of politics with theorising politics as if theorising were not itself a practice. The practice of politics involves practical reasoning about what to do and how to act in one range of settings and, no less, the practice of political analysis involves practical reasoning in another range of settings. The practice of theory and analysis cannot suspend the necessity to make the usual risky and uncertain choices about the practical and political consequences of one's theorising and analyses.

Using distinctions between forms of reasoning familiar since Aristotle, and taking into account Marx's notion of a critical science (refracted through the work of Horkheimer and the early Frankfurt School), Habermas' (1972; 1974) theory of knowledge-constitutive interests aimed to show that science is always guided by one or another knowledge-constitutive interest (interests which give form to the way knowledge is constituted): characteristically, the empirical–analytic sciences express a technical (or instrumental) interest; the hermeneutic (interpretive) sciences a practical interest; and the critical sciences an emancipatory interest. Can Foucault, or Popkewitz, reasonably claim to have avoided choosing one or another from among this range of choices? I do not think so.

The forms of reasoning Popkewitz and Foucault have actually employed in *doing* (practising) their theorising, have clearly involved them in practical reasoning about what to do and how to act wisely and prudently in the light of their circumstances. *In addition to* this practical reasoning, they may or may not have seen themselves as engaged with others in critical reasoning about the actual reconstruction of the terms to be used in the debates in which they were engaged, and also in the reconstruction of the ways in which these debates were to be conducted — if so, then they would seem to have been engaged in critical forms of reasoning. There can be little doubt that both Popkewitz and Foucault would reject the notion that theirs is simply a technical interest in developing new forms of control of social life through their work (though the quotation from Foucault does evince an interest in 'the strategies which will make it possible to modify the relations of force, to coordinate them in such a way that such a modification is possible and can be inscribed in reality'); indeed, there is much to suggest that their work has the interpretive and hermeneutic quality characteristic of work guided by a practical interest (in promoting wise and prudent judgment in practical circumstances). Beyond this, it may be that they also have a critical interest in reconstructing — in thought and theory at least — the nature and conditions of politics and political analysis, though they are at pains to *dissociate* this from the view that it is part of some wider, more general emancipatory project, perhaps on the grounds that the notion of emancipation has too often been captured, domesticated and trained to kill in the repressive politics of world politics. Regarded in this way, a commitment to 'emancipation' might well seem to imply adopting a rigid and 'pre-formed' political position.

It seems to me that, far from being at odds with critical theory on this point, Foucault and Popkewitz are at one with it. Critical theory, at first in response to an increasing dissatisfaction with turn-of-the-century Marxist theorising and political programs, and later (especially through Habermas' early work) in response to the ideological tendencies within science itself, extended the range of the emancipatory project to include a critique of the ideology of science. Though in some ways very distinct from critical theoretical perspectives, it is nevertheless reasonable to suggest that the work of Foucault and Popkewitz shares something of *this* emancipatory interest[13] — though it remains (as do other critical perspectives) suspicious of particular political *programs* which announce themselves as 'emancipatory'.[14] The question is: can one retain any faith in the aspiration of emancipation without being a dupe of these wider interests?

A critical view of education, unlike the kinds of views represented by Foucault and Popkewitz, does not distance itself from the possibilities for social transformation. It makes no apologies for its engagement in an emancipatory project like the one Freire described as 'cultural action for freedom'. It has doubts about speaking on behalf of others, to be sure, but its intention is *not* to speak *on their behalf;* rather, it intends to create conditions under which they can speak *for themselves*. Recognising that the circumstances of the lives of many oppressed people deprive them of the conditions under which they can speak for themselves, it aims to break open 'the culture of silence' in which and through which social relations of dominance and dependence are reproduced.

There are many parts of the world where 'the culture of silence' continues to characterise lived social relations, not only in the Third World, but also in new and developing forms in the First. It is too easy, perhaps, to generalise from the conditions of one culture to another, and from the cultures of tradition-based societies to those in which 'the postmodern condition' has changed the face of lived reality for many people. Nevertheless, the new, globally intrusive forms of the late modern age, or of late capitalism, have changed the character of social relations, and they have produced new, 'silenced' majorities — in the sense that they have produced a 'depoliticisation of the masses' (as Habermas [1979] described it), and produced a change of the locus of political action so that social movements, in a sense at the margins of — though also intricately interwoven with — 'official' politics, become even more important elements of political life.[15] In the face of such challenges, it seems to me that the need for emancipation continues to exist, though what counts as 'emancipation' itself needs critical reconstruction if we are to avoid the consequences of some of the political programs that have taken its name.

My view is not shared by the advocates of some postmodernisms, however.[16] For some, the justification for the emancipatory project has collapsed not only in practice and politics, but also in theory.

Lyotard is one such postmodernist. In the context of cultural politics, he argues that the 'metanarratives' of 'universal history' (for which we may read 'emancipation') are a form of cultural imperialism. Describing Lyotard's view, Connor (1989: 36–37) writes:

> More recently ... Lyotard has turned his eye to issues of cultural politics. Here the question of the decline of metanarrative has less to do with the possibilities or not of scientists agreeing with one another, or knowing why they do, and more to do with questions about the relationships within and between cultures. In an essay entitled 'Missive on universal history' Lyotard (1987) has mounted an attack on the cultural imperialism of metanarrative by means of a linguistic argument. He argues that if we ask, or attempt to ask a question such as 'Should we continue to understand the multiplicity of social and nonsocial phenomena in the light of the Idea of a universal history of mankind?' the central problem lies in the very use of the word 'we'. This 'we', he writes, is a form of grammatical violence, which aims to deny and obliterate the specificity of the

'you' and the 'she' of other cultures through the false promise of incorporation within a universal humanity. We must therefore wean ourselves away from the 'we', that grammatico–political category that can never exist except as a legitimating device in the service of appropriative and oppressive cultures. Instead, we must embrace and promote every form of cultural diversity, without recourse to universal principles.

On first reading, Stuart Hall (quoted in Connor 1989: 195) seems to echo this view, indicating that there are problems for marginal groups who get caught up in global culture:

In the last ten or fifteen years, marginality has become a very productive space. People are speaking up from the margins and claiming representation in ways in which they probably didn't twenty or thirty years ago. But now the problem of putting your head up above the parapet, so to speak, is to be instantly swept up by this global culture which precisely because it is more sensitively oriented towards difference, diversity, pluralism, eclecticism sweeps you in. Whatever new voice, they say, yes, you can be part of the global culture. And before you know where you are an Aboriginal painter is just one slot in somebody else's heroic portrait and has lost the sense of a relationship to a culture.

For Hall, however, the issue is more dialectical than Lyotard's references to 'universal principles' suggest. Hall sees the kind of view Lyotard defends as being just as dangerous as the one he (Lyotard) rejects. For Hall (see particularly Hall 1986a), there is a present and real risk that the interdependence of the circumstances of the rich and the poor, the healthy and the sick, women and men, nature and culture, will be swept aside in the grand assertion that all discourses are fragmentary, partial and self-interested.[17] In Hall's view, it is the task of social theory to identify and articulate such interdependencies and the contradictions which structure social divisions and fragmentation, and to find ways of articulating them so that people can act on them, in the interests of those who suffer most from the consequences of such contradictions.

Edward Said (1983), too, takes the view that there are more dangers than those of Lyotard's 'universal history' in cultural politics; there are also dangers in leaving the field of cultural politics to the information industries of the postmodern age:

... the politics of interpretation demand a dialectical response from a critical consciousness worthy of its name. Instead of non-interference and specialization, there must be *interference,* crossing of borders and obstacles, a determined attempt to generalize exactly at those points where generalizations seem impossible to make. One of the first interferences to be ventured, then, is a crossing from literature, which is supposed to be subjective and powerless, into those exactly parallel realms, now covered by journalism and the production of information, that employ representation but are supposed to be objective and powerful.

Much of the world today is represented in this way: ... a tiny handful of large and powerful oligarchies control about ninety percent of the world's information and communication flows. This domain, staffed by experts and media executives, is ... affiliated to an even smaller number of governments, at the very same time that the rhetoric of objectivity, balance, realism and freedom covers what is being done. And for the most part, such consumer items as 'the news' — a euphemism for ideological images of the world that determine political reality for a vast majority of the world's population — hold forth, untouched by interfering secular and critical minds, who for all sorts of obvious reasons are not hooked into the systems of power.

This is not the place, nor is there time, to advance a fully articulated program of interference. I can only suggest ... that we need to think about breaking out of the disciplinary ghettos in which as intellectuals we have been confined, to reopen the blocked social processes ceding objective representation (hence power) of the world to a small coterie of experts and their clients, to consider that the audience for literacy is not a closed circle of three thousand professional critics but the community of human beings living in society, and to regard social reality in a secular rather than a mystical mode, despite all protestations about realism and objectivity...

[In such ways we may recover] ... a history hitherto either misrepresented or made invisible ... [I]n having attempted — and perhaps even successfully accomplishing — this recovery, there is the crucial next phase: connecting these more politically vigilant forms of interpretation to an ongoing social and political praxis. (Said 1983: 157–58)

For Said, cultural politics offers the possibility of critical resistance to the homogenising tendencies of global culture — and clearly his use of the notion of 'critical resistance' implies an affiliation with a notion of emancipation, though it may be more self-conscious and more hesitant than is to be found in some rhetorics of emancipation.

The rhetoric of emancipation that Paulo Freire employed, of 'utopian pedagogy', and of 'denunciation and annunciation' (1970: 39–42), may have been insufficiently cautious about its own limits in articulating views of what the better future it announced might be. Sympathetic critics of Freire, like feminist authors Kenway and Modra (1992), refer to unheeded critical analyses of conscientisation as it has been practised in some programs inspired by Freire (and to the potential for manipulation in 'Freirean work'), and warn of the danger of allowing uncritical views of Freire's work ('Freirean idolatry') to take 'the place of the development of critical consciousness *in the very project of liberatory education itself'* (1992: 157; emphasis in original). As Kenway and Modra suggest, we must take a critical view of the project of emancipation: it makes no sense to rely on Freire's particular theoretical perspectives and particular practical educational proposals as if they stood above the vicissitudes of history. It is the task of new groups and rising generations to re-make emancipatory theory and practice — including the notion of 'emancipation' — anew, in response to changed times and circumstances.

It seems, then, that the conceptual space to be occupied by 'emancipation' is not so wide or so welcoming as once it seemed to be. While there is a clear practical need for a diverse range of educational, cultural and political programs of 'emancipation-from' various forms of irrationality, suffering and injustice, the territory of 'emancipation-for' is narrowing — as properly it should. Emancipation, as I understand the term, does not announce any particular positive program; it is a critical concept whose power is in *critical negation*. It may 'denounce' structures of oppression, but it is not required or designed to offer, in addition, a clear, positive, universal vision of what the release from suffering, irrationality, injustice and inequity will be like, though we can, at any historical moment, in any particular group, readily imagine some of the forms a better life can or should take. Freire's genius was in offering an image of what some of those possibilities might be, at certain particular moments in history and for certain particular groups. Many of those specific historical conditions — problems to which his ideas of 'utopian pedagogy' and 'cultural action for freedom' were a response — continue to exist today, and there may still be a *prima facie* case for considering the appropriateness of some of his responses to such problems. Our task in reconceptualising 'emancipation' and what is 'critical' about a 'critical' perspective will need to be different today, as we face changed circumstances and new problems — even though we may learn from responses to past circumstances and past problems.

Conclusion

A variety of analysts of contemporary social conditions make a compelling case that there have been significant shifts in the forms and structures of contemporary social life. While some shrink from the labels 'postmodernity' and 'the postmodern condition', favouring instead 'late modernity', 'high modernity' or 'late capitalism', there is widespread agreement that received social and educational analyses — whether of theory, policy or practice — do not equip us adequately to deal with contemporary problems. There is sharp disagreement, however, over the kinds of theoretical resources which might help us to analyse and interpret these problems — disagreements over the potential and limitations of various postmodernisms and reconstructed modernisms. There is also disagreement about how these theoretical resources might orient us to the problem of change — whether by offering new forms of technical–instrumental reasoning, new forms of practical–interpretive reasoning, or new forms of emancipatory–critical reasoning. In terms of theoretical resources, I have concentrated here on the competing claims of certain particular poststructuralist postmodernisms (the views of Foucault and Lyotard, for example), various reconstructed modernisms (the views of Jameson, Kellner, Hall and Said, for example) and the reconstructive modernism of Habermas. In terms of perspectives on change, I have attempted to argue against the quietism or conservatism of some postmodernisms, and in favour of a continuing commitment to emancipatory–critical perspectives.

Despite Lyotard's view that it is 'grammatical violence' to speak in terms of 'we', I regard this 'we' as indispensable to the project of emancipatory–critical social and educational theorising. When this 'we' is used in purportedly emancipatory–critical theorising as a universal category, there is no doubt that it involves a 'prodigious abstraction' (Habermas 1990a: 212–13) which obscures differences between people, groups, cultures and interests. In concrete communicative contexts of establishing uncoerced agreements and shared commitment to transformative action, however — when groups of people decide to analyse their shared situations and to take action to overcome irrationalities, injustices and sufferings that disfigure their lives — to use the first person plural ('we', 'us') is not to perpetrate grammatical violence or to obscure difference behind the veil of a prodigious abstraction; it is a mark of solidarity. In such contexts, to use the term 'we' is not to obliterate difference or disagreement, but to engage it — communicatively, productively, politically and personally.

There is a danger that sensitivity to difference is being fetishised in social theory, policy and practice today, making us more than reasonably hesitant about the possibility of solidarity and shared commitment to social action capable of changing our circumstances. At times, this attitude can itself be imprisoning: like-mindedness has its own dangers, including the danger of being divided and conquered. In their very different ways, Alasdair MacIntyre, Stephen Toulmin, Raymond Williams (1983; 1989), Alain Touraine (1981), Stuart Hall, Edward Said, Seyla Benhabib, Anthony Giddens and Jürgen Habermas are among those who suggest that the dynamics and circumstances of contemporary social life are such that we are already divided and fragmented by the social relations of bureaucracy, expert systems, and the apparatus of the modern state. And each of these authors, without invoking outmoded and romantic notions of the *gemeinschaft* community (Tonnies 1957), argues that resources for resisting the incursions of these system relationships into our lifeworlds and consciousness are to be found in communicative relationships, collaborative endeavour and engagement in the politics of social movements.

As we, as educators, address the problems of curriculum reconstruction appropriate to our late modern or postmodern era, we should consider how we can take such advice to heart. Of course we are obliged by the system structures of contemporary education to participate in the very social relations that divide and fragment the social world, but we may also consider how our locations in these systems offer us opportunities for connection and solidarity across these divisions. We may want to consider how our social practices as educators — social practices of curriculum, educational administration, teacher education and educational research and evaluation — offer opportunities to increase participation by and collaboration among those whose lives and work constitute these practices. We may want to consider how our work contributes — often simultaneously — to processes of inclusion and processes of exclusion, and to consider how the two are mutually constituted, and what the consequences of these inclusions and exclusions may be. In some recent times, and in some places, the politics of inclusion have also fostered exclusion — for example, in some of the politics of 'inclusive curriculum' in Australia in the 1980s, which produced division between those pursuing more inclusive cultural values and those pursuing the differentiating and potentially exclusive values of education for economic reconstruction. As we have seen, holding these together takes more than the rhetorical flourish that sloganises potentially conflicting values like those of 'social justice' and 'economic development' in an educational policy.

Overcoming such contradictions is not a matter of finding more or better words to express such policies. Perhaps it is the very act of policy-making — and certainly it is the hyper-rationalisation of policy (Wise 1977; 1979) — that contributes to the contradiction. It seems to me likely that developing better theories may help us, however — especially if we understand better theories to be those which engage, challenge and develop people's (students', teachers', parents', administrators') actual understandings and interpretations of their circumstances. The point, however, is not merely the improvement of theories; it is to contribute to the improvement of the social practices of education — curriculum, educational administration, teacher education, educational research and evaluation — the practices which frame almost every activity of teaching and learning in educational institutions today. And this requires engaging the attention and commitment of every teacher and learner, every curriculum developer, every administrator and policy-maker in the task of critical reconstruction of education. It requires of each of us that we consider the kinds of relationships I sketched in Table 12.3, to work out how, in our understandings, in our practices, in our settings, these relationships are expressed, and how they are constituted, and to work out how we may participate in the process of reconstituting them differently so that we can reproduce those aspects of our social lives that are of value, and transform those that contribute to our difficulties. This critical task, I suggest, is a practical task for all of us, and for each of us. In our contemporary circumstances — the circumstances of late modernity or postmodernity — it is a task too intimate and too important to be left to policy, and to education systems.

References

Althusser, L. (1971) trans. B. Brewster. *Lenin and Philosophy and Other Essays*. New Left Books, London.

Angwin, J. (1992) The changing workplace: the effect of change on teachers' work in adult language and literacy programs. *Critical Forum* 1 (3), 48–77.

Baudrillard, J. (1983) trans. P. Foss, P. Patton and J. Johnston. *In the Shadow of the Silent Majorities ... or, The End of the Social*. Semiotext(e), New York.

Benhabib, S. (1992) *Situating the Self: Gender, Community and Postmodernism in Contemporary Ethics*. Polity Press, Cambridge.

Bennett, T. (1979) *Formalism and Marxism*. Methuen, London.

Bloom, B.S. (ed.) (1956) *Taxonomy of Educational Objectives, the Classification of Educational Goals: Handbook I, Cognitive Domain*. Longmans Green & Co., New York.

Carr, W. and Kemmis, S. (1986) *Becoming Critical: Education, Knowledge and Action Research*. Falmer Press, London.

Cherryholmes, C. (1988) *Power and Criticism: Poststructural Investigations in Education*. Teachers' College Press, New York.

Connor, S. (1989) *Postmodernist Culture: An Introduction to Theories of the Contemporary*. Basil Blackwell, Oxford.

Derrida, J. (1978) *Writing and Difference*. University of Chicago Press, Chicago.

Flax, J. (1990) *Psychoanalysis, Feminism and Postmodernism in the Contemporary West*. University of California Press, Berkeley, California.

Foucault, M. (1970) trans. Alan Sheridan-Smith. *The Order of Things: An Archaeology of the Human Sciences*. Random House, New York.

—— (1972) trans. Alan Sheridan-Smith. *The Archæology of Knowledge*. Harper and Row, New York.

—— (1977) History and systems of thought. In D.F. Bouchard (ed.) *Language, Counter-Memory, Practice: Selected Essays and Interviews with Michel Foucault*. Cornell University Press, Ithaca, N.Y., 199–204.

—— (1978) trans. Robert Hurley. *The History of Sexuality, Volume I: An Introduction*. Random House, New York.

—— (1980) Truth and power. In C. Gordon (ed.) *Power/Knowledge: Selected Interviews and Other Writings 1972–1977 by Michel Foucault*. Harvester, Brighton, Sussex.

Freire, P. (1970) *Cultural Action for Freedom*. Center for the Study of Social Change, Cambridge, MA.

—— (1972) *Pedagogy of the Oppressed*. Penguin, Harmondsworth.

Giddens, A. (1979) *Central Problems in Social Theory: Action, Structure and Contradiction in Social Analysis*. Macmillan, London.

—— (1990) *The Consequences of Modernity*. Stanford University Press, Stanford, Cal.

—— (1991) *Modernity and Self-Identity: Self and Society in the Late Modern Age*. Stanford University Press, Stanford, Cal.

Gordon, C. (ed.) (1972) *Power/Knowledge: Selected Interviews and Other Writings by Michel Foucault*. Random House, New York.

Green, B. (1992) Literacy studies and curriculum theorizing. In B. Green (ed.) *The Insistence of the Letter: Literacy Studies and Curriculum Theorizing*. Falmer Press, London, 195–225.

—— (ed.) (1993) *Curriculum Technology and Textual Practice*. Deakin University Press, Geelong, Victoria.

Habermas, J. (1972) trans. Jeremy J. Shapiro. *Knowledge and Human Interests*. Heinemann, London.

—— (1974) trans. John Viertel. *Theory and Practice*. Heinemann, London.

—— (1979) trans. Thomas McCarthy. *Communication and the Evolution of Society*. Beacon Press, Boston.

—— (1981) Modernity versus postmodernity. *New German Critique* 22 (Winter), 3–14.

—— (1983) Modernity — an incomplete project. In H. Foster (ed.) *Postmodern Culture*. Pluto Press, London.

—— (1984) trans. Thomas McCarthy. *Theory of Communicative Action, Vol. 1: Reason and the Rationalization of Society*. Beacon Press, Boston.

—— (1987a) trans. Frederick G. Lawrence. *The Philosophical Discourse of Modernity: Twelve Lectures*. MIT Press, Cambridge, MA.

—— (1987b) trans. Thomas McCarthy. *Theory of Communicative Action, Vol. 2: System and Lifeworld: A Critique of Functionalist Reason*. Beacon Press, Boston.

—— (1990a) Apologetic tendencies. In J. Habermas, *The New Conservatism: Cultural Criticism and the Historians' Debate*. MIT Press, Cambridge, MA, 212–28.

—— (1990b) Taking aim at the heart of the present: on Foucault's lecture on Kant's 'What is enlightenment?'. In J. Habermas, *The New Conservatism: Cultural Criticism and the Historians' Debate*. MIT Press, Cambridge, MA, 173–79.

—— (1992) trans. William Mark Hohengarten. *Postmetaphysical Thinking: Philosophical Essays*. MIT Press, Cambridge, MA.

Hall, S. (1986a) History, politics and postmodernism: Stuart Hall and cultural studies (an interview with Lawrence Grossberg). *Journal of Communication Inquiry* 10 (Summer), 61–77.

—— (1986b) On postmodernism and articulation (an interview by Lawrence Grossberg). *Journal of Communication Inquiry* 10 (2), 40–56.

Holub, R.C. (1991) *Jürgen Habermas: Critic in the Public Sphere*. Routledge, London.

Jameson, F. (1983) Postmodernism and consumer society. In H. Foster (ed.) *Postmodern Culture*. Pluto Press, London.

—— (1984) Postmodernism: or, the cultural logic of late capitalism. *New Left Review* 146 (July/August), 53–92.

—— (1991) *Postmodernism: or, the Cultural Logic of Late Capitalism*. Duke University Press, Durham, North Carolina.

Kellner, D. (1988) Postmodernism as social theory. *Theory, Culture and Society* 5 (Special nos. 2–3), 239–69.

—— (1989) *Critical Theory, Marxism and Modernity*. John Hopkins University Press, Baltimore.

Kemmis, S. and Fitzclarence, L. (1986) *Curriculum Theorising: Beyond Reproduction Theory*. Deakin University Press, Geelong, Vic.

Kenway, J., and Modra, H. (1992) Feminist pedagogy and emancipatory possibilities. In C. Luke and J. Gore (eds) *Feminisms and Critical Pedagogy*. Routledge, New York.

Lundgren, U.P. (1983) *Between Hope and Happening: Text and Context in Curriculum*. Deakin University Press, Geelong, Vic.

—— (1991) *Between Education and Schooling: Outlines of a Diachronic Curriculum Theory*. Deakin University Press, Geelong, Vic.

Lyotard, J.-F. (1984) trans. G. Bennington and B. Massumi. *The Postmodern Condition: A Report on Knowledge*. Manchester University Press, Manchester.

—— (1987) *Le Postmoderne Expliqué aux Enfants: Correspondance, 1982–85*. Galilée, Paris.

MacIntyre, A. (1983) *After Virtue: A Study in Moral Theory*. 2nd edn. Duckworth, London.

—— (1990) *Three Rival Versions of Moral Theory: Encyclopædia, Genealogy and Tradition*. Duckworth, London.

Popkewitz, T. (1991) *A Political Sociology of Educational Reform: Power/Knowledge in Teaching, Teacher Education, and Research*. Teachers College Press, New York.

Rabinow, P. (ed.) (1984) *The Foucault Reader*. Pantheon, New York.

Reid, W.A. (1978) *Thinking About the Curriculum: The Nature and Treatment of Curriculum Problems*. Routledge and Kegan Paul, London.

Rorty, R. (1989) *Contingency, Irony and Solidarity*. Cambridge University Press, Cambridge.

Said, E. (1978) *Orientalism*. Pantheon, New York.

—— (1983) Opponents, audiences, constituencies and community. In H. Foster (ed.) *Postmodern Culture*. Pluto Press, London.

—— (1993) *Culture and Imperialism*. Chatto and Windus, London.

Schwab, J.J. (1969) The practical: a language for curriculum. *School Review* 78, 1–24.

Stenhouse, L.A. (1975) *An Introduction to Curriculum Research and Development*. Heinemann, London.

Tonnies, F. (1957) *Community and Society*. Michigan State University Press, East Lansing, Michigan.

Toulmin, S. (1990) *Cosmopolis: The Hidden Agenda of Modernity*. The Free Press, New York.

Touraine, A. (1981) Trans. by Charles Duff. *The Voice and the Eye: An Analysis of Social Movements*. Cambridge University Press, Cambridge.

Tyler, R.W. (1949) *Basic Principles of Curriculum and Instruction*. University of Chicago Press, Chicago.

Williams, R. (1983) *Towards 2000*. Chatto and Windus, London.

—— (1989) *The Politics of Modernism: Against the New Conformists*. Verso, London.

Wise, A.E. (1977) Why educational policies often fail: the hyperrationalization hypothesis. *Journal of Curriculum Studies* 9, 17–28.

—— (1979) *Legislated Learning: The Bureaucratization of the American Classroom*. University of California Press, Berkeley, Cal.

Notes

1   This paper was originally prepared as a keynote address to the conference 'Curriculum changes in Hong Kong: the needs of the new era', The Chinese University of Hong Kong, 29–30 April 1994; it appeared subsequently in the Triangle Publications journal *Curriculum Studies*. Grateful acknowledgment is made to the publishers and editors of *Curriculum Studies* for their permission to reprint the article in this collection.

2   In this chapter I discuss social media in terms of language (and discourses), work and power.

3   For a good account of the nature of social practices (and their relationships to traditions, values and the virtues), see MacIntyre 1983, especially pp. 175–89. For a contrasting, sharply materialist, view of practices, see Althusser 1971. Althusser has this to say of practices: 'By practice in general, I shall mean any process of *transformation* of a determinate given raw material into a determinate *product,* a transformation effected by determinate human labour, using determinate means of production.' (quoted by Bennett 1979: 111)

4   Putting this brief quotation in context may help to clarify the relationship between practices and institutions: 'Practices must not be confused with institutions. Chess, physics and medicine are practices; chess clubs, laboratories, universities and hospitals are institutions. Institutions are characteristically and necessarily concerned with ... external goods. They are involved in acquiring money and other material goods; they are structured in terms of power and status, and they distribute money, power and status as rewards. Nor could they do otherwise if they are to sustain not only themselves, but also the practices of which they are the bearers. For no practices can survive any length of time unsustained by institutions. Indeed, so intimate is the relationship of practices to institutions ... that institutions and practices characteristically form a single causal order in which the ideals and the creativity of the

practice are always vulnerable to the acquisitiveness of the institution, in which the cooperative care for common goods of the practice is always vulnerable to the competitiveness of the institution' (p. 181).

5   Cf. the dialectic of 'social integration' (involving reciprocity, and relations of autonomy and independence, between actors) and 'system integration' (involving reciprocity, and relations of autonomy and independence, between groups or collectivities) in Giddens' theory of structuration (1979: especially pp. 76–81).

6   This trend or tendency is strikingly exemplified in a study now being completed by Jennifer Angwin of the Centre for the Study of Education and Change at Deakin University. (For a report in progress, see Angwin 1992.) Her investigation of the changing forms of curriculum and educational policy in the area of Teaching of English to Speakers of Other Languages (TESOL) in Australia suggests that the rationalisation of approaches to TESOL curriculum, policy and staffing has proceeded so far that: (a) learners can no longer be guaranteed articulation between short courses designed to meet 'their' (generalised) needs; (b) teachers on short contracts to serve these courses can no longer sustain a viable career in the field; (c) professional development in the field (to the extent that it remains available at all) can no longer maintain TESOL teaching as a mature specialism within the teaching profession; and (d) TESOL curricula have been fragmented into atomised 'competencies' which can barely hope to meet the well-known diversity of needs and circumstances of the learners for whom TESOL courses are intended. In part (following Habermas), she is interpreting these phenomena in terms of 'the colonisation of the [TESOL] lifeworld' by system values.

7   Robert Holub, in the first chapter of his (1991) book *Jürgen Habermas: Critic in the Public Sphere,* describes the dialectical relationship between Habermas' philosophical and social theoretical work, on the one hand, and his engagement in the public debates of the day (for example, in his social commentary in newspaper articles), on the other.

8   Habermas writes: 'The theory of modernity that I have here sketched in broad strokes permits us to recognize the following: In modern societies there is such an expansion of the scope of contingency for interaction loosed from normative contexts that the inner logic of

communicative action "becomes practically true" in the deinstitutionalized forms of intercourse of the familial private sphere as well as in a public sphere stamped by the mass media. At the same time, the systemic imperatives of autonomous subsystems penetrate into the lifeworld, and, through monetarization and bureaucratization, force an assimilation of communicative action to formally organized domains of action — even in areas where the action-coordinating mechanism of reaching understanding is functionally necessary. It may be that this provocative threat, this challenge that places the symbolic structures of the lifeworld as a whole in question, can account for why they have become accessible to us' (1987b: 403).

9   Cf. Rorty 1989: 8n — 'Nietzsche has caused a lot of confusion by inferring from "truth is not a matter of correspondence to reality" to "what we call 'truths' are just simple lies". The same confusion is occasionally found in Derrida, in the inference from "there is no such reality as the metaphysicians hoped to find" to "what we call 'real' is not really real". Such confusions make Nietzsche and Derrida liable to charges of self-referential inconsistency — to claiming to know what they themselves claim cannot be known.'

10   Holub (1991) believes that Lyotard is led into 'a performative contradiction that is typical of postmodernist thought. Lyotard presents his theory as a criticism of Habermas's notion of consensus, and posits as an alternative that dissension is the trajectory of speech acts. If we assume that Lyotard is correct and that dissension is the *telos* of speech, then we are unable to account for the status of his own statement. We cannot agree with the propositional content of his statement without simultaneously denying the validity of the statement.' (143)

11   An interesting point: is it the case that in seeking to deconstruct and, in a sense, re-write the texts of others, poststructuralists like Derrida also form first-person relationships with the authors of those texts? Building on the insights that to read a text is, in a sense, to rewrite it for oneself, and that to comment on a text is, in a sense, to rewrite it for others, do such authors form a kind of (intertextual) solidarity with other authors which places them in a first-person plural ('we', 'us') which is a solidarity of authorship, to be distinguished from the society of those who do not read or do not write about the particular matters being written about? If this is so,

then does not this presuppose the first-person relationships of emancipatory narratives which the content of their texts denies?

12 See J. Habermas (1981) Modernity versus postmodernity. *New German Critique* 22 (Winter), 3–14; and *Lectures on the Philosophical Discourse of Modernity.* MIT Press, Cambridge, Mass. For a brief critical analysis of Habermas' views, see D. Kellner (1988) Postmodernism as social theory. *Theory, Culture and Society* 5, (special nos. 2–3), 239–69. In Kellner's view, Habermas and some of his followers have taken too defensive a line on postmodernity, breaking the Frankfurt School critical theory tradition of vigorously accepting the theoretical challenge of developing new theoretical approaches for the analysis of changed cultural conditions; the criticism seems to me unwarranted since for more than a decade, Habermas has clearly been concerned (a) to provide an analysis of the changed social conditions of late modernity, and (b) to develop critical philosophical and social–theoretic resources which will not only allow us to interpret this new world but also to change it.

13 Perhaps this takes up one element of Habermas' (1990b) point (in his essay on 'Foucault's lecture on Kant's *What Is Enlightenment?*') that Foucault's lecture — his last work — also demonstrates a connection with 'the philosophical discourse of modernity'.

14 On this point, Freire, too, attempts to avoid too close an identification with some of the specific programs of revolutionary action in South America. In *Cultural Action for Freedom,* he attempts to distinguish the 'true' revolutionary consciousness from some of the specific forms being adopted by in South America, though in celebrating Che Guevara's revolutionary ideals he risks having this specific *program* treated as a model for 'the' revolution. Since Freire offers a critique of aspects of the revolutionary program of the left at the time, it may be possible to distinguish between Freire's *educational* interest in emancipation and what he sees as the cultural–revolutionary perspective which frames it, on the one hand, and, on the other, his practical–political interest in the possibilities of specific programs for 'cultural action for freedom'.

15 On the dialectic of social order and social movement, see, for example, Touraine (1981); on the possibility of a 'life politics', see Giddens (1991). Habermas' (1987b) comments on the possibilities for protest are also relevant here.

16   This is not the view of those theorists of the postmodern who aim to develop responses to the cultural, economic and political transformations of 'the postmodern age' which sustain a commitment to emancipatory perspectives, while at the same time acknowledging that the nature and form of emancipation needs to be understood in new ways — authors like Jameson (1991), Said (1983) and Hall (1986a; 1986b).

17   This view is echoed by Seyla Benhabib (1992) in the chapter 'Feminism and the question of postmodernism'.

Chapter 13

Issues for Participatory Action Researchers[1]

Robin McTaggart

Abstract

This chapter contests the emergent contention that participatory action research has not been and cannot be emancipatory and reasserts the prospects for personal agency amidst new coalitions in action research. Presenting a short personal account of the author's introduction to participatory action research theory and practice, the chapter outlines several issues arising from the literature of social theory and from action research theory and practice itself. The pessimistic views of social theorists who can see nothing in the enlightenment project but lack of achievement, lack of sustainable ideas and lack of the capacity to change things are challenged. Instead action research is seen to have engaged with some success the very objections made, and to have confronted both new and perennial obstacles to its emancipatory aspirations. Further, the principles of action research coupled with new strategic alliances provide a way forward.

Introduction

There is too much pessimism about the potency of participatory action research. This stems from two main sources. First, there is unjustified optimism about the pace with which even the most obviously unjust social practices can be dismantled. Most injustice is sustained deliberately, systematically and hegemonically by longstanding social practices which promote advantage as well as disadvantage. The latter are not completely complementary, but are significantly so, and advantage is very reluctantly surrendered. It follows that disadvantage is persistently difficult to redress. Further, the multiple causal chains of injustice are notoriously difficult to simultaneously influence enough to effect lasting change. There is a pressing need to heed the literature of innovation and to vitalise more complex networks of 'participants' to work on the most pressing problems. Second, there is a proliferation of theorising, sponsored by the commodification of knowledge in the academy, which makes a fetish of the new and privileges critique over social impact. This is not to say that new ideas are not useful or necessary, but that new coalitions and new practices are more important than new ways of labelling problems people have made some progress towards solving. Social progress requires personal progress, and that requires attention to the pedagogies of reform, some of which are clearly not working to secure collaboration among diverse groups and across institutional hierarchies. People come to social issues with different backgrounds, different skills, and different views; there is a need for advocates for change to work more generously, tolerantly and strategically.

Coming to emancipatory action research

Like many people in Australia of my age interested in educational research, I was once trained in educational measurement. Though my motives in teacher education were to ensure that educators knew what could and could not be achieved by natural scientific methods and to help teachers to improve quantifiable assessments, I became tired of inducting educators into that discourse. I began working with Stephen Kemmis, Colin Henry and others at Deakin on the ideas of action research. My own route into those ideas was through Joseph Schwab's work in curriculum. Whilst it is a commonplace in the sociology of knowledge now, for me Schwab made the 'disciplines' seem much more like vulnerable human inventions and teaching much more complex than inducting students into the disciplines' own views of themselves. As a former biology teacher, I wondered why the Lysenko tragedy was featured in Biological Sciences Curriculum Study (BSCS) curricula as an example of state interference in science, when high energy physics was sponsored everywhere at the expense of research and other efforts which might ameliorate human suffering. I began to discover that the hidden curriculum was like the familiar Russian dolls — there was always another one underneath. And one of them was always an issue to do with social justice.

Since those days, I have taught and worked in action research projects (and these days I have learned how important it is to say *participatory* action research) in a variety of formal and informal settings, and in different cultures. Like most teaching I have done, this is a mixed bag of success and failure, but I am dismayed when people dismiss action research as if it had contributed little to improving the rationality, justice, coherence and satisfactoriness of educational and other forms of work. These dismissals seem to be based on an assumption that action research has not always been successful as an 'emancipatory' project, in the terms of critical social science, or from some other point of view. Almost always they are based on an implicit assumption that 'emancipation' is some ideal state to be achieved. This is *not* the aspiration of participatory action research, which works on critique of current conditions and more or less immediate attempts at concrete improvement. Its referent is 'Are things better than they were?', not 'Are we emancipated yet?'

There is also too much baggage added to the notion of 'emancipation'. Some folks speak about it as if nothing short of the revolution will do. This is not merely defeatist, it can also induce that paralysing version of ideological soundness which nurtures sniping ahead of genuine attempts to improve things. Action researchers must simply ask regularly whether things are a little more rational (or reasonable), coherent, just, humane and satisfying for participants and others than they were. The political, cultural and linguistic practices which make the world an unsavoury place for many people did not arise overnight, and will take sustained effort and tolerance of slow progress and setbacks. Perversely, military technologies and less controllable features of our lives can make things worse suddenly, and much effort is expended on avoiding regression.

Whether things are better is not always an easy question to answer, as the story towards the end of the paper shows, but it is the primary question participants in an action research program need to answer for themselves when they are deciding whether to continue. Many of the people I have worked with are quite adamant that they have made progress of various kinds. Most would not lay claim to 'emancipation', largely because they would regard such talk as self-regarding. But many, even those who viewed action research with some suspicion, talk about the experience as changing their work irreversibly and in ways valued by them and by me. I don't claim any credit for this — the ideas I have I learned from others — but the point is that people can present evidence that their lives have improved in one way or another. Obviously, there are some lessons action researchers can learn from recent theoretical positioning and from the difficulties experienced in confronting the conditions which disfigure our lives, but learning from our own and others' experience has always been an explicit feature of action research. I am optimistic that some ways of working developed by participatory action researchers may help to address some of the trenchant criticisms advanced in recent times in critiques of social science theory and practice.

Theoretical issues

Much of the critique which might impact on action research is not based upon what action researchers do in practice, but on the theoretical and metatheoretical positionings like critical theory, neo-Aristotelianism and some forms of feminism which might be argued to develop the epistemological bases for action research. Some authors from the participatory research movement, however, regard such debates as somewhat ephemeral to their concerns.

Popular knowledge and academic 'legitimation'

One of many issues which predates the current fervour in postmodernism and poststructuralist writing, themselves partly energised by the commodification of knowledge in the academy, concerns the status of what is often termed 'popular knowledge'. The issue appears in the participatory action research literature in the work of Budd Hall (1979; 1981) and Rajesh Tandon (1988; 1989) who dispute the need for popular knowledge to be vindicated epistemologically by approval from the academy. Others, like Orlando Fals Borda (with Rahman 1991), have recognised the issue, but have worked to establish complementarity and reciprocity between 'popular' and 'academic' knowledge. Nevertheless, there are genuine dangers inherent in the 'naming' of concerns by different parties, and the issue of the relationship between forms and forums of knowledge (and the danger of intellectual imperialism on the one hand, and reinventing the wheel on the other) is longstanding.

Postmodernism (or epistemological bungee-jumping with rubber bands of unmeasured lengths)

The issue outlined above reappears in several guises in the 'challenges of postmodernism' debate, which we can give a more coherent structure. This debate is finely captured by Seyla Benhabib (1992, esp. pp. 211–55) in her analysis of its impact on the emancipatory project of feminism. Benhabib dismantles the 'strong theses' proposed by Jane Flax (1990), summarised as the *death of the subject* (and agency), the *death of history* (and the possibility of progress and emancipation) and the *death of metaphysics* (and the possibility that science and reason are anything other than a mask for control of the social and natural worlds). Benhabib then proposes a 'weaker' version of each thesis which sets an agenda for feminist praxis, which may also be used as an analogy for all so-called emancipatory projects such as participatory action research. The issues these pose for action researchers may be summarised in the following ways:

1   *Subjectivity*: What evidence/arguments can be adduced to support (or contest) the contention that action researchers can be regarded as autonomous and responsible agents of change (individually or in a group) and as persons autonomously capable of constructing knowledge which can guide their own reconstructive activities (as opposed to being merely reactive creatures of the discursive formation of subjectivity, 'merely another position in language')? This is a question which has been of practical concern in the action research literature, especially in relation to the relative roles of action researchers and the 'facilitators' of action research who are sometimes regarded as (intentionally or unintentionally) pre-forming the critical work done by participants as they study their own ideas, practices and situations.

2   *History:* What evidence/arguments can be adduced to support (or contest) the contention that participants' readings (understandings) of 'progress', 'improvement' and 'emancipation' shaped by their own (self-)interests and their own perspectives, rather than by 'regimes of truth' and 'discursive practices' which pre-form participants' ways of viewing themselves, their understandings, their practices and the settings in which they work? For example, if they resist dominant discourses and ideologies, is their resistance based on a rational, critical reconstruction of their situation, or is it merely the expression of their being (just as much) 'captured' by an alternative or emerging counter-discourse? This is a question of practical concern in the action research literature about the nature and sources of practitioners' ideas about 'improvement' (and 'progress' and 'emancipation') through action research, in relation to other ideas (for example, from research literatures, from other action researchers' reports, from 'facilitators' ...), and about the ways practitioners relate to the social structures of their settings (for example, as contributors to the improvement of work in their settings, as critics, as members of social movements with sources outside their own settings, as the dupes of 'radicals' ...).

3   *Metaphysics*: What evidence/arguments can be adduced to support (or contest) the contention that action researchers' representations of themselves, their understandings, their practices and their

situations may be regarded as socially and historically constructed and reconstructed through communicative action (cf. 'the philosophy of consciousness' or ' ... of the subject' versus contemporary, 'postmetaphysical' views of critical social science and communicative action) and as amenable to (systematic) 'objectification' (cf. objectivist, empiricist and 'value-free' views of science) and to (disciplined) 'subjectification' (cf. interpretivist views) as part of a reconstructive program? This has been of practical concern in the action research literature in relation to such issues as the kinds of evidence to be collected in action research projects, the relative roles of observational and autobiographical (journal-based) evidence, the modes of analysis of evidence appropriate in action research, and the place of (self-) reflection and collaborative analysis in interpreting evidence in action research.

Teaching issues

Action research as procedure

How do we confront the problem of the 'action research spiral' becoming the 'procedure' of action research? The Lewinian (1946; 1952) spiral has created serious confusion about the idea of action research, the fundamental feature of which is collective reflection by participants on systematic objectifications and disciplined subjectifications of their efforts to change the way they work (constituted by discourse, organisation and power relations, and practice) (McTaggart & Garbutcheon-Singh 1986; 1988; Kemmis & McTaggart 1988).[2] It is a mistake to think that slavishly following the 'action research spiral' constitutes 'doing action research'. The most crass of these misinterpretations is the view that a masters thesis might involve only 'one cycle' but a PhD several. Action research is not a 'method' or a 'procedure' for research but a series of commitments to observe and problematise through practice a series of principles for conducting social enquiry (the praxis of a critical social science?).

Understanding the historical location of the spiral metaphor is important: in my view, Lewin was not specifying the method (or even *a* method) for research but, albeit obliquely, was trying to suggest that action research was different from traditional empirical–analytic and interpretive research in both its dynamism and its continuity with an emergent practice. However, we should be mindful that Lewin actually referred to the spiral as a method for 'rational social management'! We can say that the spiral makes explicit the need for acting differently 'within the study' as a result of progressively learning from experience. The other features of action research are obviously more important than Lewin's simplistic iconography suggested. However, it is also true that the 'spiral' is sometimes useful as a heuristic for people starting to research their own practice. Unfortunately, all too often we are hoist by our own heuristic.

Do teachers yet identify with 'doing' research?

For many years we have taught action research units in mid-career professional development with the term 'action research' in the title, but have not attracted large numbers of Australian students. Thousands of Australian teachers use the term and describe many of their staff development activities in this way. *The Action Research Planner* (Kemmis & McTaggart 1988) has sold around 10 000 copies (internationally, not counting Thai and Spanish translations, and French and Malaysian interpretations); Yoland Wadsworth's book, *Do it Yourself Social Research*, has sold 27 000 copies. Are Australian educators shying away from the claim that what they do counts as research and as a contribution to other teachers' knowledge as well as their own? If they are, perhaps it is because we have not yet generated a literature (if indeed, a literature is what is required) to which teachers can confidently turn as a platform for their own enquiries. McGaw's (1992) review of educational research in Australia suggests that this may be so. Years ago, David Hamilton suggested we could quarantine a method for educational research, avoid being deflected by the battles of social science and engage educators more readily by calling what we now do 'curriculum enquiry'. In fact, the first versions of Deakin University action research courses were called *Curriculum Research*. Given the support and enthusiasm for action research beyond curriculum (and other interesting methodological developments in the curriculum field), that suggestion was probably best not heeded. But how strong is the explicit identification of educators with action research methodology? And what are the forums and modes of presentation of teachers' knowledge claims, if indeed this is the appropriate language for a discourse of praxis?

Action research as commonplace, co-option or co-opted?

The term 'action research' is now one of the commonplaces of professional[3] education, and I find it refreshing to find it in both common and uncommon places. In the last twelve months or so, I have talked about action research with community medicine specialists, nurse educators and teacher educators in Thailand, with business 'trainers' and process management folks in Brisbane, with instructional designers in Telecom in Melbourne, with community development workers and activists in Ross House in Melbourne, with teachers in Footscray, with business managers in Singapore and Hong Kong, and with Indonesian teacher educators and agricultural scientists in Yogyakarta. The proliferation of 'action research' marks a significant shift in both the kinds of relationships researchers from the academy have with others and in the locus of knowledge production about professional and community practice.

Proliferation has also led to the diversification and articulation of action research theory and practice. This has led in turn to more substantial versions of action research, but also to versions which seem to have lost their way (or were lost to begin with). Not all good things in the world are action research, and many versions of action research might be strategic versions of aspirations with a broader and more justifiable social agenda, but how can we sustain the debate across different practices claiming to be action research to ensure mutual and reciprocal critique? We live in glass houses, because many of our own efforts fall short of our aspirations for emancipatory action research, though our efforts may pass muster against less demanding or different criteria. There is, for example, an urgent need for educational action researchers who take a critical theoretical perspective to engage in thoughtful dialogue with advocates and practitioners of action learning, soft systems methodology, process management, total quality management, quality circles and the like, which for many years have used the rubric of 'action research'.

Case studies as models of action research

The quest for methodological unity in the natural sciences is emulated in the social sciences in the arguments for finding molar causal laws where correctly following a standardised model procedure is a guarantee of quality. Quality is a particular kind of 'validity' linked to causal inferences made by the researcher (privileging the interpretation of the researcher over those of the reader). Adherence to the model produces quality. In action research, *cases* are much more likely to be instructive about quality. That is, the best models are our best cases, not summary procedural abstractions (like the 'spiral of action research'). Methodological and substantive insight is more likely to depend upon 'naturalistic generalisation' (Stake & Trumble 1977), learning from the particulars of the case in the light of one's own situation and experience. Case studies are available, but they are notoriously difficult to access. How are we to improve the accessibility of accounts of cases? Or is it the accessibility of participants in cases and dialogue which we mean here?

What is the nature of action in action research?

One of our colleagues in nursing education is conducting an action research project in institutional care for the elderly (Crane 1994). She works with the care-providers on a regular basis and recently taught them aromatherapy to assist patients. It is too early to understand why the aromatherapy helped to 'bond' the group with the 'outsider', but it appears to have helped significantly. Let us suppose it did help — why then did *this* 'strategic action' actually 'work' to consolidate the group and its commitment to improve care together? Without lapsing back into the fruitless 'insider/ outsider' distinction, we might ask how 'action' is understood — how 'individual' action and 'collective' action confirm and confound each other and just what it is that ultimately helps groups to come together and stay working together on problems of mutual concern and consequence. What 'action' is justified? When we 'teach' action research, what is the nature of our action, our involvement in students' lives and projects, and their role in ours?

What is the biographical nature of changing a practice?

Action research focuses on 'practice'; in the Deakin University versions of action research we usually employ MacIntyre's (1981) notion of practice. 'Education' (but not schools or schooling) in this sense is a practice. This gives considerable scope, but also considerable justificatory demand, for deliberate and informed action for change. Suppose one wants to explore gender issues in the classroom using action research methods. At one level, it is a reasonably straightforward thing to do. But one's own identity as a gendered subject is also on the line.[4] Taking Frigga Haug's (1987) memory work as an example of a research process by which the gendered subject as self is understood to be learned (constructed and positioned) and submerged over time, this makes the possibility of informed 'first action steps' somewhat tricky. Action research takes it as fundamental that trying to *change* things is a way to discovery. But what is the balance between extended introspection and first moves to change 'practice'? Which practice? The practice of feminist politics? Where and *when* would one make a start? We could call all of this 'reconnaissance', extending the meaning of that term to take account of individual, personal concerns, as some action research writers have urged (Nias & Groundwater-Smith 1988), but I make a different point. When you really do get down to thinking about your work in relation to your 'self', just where you might elect to take a first (second ...) step towards change, may not be quite where you began. The change in cultural practice you seek might be occurring somewhere else altogether. This is no bad thing, and people can work in more than one sphere of influence at a time, and perhaps that is the point at issue. Nevertheless, there is a danger that a search for confidence can become an extended search for ideological purity which is immediately and ultimately paralysing.

What is the relationship between educational action research and the other cultural practices with which people are engaged? I have argued elsewhere that action researchers need to identify with social movements extending beyond education (McTaggart 1991b), but the intersection of these activities and educational action research, and action researchers' support networks, knowledgeability, confidence, potential spheres of action and personal development (in the politicised sense of the term) are not well understood. Some might say that all this means that action research is 'undertheorised'. I am not sure that I know what that means since we work on the problem unremittingly, but I am sure that action research is 'under-practised', especially by many of its critics.

A story about progress

Some time ago now, some Deakin colleagues and I worked with Aboriginal educators in the Northern Territory of Australia using a participatory action research approach to support them in developing what they sometimes called 'both ways' education, but later called 'Aboriginal pedagogies' (in English translation). After a very long, thoughtful and sometimes harrowing discussion, the group decided that it would allow publication of their own accounts of this work. The teachers imposed a significant condition on the publication — that it would not be 'edited' by the Northern Territory education department personnel (one of whom had indicated that it was their responsibility to put things in ways which would not offend people).[5] The decision was a courageous one because as well as affirming the nature of Aboriginal pedagogy for each community represented, the case studies indicated how the Western education system, both state and private, impaired Aboriginal teachers' efforts to give expression to their own culture in the schools in which they were teaching the Aboriginal children of their own communities.

The publication went ahead some time later and, as expected, did create the strife the teachers knew it would. One teacher suffered more than the others, and explored the possibility of withdrawing the publication. The teacher agreed that withdrawal would not solve the problems she was experiencing, and allowed the publication to stand. A few months later, the same teacher contacted us to arrange for the supply of multiple copies of the book for distribution among other Aboriginal teachers. The book was then and still is being used as a key reference for Aboriginal students in teacher education in the Northern Territory. The teacher's problem has not gone away, but there is now a strong sense of accomplishment in the work, and still a strong commitment to the ideas expressed in it. Aboriginal teachers throughout the Northern Territory know of the work, but it is a moot point whether being an Aboriginal teacher in the Northern Territory has been made easier or more difficult by the program and the publication, or indeed by association with us. Progress *is* difficult to estimate.

Conclusion

Participatory action researchers face some considerable practical, theoretical and organisational challenges. Their work has been sold short by some explicit and implicit criticism. In fact, their achievements across the broad family of action research approaches have not been inconsequential, and there is good reason to believe that the issues identified here are already being engaged with success under quite difficult circumstances. Good ideas and theory are necessary, but a bit more concrete help and documentation of enlightening cases would not go astray in the current debates of social theory and practice.

References

Benhabib, S. (1992) *Situating the Self: Gender, Community and Postmodernism in Contemporary Ethics*. Polity Press, Cambridge.

Crane, S. (1994) Action research in a nursing home: critical and feminist perspectives arising. Paper presented at the Fifth Annual Critical and Feminist Perspectives in Nursing Conference. Bothell, Washington.

Fals Borda, O. and Rahman, M.A. (1991) *Action and Knowledge: Breaking the Monopoly with Participatory Action Research*. Apex, New York.

Flax, J. (1990) *Psychoanalysis, Feminism and Postmodernism in the Contemporary West*. University of California Press, Berkeley CA.

Hall, B.L. (1979) Knowledge as a commodity and participatory research. *Prospects* 9 (4), 393–408.

—— (1981) Participatory research, popular knowledge and power: a personal reflection. *Convergence* 14 (3), 6–19.

Haug. F (ed.) (1987) *Female Sexualisation*. Verso, London.

Kemmis, S. and McTaggart, R. (eds) (1988) *The Action Research Planner*. 3rd ed. Deakin University Press, Geelong, Australia.

Lewin, K. (1952) Group decision and social change. In G.E. Swanson, T.M. Newcomb and E.L. Hartley (eds) *Readings in Social Psychology*. Henry Holt, New York, 459–73.

—— (1946) Action research and minority problems. *Journal of Social Issues* 2, 34–46.

McTaggart, R. (1991a) Western institutional impediments to Aboriginal education. *Journal of Curriculum Studies* 23 (4), 297–325.

—— (1991b) Community movements and school reform: a new coalition for action research. Keynote address to the Biennial Conference of the Australian Curriculum Studies Association, Adelaide, July.

McTaggart, R. and Garbutcheon-Singh, M. (1986) New directions in action research. *Curriculum Perspectives* 6 (2), 42–46.

—— (1988) Fourth generation action research: notes on the 1986 Deakin seminar. In S. Kemmis and R. McTaggart (eds) *The Action Research Reader*. 3rd edn, Deakin University Press, Geelong, Australia.

Nias, J. and Groundwater-Smith, S. (1988) *The Enquiring Teacher: Supporting and Sustaining Teacher Research*. Falmer Press, London.

Stake, R.E. and Trumble, D.J. (1977) Naturalistic generalizations. *Review Journal of Philosophy and Social Science* VII (1–2), 1–12.

Tandon, R. (1988) Social transformation and participatory research. *Convergence* 21 (2–3), 5–14.

—— (1989) Movement towards democratization of knowledge: reflections on participatory research. Paper presented at the Tercer Encuentro Mundial Investigacion Participativa (Third World Encounter on Participatory Research), September. Managua, Nicaragua.

Notes

1   An earlier version of this paper was presented as background to a discussion in a symposium entitled 'Personal, professional, political: international perspectives on the teaching and doing of action research' at the Annual Meeting of the American Educational Research Association, New Orleans, April 1994.

2   Stephen Kemmis and I must take these criticisms on the chin. We have been trying press the dynamism home in the same way, in the

hope of having the students in our distance education programs initiate action research rather than become stranded in what Lewin called the 'reconnaissance phase' of action research. Mea culpa.

3   I acknowledge that this term denotes a privileged group. I sometimes use 'worker', but in professional contexts people sometimes think this does not apply to them. The term 'practitioner' might be helpful, but not always, partly because researchers and theorists sometimes think they are not practitioners when in fact they are. Unfortunately there is no convenient universal term to label anyone engaged in a 'practice', but perhaps that's a good thing.

4   The example has some obviously distinctive features, but we are also 'taught' subjects, for example.

5   See McTaggart (1991a) for my own observations of these obstacles.

Author Index

Adelman, C., 54, 146
Adorno, Theodor, 142
Alexander, R.J., 54
Althusser, L., 193
Altrichter, H., 54, 123, 132, 127, 129
Alvesson, M., 132
Arendt, Hannah, 110
Argyris, C., 83, 84
Aristotle, 225
Aronowitz, S., 54, 55
Barthes, R., 188
Bataille, Georges, 223
Baudrillard, Jean, 168, 176, 177, 178, 203, 223
Bawden, R., 50, 53
Beer, M, 83, 84, 93, 94, 95
Benhabib, Seyla, 109, 110, 203, 232, 246–48
Benton, P. , 67, 68
Bernstein, R., 167, 168
Blanchard, K.H., 55
Bloom, Benjamin, 205
Boston Consulting Group, 100
Boud, David, 157, 158
Bourdieu, P., 126, 128, 130
Boyne, R., 187
Bunning, Cliff, 83, 92
Burns, J., 55
Burrell, G., 132, 170, 176
Bussey, Kay, 35
Candy, P.C., 50, 51, 52

Capra, F., 37
Carr, W. , 4, 53, 84, 94, 146, 148, 166, 211
Carter, C., 100
Castenada, Carlos, 33–35, 38
Chadbourne, R., 114, 115, 117, 118
Cherryholmes, C., 207, 224
Chisholm, Lynne, 155, 156
Clarke, R., 114, 115, 117, 118
Clegg, St., 133
Codd, J., 55
Connor, Steven, 203, 227
Coombe, R.J., 167
Cooper, R., 170, 176
Corben, J., 85, 107
Corey, Stephen, 146
Crane, S., 251
Crawford, J., 67, 68
Cunnington, Bert, 55, 100
Deetz, St, 132, 133
Derrida, Jacques, 176–77, 178, 220, 223
Descartes, René, 209
Devereux, G., 75
Dreyfus, H., 174
Edwards, R., 168, 175, 177
Elliot, John, 146
Ellsworth, Elizabeth, 113, 153, 154–55
Fals Borda, Orlando, 246
Farquhar, Mary, 88
Fitzclarence, Lindsay, 53, 54, 69, 206

Flax, Jane, 203, 246
Foucault, Michel, 127, 151, 170, 171, 173, 174, 175, 176, 179, 208, 220, 221, 223, 224, 225, 226, 231
Freire, Paulo, 53, 144, 183, 184, 219, 224, 230
Fromm, Erich, 142
Garbutcheon–Singh, 248
Gault, U., 67, 68
Gee, J., 171, 172
Gibson, R., 148, 149, 150
Giddens, Anthony, 36, 127, 128, 133, 167, 199, 203, 209, 216, 217, 218, 232
Giroux, H.A., 54, 55
Glaser, B., 5
Gorbach, St, 122
Gordon, C., 220, 225
Gore, J., 179
Graham, Anne P., 165–81
Green, Bill, 208
Greenwood, J., 167
Gron, P., 55
Groundwater-Smith, S., 251
Grundy, Shirley, 5, 106–20, 108, 166
Gstettner, P., 123, 132
Guba, E.G., 50
Haag, F., 123
Habermas, Jürgen, 50, 54, 106, 109, 110, 111, 112, 124, 125, 128, 137, 142, 143, 146, 154, 167, 169, 170, 199, 203, 209, 211, 216, 218, 220, 223, 224, 225, 226, 227, 232
Hall, Budd, 246
Hall, Stuart, 203, 228, 231, 232
Hall, Susan, 28–48, 29
Hamilton, David, 54, 249
Hannah, M., 157
Hassard, J., 168, 169
Haug, Frigga, 67, 68, 251
Hegel, 110, 140, 147, 149
Heinze, Th., 128
Henry, Colin, 244
Hershey, P., 55
Holub, R.C., 218

Horkheimer, Max, 142, 225
House, E.R., 54
Howell, Faith, 88
Hughes, C., 52, 55
Hume, David, 195
Iococca, Lee, 55
Jäger, 76
Jameson, Frederic, 167, 178, 200–201, 203, 209, 231
Jennings, Leonie E., 165–81
Jonas, Hans, 223
Kant, 220
Kappler, E., 123
Karr, Alphonse, 218
Keep, E., 122
Kellner, Douglas, 203, 209, 231
Kelly, A.V., 54
Kelly, G.A., 5, 85, 86
Kemmis, Stephen, 4, 5, 32, 35, 50, 51, 52, 53, 54, 55, 84, 94, 146, 148, 166, 199–242, 206, 211, 244
Kenway, J., 230
Kippax, Susan, 68, 69
Laske, Stephan, 121–36
Lather, P., 30, 37
Lewin, Kurt, 83, 97, 99, 146, 192, 248, 249
Limerick, David, 55, 100
Lowenthal, Leo, 142
Lundgren, Ulf, 53, 204, 206
Lyotard, Jean-François, 167, 170, 176, 178, 203, 219–20, 221, 223, 227, 228, 231
MacIntyre, Alisdair, 199, 203, 214, 223, 232, 251
Marcuse, Herbert, 142
Marshall, J., 55, 179
Marx, Karl, 140, 147, 149, 225
McDonald, Rod, 157, 158
McGaw, 249
McKay, Penny, 88
McNiff, J., 147
McTaggart, R., 147, 166, 243–55, 248, 249, 252

Melrose, Mary-Jane, 49–65, 56
Mezirow, Jack, 143–44, 145
Miles, R., 75
Miller, M., 125
Minh-ha, 155
Modra, H., 230
Moser, H., 123, 126, 129, 132
Neuberger, 129
Nias, J., 251
Nichols, A., 53
Nietzche, 175
Noxon, J., 195
Onyx, J., 67, 68
Parlett, M., 54
Passeron, P., 126
Peters, M., 55
Peters, T., 179
Pieper, R., 123
Plato, 140
Popham, W.J., 54
Popkewitz, Tom, 224, 225, 226
Power, M., 168
Print, M., 53
Rabinow, P., 174, 220
Rahman, M.A., 246
Reid, W.A., 206
Rolph, J. , 54
Rorty, R., 213
Ruby, J., 31–32, 35, 37, 38
Said, Edward, 203, 228, 229, 231, 232
Sanger, Jack, 182–98
Schmitz, E., 126
Schneider, U., 124
Schön, Donald, 66, 84
Schratz, Michael, 66–80, 184
Schwab, Joseph, 53, 206, 224, 244
Scriven, M., 54
Selsnick, P., 55
Senge, P., 84, 91
Shapiro, S., 167, 177
Sheehan, J., 53
Silverman, D., 32, 36
Simon, H.A., 107
Skilbeck, M., 53

Smart, B., 168
Smyth, J., 55
Spaemann, Robert, 223
Stake, R.E., 250
Stenhouse, L., 54, 206
Storey, J., 122
Strauss, A., 5
Strauss, Leo, 85, 223
Strohmayer, U., 157
Taba, H., 53
Tandon, Rajesh, 246
Thompson, J.P., 128, 129
Toffler, 55
Tonnies, F., 232
Toulmin, Stephen, 203, 208, 223, 232
Touraine, Alain, 213, 232
Townley, B., 122
Trumble, D.J., 250
Tyler, Ralph, 53, 54, 206
Usher, R., 168, 175, 177
Wadsworth, Yoland, 249
Walker, D.F., 53
Walker, M., 184
Walker, Rob, 69
Waterman, R., 179
Watkins, P., 108
Wawn, T., 100
Webb, G., 50, 51, 52, 137–61, 139, 150–51, 153
Weiskopf, Richard, 121–36, 122
Wheeler, D.K., 53
Whitehead, Jack, 152
Williams, Raymond, 108, 232
Winter, Richard, 13–27
Wise, A.E., 233
Wolf, Naomi, 74
Wünsche, K., 132
Yeatman, A., 107
Zuber-Skerritt, Ortrun, 3–9, 4, 53, 83–104, 84, 85, 86, 88, 92, 100, 151, 152, 184

Subject Index

academic legitimation, 246
accountability, 86
action research
  acceptance, 148
  action in, 3, 251
  as procedure, 167, 248–49
  case studies, 250
  definition, 14, 146
  discourse, 172, 173
  ideology, 17–18, 172
  methods, 15–17, 147, 167
  paradigms, 89
  spiral, 249
  see also critical action research,
    emancipatory action research
analysis of data, 34
  researcher's influence on,
    34–35
anti-modernism, 223
appraisal, 182–98
  and causality, 195–96
  project philosophy, 190–95
  project structure, 190–95
  project style, 190–95
  system, 185, 189, 197
Aristotle, 52
attitudes, 53
audiences, for research reports, 26–27
authority, sources of, 35
authorship, 116, 182, 185, 186
automated decision-making,
  107–08

autonomy, 186, 190
both–and, 168
bureaucratic model, 93
case studies, in action research, 250
causality, 196
challenge, 186, 190
  coping with threat of, 118–19
change, 84, 210–13; barriers to, 93–
  95
charismatic leader, 112
class struggle, 140
classification, 34
collaboration, 13, 24, 109
  collaborative inquiry, 66–82, 182
  collaborative process, 22–23
  collaborative resource, 21–23
commitment to change, 93, 94
commodification of knowledge, 246
communicative action
  model, 125, 131
  theory of, 223, 224
communicative community, 111
communicative competence, 109,
  110, 112, 115, 117
  concept of, 111–14
communicative practices, 110, 111
communicative rationalisation, 124,
  170
community of action researchers, 172
community of scholars, 5, 85
competencies, developing new, 93, 94
conflict, 130

conformity, 137
consensus, 121, 127, 128, 132, 150
  orientation, 129
construction of difference, 157
consultant, 126
consultation, 108
continuity, disruption of, 178
control, 212
cooperation pact, 121, 131, 132
coordination, for change, 93, 94
corporate training, programs, 122
CRASP model of action research, 85,
  86
  applications, 86–87
credibility, 28
critical action research, 166
  postmodernism and, 8
  principles for, 6
  problems in, 7
  procedures for, 6
critical attitude, 86
critical awareness, 144
critical consciousness, 144
critical negation, 230
critical paradigm, 49, 52–54, 55
critical pedagogy, 153, 154, 155
critical reflection, 169
critical resistance, 229
critical theory, 29, 51, 53–54, 123,
  141–43
  criticism of, 199
  in education, 143–46, 219–31
  origins, 137
  relevance of, 199
critical transformation, 56
critical world view, 50, 51–52
critique, 23
cultural politics, 229
culture, contemporary, 202
  for change, 91
  nature of, 202
  of silence, 227
curriculum, 204, 207
  critical perspective on, 208–10
  development, 49, 53

evaluation, 49, 53
  leadership, 53, 60–65
  models, 56
  paradigms, 53–54
  practices, 214
  technical view of, 206–8
cybernetic loops, 92
  cycle of action research, 84, 166;
    see also CRASP cycle
data, 29
data gathering, 15
  methods of, 15–16
death of history, 246, 247
death of metaphysics, 246,
  247–48
death of the subject, 246, 247
deconstruction, 153, 178–79
deconstructive approach, 176
delegation, 186
deliberation, 4
democracy, 151
democratisation, 123
devolved decision-making, 109, 114
dialectics, 20, 140
  dialectic critique, 13, 20–21, 23
  dialectical reasoning, 54
dialogue, discipline of, 92
difference, 185, 190
disciplinary society, 173
discourse, 143
  analysis, 171
  exposure through action research,
    165–81
  innocent, 127
  role of subject in, 127
discursive consciousness, 128
discursive practices, 171, 173, 208
disembedding mechanisms, 217
dissensus, 176
disturbance, risking 14
double-loop learning, 84, 90–91
education, as gatekeeper to privilege,
  146
  action research in, 168
  administration of, 215

and postmodernism, 168
critical theory of, 219–31
evaluation, 215
functionalist view of, 204–6
institutions, 214–15
lifeworld, 215–16
policy and practice of, 213
practices, 214–15
research, 215
systems, 213–17, 218
educational framing, 217
efficiency orientation, 107
  as barrier to action research, 91
either–or, 168
elites, 130
emancipation, 182, 183, 184,
  222–31, 245
emancipatory action research,
  83–105, 82
and personnel development, 121–36
barriers to, 90–91
definition, 3, 5, 84–85
problems with, 121
emancipatory aspirations,
  199–242
emancipatory dialogue, 124
emancipatory paradigm, *see*
  transactional paradigm
empowerment, 85, 106, 182, 183, 184
  of leadership, 106–20
epistemology, 29, 30, 171
equality, 148
  principle, 112
ethics, of action research methods,
  16–17, 29
ethnographic description, 44
ethnomethodology, 29
evaluation, paradigms, 54–55;
  tools, 49
evidence, 186, 191
excellence, 92
Excellence in University Education
  program, 87–88
experts
  dependence on, 91

expert knowledge, 130
  subject, 184
false consciousness, 137, 145, 149
feedback, 41
feminism, 68, 155, 246, 251
fieldwork
  principles for, 16–17
  problems, 17
fifth discipline, 91
findings, implementation of, 24
flat management structures, 108
flat organisations, 186
flexibility, 186, 191
  in management, 108
Foulcauldian rupture, 187
Frankfurt School of Critical Theory,
  3, 84, 141, 152, 153, 225
functional paradigm, 49, 53, 54, 55
fusion model of action research, 131,
  132
future shock, 55
global culture, 228
global unification, 202
globalisation, 209
grand narratives, 176, 224
grounded theory, 5, 85
group privileging, 137, 152, 153
group process, 150–51
group–individual tensions, 149
Hegel, 140–41
hermeneutics, 139, 142, 143, 150
hermeneutic world view, 50–51
hierarchies, 130
historical perspective, 53
Hitler, 141
human resources
  emancipation in, 122
  investment in, 122
  management, 122
hyper-reality, 176
hypothesising, 39
ideal speech situation, 143, 145
identity, group and individual, 137
ideology, 170
  of action research, 17–18, 172

imagining, as empowerment tool,
    106–20
  art of, 106, 114–16
impact, 186, 191
individual, 51
  as subject, 174
  freedom of, 123
inevitability, 141
information industry, 203
information sharing, 116
institutional reflexivity, 199,
    216–19
institutions, 199
instrumentalism, 50
intercultural learning, 69
internalisation, of theory and practice,
    14
internationalisation, 202
interpretive paradigm, 50, 55
interpretivism, 205
interviews, 16
irrationalism, 141
job rotation, 100
judgments, 19
knowledge, 142, 205, 207, 210
knowledge-constitutive interests, 142,
    144
language, 143, 172
  of community, 169
late capitalism, 209
leadership, 111, 112
  and imagining, 114–16
  models, 50, 56
  paradigms, 55
  power of leader, 116
  theory and practice, 49
learning community, 54, 55;
    critical, 56
learning organisation, 84, 91–93
Lenin, 141
lies, 35
life politics, 218
lifeworld, 199
line management, 106, 108
lines of accountability, 109

management, development,
    83–105, 100–101
  education, 100–101
  intervention for change, 94
  practices, 100
management–action relationship, 186
Marx, Karl, 138, 140–41
Marxism, 151
mechanistic world view, 37, 38
media, 203
  images, 202
memories, shared ownership of, 79–
    80
memory work, 66–82
  as research method, 67–68
  collective, 67
  groups, 67–68
  texts, 68
mentoring, 100
meta-narratives, 169, 227
meta-reflection, 55
meta-view, 183
methodology, debates in, 219
MID, 123–32
modernism, 166, 188, 209
modernist action research, 166–67
modernist assumptions, 188
modernity, 209
moving, 97, 98
mutual dependence, 129
mutual learning, 124
narrative, 188, 197
  as discourse, 178
necessity, 141
negotiation, 44, 55
neo-conservatives, 223
networks, 244
objectification of meanings, 137
objectivity, 38, 157, 196
observation, 3, 16, 45, 174
operational issues, as barrier to action
    research, 91
organisational change, 83–105
  action research model of, 6,
    95–100

defences and barriers to, 83–84
management of, 92
models of, 83
models, 98
task-alignment model of, 95, 96
organisational culture, 93
organisations, multiple realities of, 55
other, 137
outcomes-based management, 108
ownership, 37, 182, 183
paradigm agreement, 56
parity, 185, 190
participatory action research, issues for, 243–54
participatory decision-making, 114, 116–18
pedagogic authority, consultant as, 126
personal scientist, 5, 85
personnel development, 121–36
personnel management, *see* human resources management
perspective transformation, 144
phenomenography, 139
plural structures, 23–24
creation of, 14
pluralism, 190
plurality of voices, 125, 202
political intervention, action research as, 129–30
politics of cultural change, 192
popular knowledge, 246
positivism, 19, 30, 50, 142
methods of, 20
positivist world view, 50
postcolonialist perspectives, 202
postmodernism, 137, 156, 157, 165, 167, 168, 176–80, 199–242
and appraisal, 182–98
and critical action research, 8, 165–66, 169–70, 171
and education, 168
discourse, 176

postmodern condition, 167, 200–204
postmodern moment, 165–66
postmodernist assumptions, 188
versus modernism, 167–68
vocabulary of, 167
poststructuralism, 30, 39, 154, 205
power, 173, 175, 207
knowledge and, 174
reconceptualisation of, 174
relationships, 125, 139, 142, 173
study of, 171
practical action research, 4
practice, 24–25, 199
practitioner action research, 14
pragmatism, 39
praxis, 52
privileged position, 37, 39
professional development, 14
professionalism, 86
programmed management decisions, 107
quality, 92
questionnaires, 16
racism, and memory work, 69–79
rate of change, 55
rational consensus, 128, 137
rationality, 137, 142, 153, 154
readers, 204
reasoning, 200, 211
critical, 211–12
instrumental or technical, 211
practial, 211
reciprocal inquiry, 66–82
reconstruction, 178
emancipatory, 212
recording, audio or video, 16
distorting effect of, 16
reflection, 3, 14, 66, 98, 172
critical and self-critical, 99
reflexive critique, 13, 18–20, 23
reflexivity, 29–32
degrees of, 35
in educational research, 37–38

interpretation of, 28, 31
need for, 35–37
partial, 32–34, 35
procedures for, 38–47
thesis of, 18
in emancipatory action research,
  see research, reflexive
refreezing, 97, 98
regimes of truth, 208
regulation, 212
relativism, 166
reporting, 32;
  reflexive, 32, 36
representation, 204, 205, 207
research diary, 45–46
research paradigms, 50–53; *see also*
  functional, transactional, critical
  paradigms
research reports, nature of, 23
research
  as value laden, 53
  methods, 30
  practice, 28
  reflexive, 28–48
researcher, role of, 4, 21–23
  constitutiveness, 28–48
  influence on setting, 30
  personal involvement, 36
  relationship with participants, 29,
    130–32
  theory-laden view of, 29
resonance, 186, 190
results-oriented organisational
  practices, 107
risk, 23
science, 47, 142
scientific management, 108
scientism, 37–38
self-actualisation, 51
self-awareness, 31
self-consciousness, 203
self-disclosure, 36
self-evaluation, 86
self-identification tool, 60–65

self-inclusion, 31
self-management, 126
self-reference, 31
self-reflection, 4, 145
self-reflexivity, 37
simulacra, 176
single-loop learning, 90–91
skills, 205
social contexts, 212
social formation, 201
social media, 207, 210
social movements, 202
social order, 219
social structures, 205, 210
social transformation, 220, 221
sponsors
  influence of, 38
  support for action research, 88
stabilisation, 212
staff developer, role of, 146
staff development, 53, 55, 145, 147–
  48
staff, empowerment of, 92
stakeholders, 54, 150
stories, writing of, 67
storyline decision-making, 106
storyline management, 116–18
straight-line management, 106, 108,
  109, 114
strategic planning, 3
structuralism, 51, 127
subjectivity, 196, 207
subject–object relationship, 183
support, 186, 191
surveillance, 173, 179
symbolic capital, 128, 130
symmetrical communication, 5, 85
system, 199
systematisation, 212
systems change, 138
systems thinking, 91
targets, 186, 191
task-driven organisation, 94
team, 55

team vision, 96
teamwork, solving problems through, 84
technical action research, 4
technical paradigm, *see* functional paradigm
texts, 204, 207, 221; of organisation, 189
textual practices, 208
theory, 24–25, 170
theory of knowledge, 158
thesis and antithesis, 140
thin-line management, 109, 110, 111, 114
time and space, separation, 216
    regularisation, 217
top management, support for action research, 88, 92
training, 100; of staff, 122
transactional paradigm, 49, 51, 52–53, 54, 55

transformation, 24–25; 202–3
triangulation, 16
trust, 118
truth, 118, 170, 175
    relativity of, 169
    multiple truths, 112
    politics of, 175
understanding, 205
undistorted communication, 125
unfreezing, 97, 98
universal history, 227, 228
utopian pedagogy, 230
validity claims, 111, 112–13
value-laden questions, 51
values, 53, 205, 210
world views, differences in, 133
writing up, of action research, 25–26